For Maril...
with lc
thanks fo:
Part of this project
Kaia xxx

REACHING ROSIE

Originally from Stroud in the Cotswolds, Kara J. Morris now lives with her husband and two children in the Midlands. By day she is a pottery teacher, but by night she loves to write. Her family is her number one priority as well as walking the dog and eating cake.

REACHING
ROSIE

from Autism to Burlesque

KARA J MORRIS

Matador
9 Priory Business Park,
Wistow Road, Kibworth Beauchamp,
Leicestershire. LE8 0RX
Tel: 0116 279 2299
Email: books@troubador.co.uk
Web: www.troubador.co.uk/matador
Twitter: @matadorbooks

ISBN 978 1 83859 245 5

British Library Cataloguing in Publication Data.
A catalogue record for this book is available from the British Library.

Printed and bound by CPI Group (UK) Ltd, Croydon, CR0 4YY
Typeset in 11pt Adobe Jenson Pro by Troubador Publishing Ltd, Leicester, UK

Matador is an imprint of Troubador Publishing Ltd

For Goldy, without whose unfailing support
we wouldn't be where we are.

★

For Andy, for being a pillar of strength and wisdom.

★

For Rosie, for showing me what it means to love.

★

For Grace, for bringing the sunshine whatever the weather.

★

To the Full Monty Girls:
Bonnie, Goldy, Ele, Alix, Emma and Nancy.
With everlasting thanks for being your cheeky, saucy, sexy,
abundantly generous selves, and giving my daughter a chance to
fulfil her potential.

★

To the people of the Stroud valleys.
For your community spirit and generosity,
and for treating us like family.

★

In loving memory of my dear friend Nick Mason,
who adored Rosie as she adored him.

INTRODUCTION

My mother always said that life is a roller-coaster ride of possibilities with only one certain outcome – so make wise choices, expect the unexpected and never take anything for granted. For me, it was good advice because my life would go in a direction neither one of us could have predicted.

It's always fascinated me how the diverging trajectories of choice and chance can shape our lives – like an infinite lottery of possibilities driving us into the unknown. All we can really do is stay alert in the present, plan for the future and hope that the odds and the gods are in our favour.

Some people breeze through life without incident and others get dealt the 'biggies'… the things we pray will never happen to us and tend not to talk about, as if mentioning them could jinx us. Most of us, though, will go through something that, for whatever reason, will rock the boat in otherwise calm seas. It could be as little as a rainstorm causing temporary discomfort, or as big as a hurricane propelling us into uncharted seas; at some point or another we will be tested – and our reaction to that test will define who we are as people and show us what we're capable of achieving.

We can see it as a burden or a blessing… in this karma-loving culture, do we take our biggest life challenges as an insult from above, or a gift to help us on the road to liberation?

And then? There's the simple answer: shit happens.

I can't say I breezed through my darkest times with any particular grace – or that the future doesn't seem daunting sometimes – so whether my past has shaped me for the better or worse, I'll let you decide.

This definitely isn't a book where I heroically overcome my adversities or break new ground. Instead, I've penned a simple invitation into my family life, during a time where chance or fate rudely interrupted my calm, carefree existence and changed everything. And the catalyst for my new-found adventure? Genetics. Well, IQSEC2 to be precise. I didn't know it then but within the first few seconds of Rosie's conception, something almost impossibly rare had taken place. A one-in-a-billion alteration in a gene that no one even knew existed at the time of her birth. This gene change has been responsible for all of the difficulties Rosie has faced, and the journey starts with her first diagnosis, one that many of us are familiar with:

Autism.

My story is as quirky as it is unlikely; mums and dads will do anything for their kids and the path I chose to help my little girl tested that premise to the extreme.

If you google 'cure autism', more than 6,870,000 results pop up on the screen and you could spend weeks (been there, done that) lost in the abyss amongst the eye-watering amounts of information to digest, following dead-end roads in search of that curative Shangri-La. From dietary intervention and specialist teaching techniques, to therapeutic dogs and Mongolian-shamanistic adventures on horseback, it's all out there and heralded as the next miracle cure. But if I've learned anything during the seventeen years since my daughter was born, it's that autism is not an 'illness' to be 'cured' and when it comes to therapy, there is no universal holy grail. Children with autism can make huge gains if the right therapy is found. For others, my beautiful daughter included, progress is slow and hard won. There are many thousands of parents who, like us, have explored every therapy, tried every diet, read every book and still struggle to see their child make significant progress. Their autism journey, like ours, has been filled with the agonies and ecstasies of small triumphs and dashed hopes. With that in mind, I can honestly say that having an autistic child can be one of the most rewarding, frustrating, lonely, funny, challenging and wonderful jobs in the world. There's never a dull moment; autism will tease out the best and the worst in you.

When it comes to defining autism, a plethora of very different and often contrasting symptoms are generalised, for the sake of diagnostic criteria, into three common areas of difficulty: communication, social interaction and imagination. You could be non-verbal and totally reliant on others for your care, or a ground-breaking scientist like Einstein… if you meet these three criteria – however they manifest – doctors will place you under the umbrella of the autistic spectrum. It's this diversity of symptoms that make it so hard to isolate the causes, let alone find the cures. They say that when you meet one person with autism, you meet *one* person with autism – and it couldn't be more true. Everyone has a different experience. This is mine.

While various genes linked to autism have been found, the precise combination of genetics and other environmental factors which cause it are still emerging. To top it all, a heady mixture of media speculation, politics and lack of clear answers is fuelling a lot of fear and superstition about autism and its causes. In fact, opinions are so conflicting and dogmatic it's almost impossible to get a clear picture and find the absolute truth, and people will fight tooth and nail to defend their theories.

For the parents of an autistic child there is only one constant in the debate: there are no words that could fully explain how terrifying and painful it is to see autism swoop in and steal your apparently healthy, bubbly child away from you.

And so the dilemma remains, for parents and professionals alike: what is causing one in every hundred children to become autistic? And more personally, what caused *my* child to become autistic and how do I help her live a full and happy life? In my case, it would take seventeen years to find out.

How this impelled me to become a burlesque stripper is still beyond me…

None of this was in my life plan.

This is my story.

CHAPTER ONE

NEW BEGINNINGS

*'Bring on the waves, for I am
learning how to sail my ship.'*
Louisa May Alcott

Trembling in their basques, five brave women stand nervously in a backstage dressing room awaiting the call of the compère.

They huddle together and join hands – a last act of solidarity before the inevitable. As they look wide-eyed from one to another, one of them, a curvaceous woman with a round, friendly face, says, 'This is it ladies! Let's get out there and have the time of our lives!'

But there is no use for words now. Nothing can quell the fear, the excitement, or the rush of adrenalin they feel as they psych themselves up to walk out on that stage. All they can do is acknowledge the fateful look in each other's eyes and wait.

Then there is stasis. And for a few stretched moments they listen to the sound of muffled cheers penetrating the dressing-room walls.

'Good evening, ladies and gentlemen!' booms the voice of a large and gregarious man into an old microphone. As he makes his way across the crowded dance floor to the stage, multicoloured disco lights dance across the sequins on his black tailcoat drawing attention from the crowd who begin to cheer loudly in anticipation.

Backstage, the women in the basques scream at one another with their hands to their mouths.

'Listen to that, they *want* us!' exclaims one, as she wiggles in her basque; causing her ample bosoms to ascend just a little bit higher and her corkscrew curls to fall decadently into her cleavage.

They line up for their introduction onto the stage.

'Here we go!' says a slender woman with dark silky hair and scarlet lips.

'I have five very special ladies for you this evening...' continues the compère, raising his arm to rouse the crowd further. 'For your PLEASURE!'

The most curvaceous lady of the group slips her leg seductively round the stage curtain, which produces a deafening roar from the waiting crowd.

'LADIES AND GENTLEMEN... PLEASE WELCOME... BONNIE... ELE... KARA... GOLDY AND ALIX... I GIVE YOU... *THE FULL MONTY GIRLS!*'

One by one they take to the stage and strut to their starting positions.

They are dressed in black suits and fedora hats, their

basques peeking teasingly from behind their lapels. The hot stage lights dazzle them, soaking them in colour, and they squint to try to make out the size of the crowd and spot a familiar face. Then they settle into position: feet hip-width apart, heads down. There is a momentary hush as both audience and performers wait for the music to start. All five women lightly hold their breath.

A couple of people shout, 'Come on, Bonnie,' and 'Goldy!'

Their hearts are pounding loudly in their chests, their mouths suddenly become paper dry, and they wait... about to embark on an unbridled leap into the complete unknown.

The eager audience begins to chant and cheer to see the dance that has been the talk of the town for weeks. The sound of the crowd is thunderous, but the women remain in position, straining for the introduction of their song. Time seems to stand still for an eternal moment, as it does sometimes when the world is hurtling beyond your control and comfort. Then, as the music penetrates the cheers, it begins.

There is nothing left to do but dance.

As the women raise their heads in perfect time and face their audience, one thought springs into all their minds, 'Oh my God. I'm actually doing this! I'm going to get naked – NAKED – in front of all these people!'

★ ★ ★ ★ ★

As you may have already guessed, I am the round-faced, curvaceous 'stripper' and the other performers are my extraordinary friends. Before this moment we were five ordinary women from ordinary lives. None of us were professional dancers – or strippers for that matter! Goldy, Bonnie and I fell under the job description of 'mother', Alix was a gardener and Ele, an estate agent. We were every different shape a woman could be from size 10 to 16. This was not a case of showing off our perfect bodies – this was a case of 'we dare to bare for a cause we believe in'.

My friends had come together to help me and my family in our time of crisis. Their naked act of bravery embodied the ultimate expression of how far one friend would go to help another. And we needed their help; my oldest daughter, Rosie, had developed severe autism and a rare and dangerous form of epilepsy that meant she couldn't go to school. She needed special therapy only available in America and my husband Andy and I were trying to raise the nearly £17,000 we needed to get her there. We needed them, we needed our community and we were overwhelmed with the generosity that now surrounded us. We were a million miles from where it had all started: a group of girls, a cup of coffee and Goldy's madcap idea to strip. Now that sleepy dream had become a reality – we were living it.

It all started, as most stories do, with new beginnings. I was having a baby. A standard life event, I know, but it couldn't have been more revolutionary. As new life grew inside me, I could never have imagined the ways in which this little person would change my life, affect the lives of those around me, bring together a town, inspire families across the nation and spread awareness to tens of millions of people around the world.

'Andy! Come here a minute,' I called in a kind of whispered shout so as not to disturb my discovery. No reply. 'Ands!' I persisted with increased volume and a pang of excited urgency. We'd just arrived and already there was scandal. 'You've *got* to have a look at this… quick!'

I heard the thud of familiar feet climbing the stairs and he emerged in the doorway holding two cups of tea.

'Quick! Look!' I giggled, pointing fervently out of our low bedroom window.

Smiling quizzically, he knelt down to see our stark-bollock-naked neighbour walking around her garden as if in the middle of a nudist colony.

'Oh my days!' he said, quickly looking away – ever the gentleman. 'Never thought I'd see that here!'

'Not in *Painswick*, darling,' I quipped in a mock posh accent.

Simultaneously we turned our heads to look out of the window then quickly looked away in case she glanced up and spotted our voyeurism. He handed me the tea and I rested it on my now huge baby bump. Our eyes met and the cheeky grin that spread across my face instantly echoed in his. Those kind olive-green eyes were my sanctuary. The eyes of a good, honest man with dreams of a new and hopeful future sparkling in his gaze. Life was suddenly changing. Together we were embarking on a new adventure into parenthood and would soon be Andy and Kara plus one. Things couldn't be better. We were young, in love and happy. The perfect cliché.

I first met Andy when I was sixteen, unromantically 'down the pub', as we call it in the West County – The

Pelican, to be precise – a hippy hangout in the Cotswold town of Stroud. Our eyes first locked onto one another over a pool table and we bonded with bottles of Grolsch. He had long brown hair pulled into a ponytail, chiselled features and those beautiful olive-green eyes. I thought he was meltingly gorgeous; he thought I was 'sexy' and that night we kissed by the door of my bedsit in the autumn rain. We instantly clicked. I loved his unconventional outlook on life, his sense of humour and his deep philosophical banter. Non-materialistic, he was never going to be a millionaire, but I thought this made him more attractive. In those days he looked a bit like an unkempt Brad Pitt – in my mind anyway.

This whole 'good-looking' thing made him a bit of a chick magnet back in the day – which would make me feel a tad insecure from time to time. But for some obscure reason he was devoted to me. We 'got' each other. Both the by-products of eventful childhoods, we saw life in the same way and luckily still do. When I was pregnant, he shaved his head, which made him look like a sexy monk. I, on the other hand, had ballooned into a frump. So, monk and frump were finally settling down and renting our first 'real' house together and we couldn't have been more excited.

We'd moved to what we thought was a sleepy rural retreat, a quaint little Cotswold town called Painswick, consisting of 80% OAPs, 20% London weekenders, Japanese tourists, and us.

Affectionately dubbed 'The Queen of the Cotswolds', houses and shops (all constructed from creamy local stone) span centuries of growth and prosperity, lining the narrow streets like members of an old stately family. Explore the town and you take an architectural journey through history. From medieval Tudor buildings, to millers' cottages, to grand Georgian-fronted homes. Our tiny rented terraced cottage was sandwiched right in the middle of it all: three stories high, one tiny room per level, with a miniscule kitchen tacked onto the back leading to a courtyard garden.

For a new family, Painswick had everything: there was a school, a pub, a village shop, and opposite our house in St Mary's Street, a popular Thai restaurant with a posh little B&B above it. Just around the corner there was a Post Office, the tiniest bank in existence, a bookshop and an up-market butcher's that sold things like pheasant and rabbit. The village church, famous for its lollipop-shaped yew trees, was a stone's throw from our house, as was the rec – a large park and playing field for the children. Next door to us was The Shetland Shop – oddly named, as there was nothing remotely Scottish about it. A hotchpotch of items were proudly displayed in its window: fossils, jewellery, toys, model boats. When we met the owners we realised that one of them was the naturist I'd spotted from our bedroom window. Looking back, perhaps it was a sign that nudity would be a theme of things to come. We were walking into a future that we could never have imagined. But that's what I love about life – its almost brazen unpredictability. You get on the train to a particular destination, but you never know what you'll encounter along the way… you could be in for a regular journey, or you could have embarked on the adventure of a lifetime.

★ ★ ★ ★ ★

The rest of my pregnancy was spent settling into village life, trying to fit in as best we could. We were the 'renters', the 'riff-raff', the 'everyday people'. We were the ones with the scruffy old beige Mini Metro. The ones who had interesting bohemian friends who were maybe a tad hip for the native middle-class Painswickian pensioner. But apart from one incident, when I parked my car and another woman, vying for the same space, ordered me to move because, 'You don't own a house here, you simply rent,' people were very friendly to us.

'Just moved in, dear? When's it due?' said an old lady one morning nodding at my whopping great bump.

'The thirteenth of June,' I replied in my poshest English accent.

'Oh lovely, a summer baby… your first?'

'Yes.'

'You're going to love it, dear. Motherhood is a wonderful gift. Cherish every moment of it. They grow up ever so quick!'

'I will,' I promised, swiftly waddling by in a 'can't stop, too busy and very pregnant' kind of way.

If I wasn't waddling about town trying to stay mobile, I was at home nesting. I would creep excitedly into our unborn baby's room (whom we had nicknamed 'Little Dave') and look at the tiny baby clothes I'd collected, carefully folding them back into neat piles around the edge of the room, as we hadn't got a wardrobe yet. In fact we had next to nothing – just a baby basket, a second-hand sofa and chair, and a small TV that rested on a cardboard box disguised with a piece of material. In our bedroom we had a wicker blanket box to store our clothes and a futon mattress on the floor for our

8

bed, which I have to say was screamingly uncomfortable when heavily pregnant. For a start, to a pregnant woman, due to decreased mobility, the floor looks very far away. Once you've bent your creaking knees and managed to lower yourself – complete with burgeoning bump – onto it, there is little chance of ever getting up again. Which is tragic because instead of moulding and supporting the whale that has now engulfed your once-agile body, a futon mattress actively resists your curves... a bit like lying on a stack of giant towels. Here I would lie with aching hips, daydreaming about my baby's future. It seemed almost inconceivable that this neat little bump would one day be five and seven and twenty-one! And, if health or luck was on their side, he or she would grow old with the memories of whatever happiness and pain had shaped their lives. I was dying to know if we were having a boy or a girl and what it looked like. Of course, like every mum-to-be, I didn't mind what sex it was, 'as long as it's healthy', and I tried not to think of the ramifications if something – God forbid – went wrong with the pregnancy. Of course, my mind was more preoccupied with maternal trivialities like eco nappies versus disposables and what outfit to dress it in first. It seemed to me this little somebody, this acorn of potential, could be absolutely anything it wanted to be, and I couldn't wait to find out what they'd do with the life Andy and I had thrust upon them. One thing, though, was abundantly clear: like all expectant mothers, I'd invested my heart in the 'easy', 'normal', 'standard' parental journey of raising a happy, healthy child. The thought of having a sick or disabled baby was one that terrified me. Our lives would surely be over. How would we ever cope?

By the end of June, a heatwave had scorched the country for a good few weeks. The roses were in full bloom and so was I. Wimbledon was in full swing and Painswick was a vision of quintessential British life. We'd turned in early but couldn't sleep. It was Friday night and there was a jazz band playing in the Thai restaurant. The music drifted into our bedroom on the gentle summer breeze, creating the atmosphere of a balmy foreign holiday. Andy leaned out of our third-floor bedroom window to spy on the festivities and I lay beached on our unyielding futon mattress like an overheated elephant seal.

The music eventually stopped and Andy watched as the last customers left the restaurant and entered the night. Shrill, happy voices exchanged farewells and drunken laughter filled the ancient Cotswold air as the final clop-clop-clopdrag-clop of high heels turned the corner and went out of earshot.

'The end of another day,' said Andy, contentedly drinking in the whispering silence that now ensued.

'Hi-ya!' shouted the voice of a young woman breaking the peace.

'Who's that?' I said in a loud whisper, but he didn't hear.

'Hi!' he replied in a friendly tone, adding, 'That was quite a night!'

'Yeah! Hey, you're having a baby! Us too! When's yours due?' A surprising Geordie accent reverberated.

'We're one week overdue!'

'Really? Poor you! We've still got three months to go. I'm Kerryann by the way…'

'Oh, hi! I'm Andy. Andy and Kara.'

'Lovely to meet you!'

'Yeah, you too!'

I felt an irrational pang of jealousy. 'Who are you talking to?' I asked, masking my possessiveness with an enthusiastic tone of voice.

'It's our neighbour… she's having a baby too!' he replied.

'Is she pretty?'

'Err yeah, I suppose so…' he said, casually gazing down at me, clearly amused. He jumped down from the windowsill with a little chuckle. 'Oh Kar,' he said parking himself beside me on the bed, 'you will always be my number-one girl, even if you are beached like a whale and can't get up to save your life.'

'Hey! I am *not* a whale!' I said, giving him a playful punch on the arm. He affectionately kissed my bump and said, 'Come on, preggers, let's get some sleep.'

'Yeah, you're right. We'd better make the most of it whilst we still can!'

Another week crawled by. I was now two weeks overdue, three stone overweight and hormonal as hell. I was irrationally starting to believe that I was stuck in my very own Groundhog Day and that the baby was never going to come. Every day more bright red stretch marks cruelly etched themselves in all directions over my once neat and beautiful bump.

I was rapidly turning into Birthzilla. An emotional, tearful and over-sensitive woman had taken over the fun, kind, smooth-skinned gal that Andy had fallen in love with seven years before. Thankfully, he had developed the compassion to accommodate my mood swings. Either that, or I had drained him of the will to live. He was tolerating me with quiet resignation, placating me with tea and chocolate and generally staying out of my way. I was trying very hard to be pleasant, and occasionally succeeding, so I was pretty certain he still held out hope that the real me was in there somewhere, having been irrationally quashed by a temporary blip in my human nature.

I was desperate for the whole pregnancy trip to be over. Every day that passed felt like a week, so we embarked on a mission to induce my labour. We'd tried all the 'bring on the baby' methods: walking, a bumpy car ride, a vindaloo, soulless and purely functional sex – but nothing had worked. How, I would ask myself, is this great big baby going to get out of me? Of course having attended sex education classes at school I knew exactly how, but as I stared down at my enormous belly it seemed a logistical impossibility.

I once read that being born is the most dangerous journey you are likely to take in your lifetime. With this in mind, most of us are doing very well; each and every one of us are the testament to a birth – the most common miracle on earth. Despite the inherent risks, an awful lot of us are born healthy and reach old age. I only had to step out of my front door in Painswick to see this.

The final stages of my journey to motherhood began on 26th June 2001, when at one o'clock in the morning my waters broke. I was in labour for what seemed like an eternity. After a night of contractions that the clearly insane midwife deemed as 'mild' (you've got to be kidding me), I was told to go home and rest.

In the morning I phoned my mum to tell her I was in labour, and then my best friend Goldy, who was also pregnant. Within ten minutes she was knocking on the door to offer some girlie support. She breezed into the living room, smiling with excitement, and with one calm and confident look instantly put me at ease. Goldy has that effect on people, an infectious, reassuring Goldyness that makes everything seem OK.

When meeting her for the first time, three attributes hit you between the eyes and can't help but leave a lasting impression: boobs, boots and curls. She's the embodiment of easy-going beauty. A natural, sexy big mama with breasts the size of Barbados. These magnificent lovelies can't help but be the first focus of your eye, insistently squeezed into a 38C bra, and emphasised by an extremely tight low-cut top. Always. Then you are struck by her mass of blonde-brown curly hair, clipped into a top-knot, ringlets cascading either side of her open friendly face. Thirdly, her big biker boots strike you, worn on every occasion from weddings to wakes, she is never without them. An unconventional free spirit with a naughty wild streak glinting in her eye; when Goldy walks down the street she quite simply owns it with her swing and swagger. Hopelessly generous by nature, selfless by instinct and sexually liberated. Think Samantha from *Sex and the City* meets Queen Latifa.

Anyway, in she breezed, short skirt, biker boots and all.

'Hi Kar,' she said warmly, giving me a huge hug and standing back a little to take me in.

'Cuppa?' said Andy, emerging from the kitchen looking flustered.

'Oooo, go on then, Ands,' she replied, smiling at him in sympathetic amusement before turning back to me. 'Now… how far apart are your contractions?'

'Sometimes five minutes, sometimes ten… they tell me I need to get as much rest as I can,' I replied, trying to look calm – a feeling quickly snatched away by another contraction. I leaned on the cold exposed Cotswold stone wall of our living room and breathed, doing my bravest, most in-control labour face for the benefit of my best friend.

She watched me for a while, thoughtfully. 'OK, we need to do something to bring on the labour,' she concluded, knowing only too well that in established labour there *is* no control and you no longer give a flying toss what you look like.

'One girl I know kept hers from going off the boil by going up and down the stairs. You need to stay upright. Let's go for a walk.'

As we sipped our tea between intermittent contractions, I looked apprehensively through my net curtains and onto the street, which was decadently bathed in late June sunshine. I did *not* want to labour in public but I squeezed my swollen feet into my sandals anyway, and we ventured onto the streets, heading for the park.

'Right, let's run,' announced Goldy as we arrived. 'That'll get you going…'

'Err…' I hesitated.

'Come on!' she shouted, the gap between us widening. 'Do you want to have this baby or not! RUN!' So I tried to run in Weeble-like fashion across the grass, stopping almost immediately for another contraction. Goldy stood next to me, hands on hips, cooking up her next plan.

'I know!' she said smiling from ear to ear. 'You need a shock. You know, like when you get hiccups…'

She began to jog away from me again, this time backwards. 'Come on, keep it up!' she yelled.

So on I waddled as fast as my legs would carry me. Suddenly she threw herself at the floor – her idea of a shock. I didn't jump, I didn't even twitch and we fell about laughing, which prompted yet another contraction.

'Just breathe… and again, breathe,' she soothed, rubbing my back.

My birthing plan was to have a nice, natural water birth at the midwife-led Stroud maternity unit where I had been born twenty-six short years previously. I wanted no intervention and no drugs. It all felt very important at the time but I now see how insignificant the drama of birth becomes. After all, the safe delivery of a healthy baby is the most important thing – the rest is just for decoration. Years earlier, Goldy had managed to give birth, drug-free, with the arrival of her first son Jo. I, however, was about to experience the exact opposite.

When Goldy went home that evening nothing had changed. The labour began stopping and starting, keeping me awake – and after another long night, still no baby. I was exhausted. The so called 'mild' contractions were getting me nowhere.

On day three I was taken to Gloucester hospital and induced. By the time the baby was ready to be born I was drugged to the eyeballs, sleep-deprived and pretty weak. After a full hour of pushing and *still* no baby, a medical team very swiftly gathered to assist the birth. It was like inviting a football team into the delivery suite. My legs were briskly strapped up and suddenly the moment of our baby's big arrival was here. Everybody gathered at my nether regions to get a good look. Normally, I'm a bit of a prude and would not appreciate an audience congregated at my vagina, but in this moment, I really couldn't have cared less… a whole damn football stadium could have been watching and I wouldn't have batted an eyelid.

The doctor put a suction cap (called a ventouse) on the baby's head and pulled with the next contraction.

'Kar…wow… I can see the head!' said Andy, peering over my hoisted-up leg. 'Whoa… it's quite blue…'

I felt a shot of fear go through me, which was quickly overridden by another urge to push.

'Come on, big push now,' said the doctor.

She assisted my efforts with another firm pull on the ventouse and out came baby. The relief was overwhelming and I craned to take a first glimpse of our child.

'It… it… it's female!' exclaimed Andy.

She was quickly put on my tummy then whisked away before I had a chance to see more than a blur.

There was then what seemed like a vast eternal silence.

'We're just clearing baby's airways with a little straw,' said the midwife in a serious voice.

My breath stilled as I anxiously looked towards where my newborn lay. The seconds ticked by in slow motion and a hushed tension hung in the air as the midwives and doctors worked swiftly with their tubes and machines. Then, finally, the cry came. That sweet cry of new life and with it, sweet relief.

The midwife wrapped the baby in a blanket and brought her to me and a very happy Andy.

'I'll leave you for five minutes,' she said.

We spent time in love… in love with the baby, in love

with each other, in amazement at this, our most wondrous achievement.

'What shall we call her?' I said, looking searchingly into his eyes and then back to her perfect little face. 'What about Rosie?'

'She does look like a Rosie…' said Andy, softly. I had never seen his face like that before. He looked completely renewed, the miracle of birth had clearly blown his mind. He had an inner glow and was wearing a gentle, somewhat relieved, smile.

The baby gazed around the room, a little distant but oh, so beautiful.

Instantly I was catapulted to the love-drenched realms of new motherhood, mesmerised by every detail of our new arrival.

I pulled back the blanket to reveal a mottled pink miniature hand and tucked it cosily back in. 'She's here, all safe and sound, ten fingers and ten toes… she's perfect! We're just so lucky!' I said in amazement.

Together we looked at her, lost in a world of complete adoration.

The midwife came back in to clear up. Suddenly, an overwhelming gratitude flooded into me. Perhaps it was the labour drugs but I couldn't stop myself from telling her how truly grateful we were for her expert help.

'Um, I love you so much… and I don't even know your name,' I clumsily announced. She was five feet tall, stocky, with spiky plum-coloured hair. In my normal life I would have put her down as a hard nut but for me, in this hormone-soaked and happy moment, she was my hero.

'I'm Dawn,' she replied, walking towards the bed smiling. I took a breath to ceremoniously announce that we would call the baby Dawn when a doctor came back in, burst the bubble and saved us from a lifetime of calling our daughter a name that neither of us would have chosen.

'You can go up to the ward now,' she said.

★ ★ ★ ★ ★

During the first few dreamy days of Rosie's life we were spellbound. Knackered, drained, sore, sleep-deprived and completely overwhelmed – but definitely spellbound. This amazing little person had effortlessly shown us a deep and beautiful love without even trying. In her every waking hour we became her captive audience. Everything she did seemed like a small miracle and we would sit for hours entranced by her every move. We couldn't believe we had created her – a living, breathing blend of us both.

I have so much video footage of those early days. I watched them back years later when a documentary was being made about Rosie and it was heartbreaking. It made me want that time back. I yearned to recapture that feeling when it was all so simple. We were a little family: together, contented and carefree. We had a beautiful bouncing baby with her whole life ahead of her: a happy, bountiful childhood, school, friends, holidays – university maybe. Then growing up, getting a job, making her way in life, marriage perhaps and children of her own. All that potential waiting to be explored. I remember that time in a sort of a golden haze, because everything was so blissfully 'normal'. Free from labels, experts and consultants. No fear of the future, no panic, no nagging guilt or swirling questions. No suffering for Rosie, no mental agony for us. Love without worry. Simple times when we were just normal parents and the world was full of possibilities.

CHAPTER TWO

THE BIRTH OF A NEW ERA

When it comes to parenting, making the transition from being an expectant mother to becoming someone's *actual* mum can bring with it a smorgasbord of emotions. The anticipation, hope, excitement and suspense felt before the big arrival is replaced in motherhood by elation, joy and relief, mixed with a healthy dose of worry and responsibility. It suddenly hits you that this vulnerable little life is totally reliant on you for its survival, so you had better get it right!

It's instinctual to establish a routine, make sure your baby is warm, fed, loved and given security, but achieving this can come as a bit of a shock to the system – especially on little or no sleep. Somehow, though, you muddle through, worrying about every little thing, celebrating every little milestone. Then suddenly, before you know it, your baby is crawling and the cosy singularity of life with a newborn opens up into a world of planning ahead:

mother-and-toddler groups, nurseries, schools, play dates – the framework around which a normal family life hangs. For most mothers this innocent and perfectly cogent life projection will be realised, but for me it was a loaded gun of expectation with the potential to cause chaos.

★ ★ ★ ★ ★

Andy and I abruptly discovered what being a parent was all about when, after two weeks of calm and blissful bonding, Rosie discovered her voice. This tiny thing, so angelic when asleep, was putting us through the seventh realm of hell when awake and we didn't know what had hit us. She began screaming blue bloody murder night and day and we could do nothing to soothe her. Worried that she was in pain, we rushed her to the doctor's but the screams were put down to colic which, we were advised, would pass in three months. Three months? How could we possibly survive that!

It was the height of a particularly hot summer so we had to keep our windows open day and night to keep Rosie cool. As her operatic screams echoed around the well-to-do Painswick streets, I wondered what the residents must be thinking as they read the daily paper or sat down to enjoy a drop of afternoon tea.

In the wee small hours Andy would take our wakeful, screaming baby out in the pram, sacrificing the peaceful sleep of the village in an attempt to calm her. This would do the trick and send her back to sleep. Eventually he would wearily trundle back to the house, open the door without a sound and painstakingly lift her back into her cot before slipping back into our warm bed.

'Well done, hun,' I'd say.

Silence would reign for a brief and blissful moment and we'd sink into it, thirsty for its restoring peace. Then the dreaded noise would recommence: 'Waaa waaa waaaaaaaa,' mercilessly forcing us awake and the whole palaver would start again.

We developed a palette of tactics to curb her crying: bouncing, rocking, walking, driving, breastfeeding. Years later, I discovered that our pregnant neighbour Kerryann was so disturbed by the relentless nature of our little foghorn that she had begun to dread her own baby's imminent arrival.

I'd had such a romantic view of parenthood before Rosie's birth but I quickly discovered that the *idea* of parenting and the *actuality* are two VERY different things. I'd thought I would be so patient, loving and kind – and I was all those things – but to my great shock I often felt angry, frustrated, controlled, exhausted and desperate as I held this red-faced yelling little bundle in my arms. I remember once, when things got really tough, I had to carefully put her down, leave the room and count to ten for fear of losing control of my temper. The feeling terrified me and it was a big reality check; motherhood can bring out the best in us all – but it can also try you to your limit. Luckily for me and a million other mothers looking after demanding little people, the unconditional love ordained in the early days of bonding remained and grew ever stronger to match her moods. When not crying, I was convinced that my baby was the sweetest on the planet. I cherished those calm, sleepy moments where I had time to drink in her sweet baby-smell and contemplate the miracle of her existence. Bursting with pride, I was certain that this innocent little bundle – my first and finest creation – was the greatest gift I could bring to this crazy chaotic world.

I loved singing to her, making her smile, feeling that magic connection that flowed between us. But sometimes I'd notice her becoming strangely detached. It felt like she'd floated away from her little body and got lost in her own little world. I had no idea of the implications, but whenever she entered this state a churning uneasiness would tug at me. I put the behaviour down to her gentle personality. 'She's just a daydreamer,' I'd tell myself. Only after having my daughter Grace did I discover that this turn of absence was unusual. I practically jumped out of my skin when she was born and our eyes first met, she was looking straight at me, totally present, awake and penetrating. The signs of the imminent journey we were about to take with Rosie were too subtle to read for a first-time mum. No doctor or health visitor noticed any problems, so how could I have known any different?

At three months, just as predicted by the doctor, Rosie stopped crying, became more aware of her surroundings and lapped up everything life had to give. We were relieved. At last we could finally find our feet and enjoy being a family.

★ ★ ★ ★ ★

I was a dutiful mum and took Rosie for all her compulsory check-ups and vaccinations. Everything seemed to be going fine and she appeared to be developing normally.

But at four months, during a routine check with the health visitor, it was noticed that her head circumference had stopped growing along the usual percentile. It had started on the 50th percentile at birth (average) but was now only at the 4th percentile (very small). Her height and weight had remained on the 85th and 91st percentiles (larger than average) so there appeared to be a notable disparity.

'I'm sure it's nothing to worry about,' said the health visitor, 'but I'll go and quickly check with the doctor, just as a precaution.'

As she slipped out of the room and the door slowly shut behind her, a shot of fear engulfed me just like the one I'd had when Rosie had been born blue. I closed my eyes for a few seconds to try and disperse it, but it remained, spreading through my body with a vice-like grip. Then I looked down at my perfect little baby, sleeping angelically, safely wrapped in her woolly blanket. Could there be something wrong? Her sudden vulnerability bore a stark contrast to her gentle pink face, so exquisite in every detail. The treatment room, still, sterile and clinically indifferent to my unease, suddenly became a holding area, a place of limbo, the potential setting for a diagnosis that could change my daughter's life forever. I stared at the clock on the wall until it faded into a blur and listened to its soft insistent tick as I bit my lip and wriggled my toes in my shoes. Then the door opened and jolted me out of my trance. In swanned Dr Johnson, an undeniably beautiful Spanish doctor, who over the years had almost become a friend.

'Hi Kara, how are you?'

'Very well, thank you. How are you?' I replied, forcing

a smile, which she returned, before focusing her attention on Rosie.

'She really is so pretty, Kara. You must be very proud,' she said, before adding, 'how's Andy? Are you getting enough sleep?'

'I… I…' I stammered.

'Well, don't worry about a thing. Her head circumference… it's perfectly normal. I remember when my youngest…' she continued, but I let her voice fade away into a jumble of words, nodding acquiescently to fake that I was listening. Because the thought that drowned out the world was this: *It's perfectly normal. Everything is going to be all right.*

For the most part, the reprieve from what had transpired drowned away any fears. But as I pushed the pushchair home through the clear, crisp autumn breeze, free-falling through my mind, like a tumbling autumn leaf, was a miniscule nagging doubt, a seed of uneasiness that begged to be recognised. Something just didn't *feel* right. I proceeded to push that doubt, that instinct, to the back of my mind. *After all*, I told myself, *I'm not a doctor, I'm just a mother.* All I wanted was the uncomplicated freedom to enjoy my baby. But the seed was planted. It could not be undone.

★ ★ ★ ★ ★

Time flew by, and apart from developing eczema and childhood asthma, Rosie had become a healthy, interactive, happy baby. With her soft blonde hair, round blue eyes and peachy skin she was a true English rose and

I felt so lucky to be able to call her mine. But after 'head-circumference-gate' I unconsciously adopted a slightly obsessive relationship (let's call it a keen interest) with the developmental milestones listed in all my baby books. According to the experts, the average baby is expected to smile by eleven weeks, sit by six to nine months, crawl by eight to ten months and walk by twelve to fifteen months. I read and reread each milestone as she grew, and observed her for signs of progress. Looking back, I can see that this was the first time that autism started to secretly steal an ordinary parental experience from Andy and me. Rosie was achieving the milestones – but only just – so when she reached eleven months of age and it was time to see the health visitor again, I decided to voice my concerns.

'Don't worry,' she said in a breezy tone, 'children all progress at different rates. Some are a little later than others, that's all.'

'Yes, I'm probably just fretting…'

'As long as Rosie's reaching those milestones in time, I'm not worried. Just relax. You'll never get this precious time again – and mark my words, before you know it she'll be at school and you'll wonder what happened!'

'I know… I mean you're right,' I replied, feeling reassured.

'Look, you're a first-time-mum – and it's only natural to worry. As far as I'm concerned, I'm happy with her development, so go home and enjoy your baby… I'll see you both again at Rosie's two-year review.'

I felt temporarily relieved but as her first birthday crept closer my doubts lingered, nagging at the back of my mind and subtly eroding my feelings of motherly contentment.

★ ★ ★ ★ ★

A frequent feature of our weekends was a trip to see Andy's grandmother, so when Rosie's first birthday came around, Granny's house was the obvious venue for a family celebration. She lived in an idyllic Cotswold stone cottage on the side of a steep valley in the picturesque village of Bournes Green, near Stroud. She had what city dwellers could only dream of: roses round her front door, an apple orchard and pin-drop silence interrupted only by birdsong. She even had her very own robin that would fly in through an open window and perch right next to her on her dusky-pink upholstered high-back chair. Granny herself was the queen of glamour. Despite her advanced years, I'd never seen her less than fully made up, with regally coiffured hair, smelling of Chanel.

The advantage of having a summer birthday is the chance of celebrating outside, and this year the weather did not disappoint. There wasn't a cloud in the sky as we opened the gate to Granny's garden and pushed past the lavender bush that spilled across her garden path. Once inside, we were greeted by Andy's bubbly blonde sister Jessica and their dad (Rosie's granddad) Richard. Granny was in her element. She loved nothing more than a good family gathering and she delighted in her role of great-grandmother. Tea was poured, presents were opened and there was much 'ooo-ing' and 'ahh-ing' over the birthday girl – but for some reason Rosie just wasn't on form…

When it was time for birthday cake, we headed into the dining room and I placed Rosie in Granny's heirloom highchair. A single candle was lit on the cake, and with cameras at the ready, I placed it before her with a feeling of triumph. The candle flame shone brightly, begging to be noticed, but Rosie didn't look up. She didn't even glance over.

'Happy birthday to you,' we all sang in unison. No response. 'Happy birthday to you.' Nothing. 'Happy birthday, dear Rosie, happy birthday to you!'

Andy picked up the cake and brought it right up to her face. She looked at it briefly, then gazed out of the window with a blank expression.

'*Rosie*! *Rosie*! Look!' called Andy's dad, trying to gain her attention. Nothing.

Together, we all counted, 'One, two, three, BLOW!' but she *still* didn't look back so Andy blew out the candle and we all cheered. Rosie appeared to be unamused by our childish excitement and it wasn't until he put the cake right on the highchair tray that she finally noticed it properly. Casually, she grabbed an iced corner of the cake and quickly stuffed it into her pink cupid's bow mouth.

'YAY!' we all praised. She briefly looked at us to see where the noise was coming from, then continued munching on her cake, crumbs escaping her hands and tumbling onto Granny's perfectly hoovered royal blue carpet.

'She's a little daydreamer,' said Jessica, gently stroking her cheek.

'Yeah, she's probably just tired,' I said, making a weak justification for her lack of interest.

'Yes. That's right,' added Granny, 'it's a long day for a birthday girl.'

None of us understood what was happening, but we were all starting to make excuses for her behaviour. Rosie was acting differently to other babies from time to time, but there'd never been any concrete evidence of a problem – nothing that couldn't be dismissed with a rational explanation.

★ ★ ★ ★ ★

By the time Rosie reached fifteen months my concerns began to gather momentum. I began to sense, by way of comparison, that something – some *je ne sais quoi* – was missing. Whenever I was in our local town, Stroud, I'd sit on a bench with Rosie on my knee and watch the other mothers walking up and down the high street with their toddlers. I couldn't help but be bemused… these tots appeared to be aware of, and reassured by, the presence and proximity of their mother. They would totter up the hill behind her, and she would turn and stop every now and then to allow the child to catch up. A special synergy existed between them – and it puzzlingly eluded Rosie and me.

In contrast, Rosie was completely unpredictable. I couldn't take my eyes off her for a second! She had very little awareness of me and wouldn't come if I called her name. Happy in her own little bubble, if my attention was distracted she could easily wander off and get lost, or worse, run over. Now that she could walk – and run – it made my job of caring for her very hard, especially if we were outside. I'd have to be on high alert at all times. If Rosie could learn to behave like the other toddlers, my life would be easier, and hers safer. I just couldn't understand how the other mothers had got their children to be so compliant. It was as if they were privy to some kind of a magical mothering formula that we'd somehow missed.

It was part of the long road to autism. Never obvious at the start, it teases you with uncertainty and undermines your confidence as a parent.

It was around this time that I took Rosie to the terribly nice and well-to-do Painswick mother-and-toddler group. With my confidence already a little dented by the *je ne sais quoi*, I had to literally force myself to go step by step up the sunlit blustery hill and in through the front door.

A group of mothers were sitting away from the children, chatting and drinking coffee and tea. I stood by the door and waved at them with a somewhat shy smile, holding Rosie on my hip. Engrossed in their conversations, they mostly ignored me, but the head of the group immediately came over and introduced herself. I can't remember her name now but for the sake of this anecdote let's call her Sophie. She was friendly, well-spoken and trim with brown straightened hair. She told me to help myself to tea and coffee and showed me where to put my £4 fee. I thanked her as charismatically as I could and put Rosie down to explore the room. I've never been good at meeting new people and I suddenly felt excruciatingly awkward, so I decided to make myself a quick tea and sit on one of the tiny chairs in the play area. That way I could be near Rosie until she got her confidence. *I'll deal with socialising later*, I told myself. Once sitting down, I was suddenly aware of my boiling cup of tea on the level of all the children but I didn't want to draw attention to myself again, so I figured I would drink it as quickly as possible. In my haste I burned the roof of my mouth. Not a good start.

I couldn't believe how relaxed the other mothers were. They just let their children 'get on with it' and only intervened if one of them bashed another on the head for no good reason or there was a kafuffle over a particular toy.

'How did these kids become so independent?' I pondered…

I supressed my social anxiety and rising confusion about Rosie under a smile, trying to look carefree, motherly and approachable. I'd known before I got there that I would have nothing immediately in common with these mums. There *would* be common ground, I was sure of that, but initially I'd have to work to find it. I glanced at them between sips of tea, wondering how I was going to start up a conversation.

Socially, I had two hurdles to get over. Firstly, Painswick mothers are mostly loaded: beautiful house, Range Rover, posh pushchairs, good hair, great clothes, children dressed in Boden. I was not of this calibre: 'homely' house, clapped-out car, second-hand pushchair and suffering from a permanent bad hair day. Secondly, I'm terrible at small talk. I'm OK with the 'Lovely/terrible day' opener, then elaborating on how that would be 'good/bad' for the garden, but then I tend to panic and either say something self-deprecating to try to be funny, or the conversation will dwindle into a tongue-tied silence accompanied by a tight-lipped smile and a shrug of the shoulders.

Rosie walked across the room and picked up a Winnie-the-Pooh toy. She clutched it in her little hands and looked around. A little boy made a beeline for it and snatched it off her with a good deal of force. I was horrified and nearly intervened but Rosie simply staggered a bit, regained her balance, then carried on towards various other toys scattered around the room. She suddenly seemed so delicate and vulnerable compared to the other children boisterously rushing around. In my heart of hearts I knew they were just being children, but for Rosie, that was just the problem; for some reason she didn't have it in her to act like them. She possessed a gentle, angelic quality – it was something we adored about her – but on the social stage it was beginning to hold her back.

I glanced again at the other mothers merrily sipping their drinks, laughing, and taking every opportunity to trumpet their child's latest milestones.

'Oliver counted to ten yesterday,' said one mother proudly. 'He can only say six other words but he can count to ten already!'

'Did he? How clever,' said another. 'Molly drew me a beautiful picture the other day – a smiley face with arms and legs coming out of it. She gave it to me and said, "It's you, Mummy." It was so adorable, I nearly cried!'

'Aw, I do love this phase,' added another. 'Every day something new happens and I think, *Slow down! I want you to stay like this forever!*'

Really? Every day, a new development? I wondered.

Due to my rising panic about Rosie's progress, these unsuspecting women were fast turning from 'mothers' to 'others'. The more they talked, the more isolated I felt. And I hated it. I wanted to celebrate my child as much as the next mum but how, I asked myself, could I do this when all their conversations were centred on their children's achievements?

The room was hot and Rosie looked a little flushed so I took off her pastel striped cardigan. I needn't have, though, because her mother-and-toddler debut was about to come to an abrupt end... As she headed over to the book area she tripped over a runaway truck and fell forward with alarming velocity, banging her head on one of the chairs. She belted out a short scream, followed by an endless breath-holding pause, before uncontrollable crying set in.

I flung the cardigan over the nearest chair and immediately ran to her aid.

'Oh Rosie. Oh no! Sweetheart!' I said, lifting her into my arms. 'Come on, let's have a look!'

She lifted her head and there was blood pouring out of her mouth. The 'other mothers' stopped drinking their tea and became a silent audience. Even the children stopped, momentarily looking up from their play to witness the noise and chaos.

As I have said before, Rosie is a foghorn and she took no prisoners on this occasion, wailing for Britain as blood poured from her mouth into my cupped hand. Sophie jumped up and handed me a tissue. Together we mopped up the blood and assessed the damage. She had whacked her tooth on the chair and gained a fat lip.

'It might have killed the tooth,' said Sophie. 'It will probably go grey now and stay that way until it falls out.'

Overwhelmed, my instinct at this point was to get the hell out of there.

'I think I'll take her home,' I replied, rubbing Rosie's back, rocking back and forth to try and soothe her now deep protracted sobs. 'We'll try again next week.'

I bundled her into her pushchair and was out of there in a flash. Door firmly shut behind me, I took a deep breath and looked out over the undulating valley, blissfully soaked in a late summer haze. We hurried away down the lane and onto the main road. Now that Rosie was calm I realised that I had left her cardigan, but too traumatised to go back, we pressed on to the sanctuary of home.

Rosie and I just don't fit in there, I thought. *But there must be something I'm doing – or* not *doing – that's making Rosie need more supervision. What the hell am I doing wrong?* My head was getting so crammed full of doubts and confusion that it was overflowing. *Surely I'm being irrational? Eighty per cent of the time she's fine*, I reasoned. *She can walk, talk a bit, babble and play like all the other kids. OK, she's not as wilful as some of the other toddlers I know, but that's just her nature…*

But anomalies were emerging and gathering momentum that could no longer be ignored. Yes, she was smiley, friendly and loved to be around people, but she had unique interests too, like a fascination with the pattern on our carpet. She was active, full of fun and engaged fleetingly with toys but she also loved exploring textures like the exposed stone on our living room wall, or the bobbles on my cardigan.

At first I thought this quirky attention to detail was curious and charming and the fact that I now know it was down to autism doesn't change that. Now I see it as a gift. Rosie was seeing the world in a unique way – a way that was entirely special to her. But as her unusual interests grew into repetitive habits, and as my mind swung between confusion and justification, the threat that challenged our chances of a normal family life also grew. It was the threat of a life that no parent would want for their daughter. The difficult life of a child with special needs.

★ ★ ★ ★ ★

I finally approached the subject of Rosie's development with Andy when she was eighteen months old. He confessed that he too had noticed that she was showing signs of slipping behind and that she possessed a 'uniqueness'.

'I think…' he paused to reconsider his reply. 'I hope… she'll grow out of it and catch up.'

'Well, I hope and pray you're right,' I replied. 'Whatever happens I know we'll be there for her but I'm scared for her – for her future – and ours too.'

'Well, don't be. We're a good team, you and I, Kar. Besides, I'm pretty sure she's gonna be fine.'

I let the comfort of his words hang in the air for a while. 'Yeah, you're probably right,' I said at last.

It was a relief to talk. Perhaps I was worrying too much, perhaps he too little. Either way we were both under more stress than we realised.

At the time, Andy had a job as a delivery driver. Rosie wasn't sleeping well and in the early hours of the morning after a bad night's sleep, he would begin his shift already exhausted. When the phone rang one morning at 5am, I instantly knew something was wrong.

'Kar,' said Andy in a grave voice, 'I've crashed the van.'

'Oh my God,' I replied, sitting bolt upright in bed. 'Are you OK?'

'No. I mean yes… but the van's totalled.'

'Bu… wha… how?' I stammered.

'They changed my round this morning and I was going along this road I didn't know... I didn't see this T-junction sign, and it was a dual carriageway on both sides. I flew right across the lot and crashed into a sign.'

'Fuck!' There was no other word for it. 'Are you sure you're not hurt?'

'No, just a bit shocked... I missed about four cars going full speed on the dual carriageway, Kar – if there had been just a moment's difference, or if I'd have braked...'

'You could have been killed!'

'Exactly.'

'Does your boss know?'

'Yes, they're on their way.'

There was a pause as I tried to take in the magnitude of what had happened.

'I was just really tired, you know? If Rosie hadn't got up all those times...'

'I know,' I interrupted. 'Just get yourself home, and we'll try to figure out what to do.'

'If they don't sack me, I've got to leave,' he said, his voice steadier now. 'Otherwise this job will be the death of me.'

★ ★ ★ ★ ★

Now that Andy was suddenly unemployed, things really began to unravel. The undercurrent of uncertainty in Rosie's development, coupled with a desperate wish for everything to turn out 'all right', put Andy and me into a melancholia that was getting hard to shake. Lack of sleep and mental exhaustion began to take their toll on our relationship. It was a gradual slide but I became more withdrawn and Andy began to drink. I hated his drinking, he found it hard to deal with my mood swings, and we began to argue. A lot. We began playing the 'who's done the most' competition. That old chestnut. The subject could be anything, but the sentiment remained the same.

Me: 'Andy. I got up at 6am. Went for a walk with Rose, tidied the house, cooked the dinner AND gave her a bath. Can you please change this one nappy.'

Andy: 'Well, I got up at 6am for *three days running* before that, and made the beds, and went food shopping, and looked for a job, and fixed the computer… so *you* do it!'

Ah, the good old days!

In an attempt to halt the descent into a full-scale family breakdown, we decided to fight against the tide and try to resolve our problems. We went for lots of family walks – just the three of us. We reconnected with old friends. We kept upbeat at home by watching episodes of *Friends* or bad romcoms accompanied by naughty puddings. Andy gave up drinking and I played more music in the house, which Rosie loved.

Andy decided to retrain as a furniture maker, so he enrolled on a course at Stroud College and got some casual work dry stone walling with his friend Rich. I got a few regular jobs cleaning for people in the village and set up a pottery studio in the coal shed in our garden. Together, we started to rebuild our lives in a more positive way.

I made friends with Kerryann, the girl from above the Thai restaurant. Her baby Georgina was a perfect playmate for Rosie and we'd often drop round for a coffee. Kerryann was a bundle of Geordie fun, full of energy with a crazy

Geordie family to match. Like me, she fitted into Painswick like a palm tree in the North Pole and I loved her for it. Outspoken, strong-minded and incredibly funny, she was good company and a loyal friend.

We approached parenting from opposite ends of the arena. She bottle-fed her baby and was strict, disciplined and organised. I was hopelessly idealistic, practised baby-led parenting and tried never to use the word 'no'. She had bleach-blonde hair with dark roots and was drop-dead gorgeous (having annoyingly snapped back into shape two weeks after giving birth). I had... well, hair, I wore glasses and I... how do I put this delicately... needed a bit of a mummy makeover. These differences never bothered us. Neither of us was particularly precious about our parenting styles and we became quite close. It was a refreshing friendship and lots of fun.

★ ★ ★ ★ ★

Goldy and her daughter Lily were also a constant in our lives. We would either hang out at my house chatting (and eating far too much cake) while the children played or we'd stroll to the park or go for long walks across the valleys.

In my opinion, Painswick Park has one of the most spectacular views in Gloucestershire. Hills undulate into the distance, made up of shapely patchwork fields speckled with solitary houses, connected by a network of hedges and lanes that lazily meander over the brow of the hill towards the creative, bohemian hub of Stroud. We loved spending time there and often took a picnic or a flask of tea.

When walking, we would set off out down Tibbiwell Lane (which was opposite my front door) and along the ancient byway to Bulls Cross at the top of Slad (the setting for the snowy murder in Laurie Lee's *Cider with Rosie*). Then, if we were feeling fit, we'd head on to the isolated and breathtakingly beautiful village of Sheepscombe. We'd hold on tightly to the pushchairs as we descended the steep hills, then tank it up the other side bending forward with straight arms, bottoms sticking out, in an attempt to put some welly behind the pushchair. At the top of the hills we'd rest, give the girls a snack and let them run about amongst the wild flowers and grasses while we took in the view.

Goldy and I were more than just friends: we were bosom buddies. Thoughts, feelings, sex lives – no subject was taboo, especially for Goldy – and these walks were privy to a good many secrets. For all my prudishness, she was the wild child. If you'd have told her she had 'charity stripper' written in her future she'd have loved it.

Apart from Andy, she was the only person who knew I had concerns about Rosie but whenever I brought it up she'd tell me not to worry. Years later she confessed that she too had had some concerns but couldn't bring herself to tell me. She also admitted that she'd stopped mentioning when Lily reached a new milestone. 'You would try to be pleased,' she said, 'but I could see in your eyes how crushed you felt as Lily caught up and then overtook Rosie in her development.'

That's the thing about autism, it doesn't just change the life of a child, it changes your world too, creating ripples that flood into the heart of everyone that loves you.

As well as my social life taking off, Andy was making more friends too. There was Alex, a tall lanky ex-public school local. He spoke in soft whispers as if the world was listening and always used the same greeting… 'All well?' said like this: 'Aaall waaal?' The only person in the world to call me by a different name, he would knock gently on the door and poke his head around saying in the softest voice, 'Hi Carla, aaall waaal?' He was a fascinating, intelligent character and Andy and I loved having him around.

Alex shared a house with Rich, the dry-stone-waller Andy was working for. Devilishly handsome – almost to Andy (Brad) standards – Rich was a modern-day dandy, the country version of a playboy with a taste for fun. Anyone who likes Mr Darcy from Bridget Jones would love Rich – he had that kind of look about him. He saw life as a great adventure and was friends with people from all walks of life. When he was working he'd work hard but he had a dazzling array of avoidance tactics, like mooching around Waitrose buying fabulous food, having coffee outside Woodruffs café in Stroud, or heading down to the Woolpack pub in Slad, to drink the local beer.

He'd often come to our house for a cuppa and relay the events and antics from his action-packed life. He was extremely well connected and his stories often involved lords, pop stars, A-list actors and famous artists. A great orator, he would have me and Andy aghast or in stitches.

On the way back from shopping one day we spotted Rich's beaten-up, ancient blue Land Rover parked on the road by our house. It was pouring with rain and as we dashed past it, laden with bags and baby, we noticed he was in it, sheltering from the rain with a pretty brunette in the passenger seat. He wound down the window to greet us and we invited them in for tea. Clearly, he'd been busy and I wanted to see who this mysterious girl was.

Two minutes later there was a knock at the door and Ele entered our lives. It was the start of a wonderful friendship and little did I know, I'd just met the third member of the Full Monty Girls.

'Hi guys, this is Ele,' said Rich introducing his new squeeze.

'Hi Ele, nice to meet you!' I said, greeting her with a kiss on the cheek. 'Give me your coat, I'll put it over the radiator.' Then I turned to Rich. 'Hi Ricky!'

'Come 'ere, me beauty,' he replied scooping me into a playful rambunctious hug as Andy hugged Ele.

'Tea? Earl Grey or normal?' said Andy, briefly putting his arm round Rich before heading into the kitchen.

'Arrr, just gi'us a narrrmal tea if yer don't moind!' joked Rich in a pretend Gloucestershire accent.

'No praablem mate,' retorted Andy. 'Ele?'

'Oh, normal for me please,' she answered politely.

Rich squatted down on his haunches and picked up Rosie. 'Hello poppet!' he said sweetly in a higher tone. 'Shall we go and see Daddy in the kitchen?'

Rosie put her finger affectionately on his lip and giggled at him as they marched off.

This gave me the chance to get to know Ele. We connected instantly. Ele had impeccable etiquette so she started the conversation by asking about Rosie, commenting on her cuteness. This got her off to a good start. Anyone who remarks on the gorgeousness of my children is a friend of mine! She was a Painswick native who, like me, had gone to the local grammar, Stroud High School for Girls, though way after my time. She was living in London during term time studying drama. Eight years my junior, she was only twenty, but I would go so far as to say she was much more mature. She was the most level-headed, non-messed-up person I had ever met. It was astonishing! If life was like a ball of thread, mine would be all tangled, colourful and frayed and hers would be pure, new, beautifully wound silk. She was perfectly proportioned, perfectly pretty, with perfect poise and posture. She had a gorgeous figure that blended curves and slenderness into feline femininity. She was well spoken, understated and classy – the epitome of country chic. Her long brown hair was always straight and glossy, but never styled. She possessed that French-style effortless beauty that you just can't fake. If you wanted someone to clone, she'd be a good candidate. A world full of Eles would be a most pleasant place to be. She had good judgement and was not fazed by anything. She was hardworking, fun, loyal, caring – the perfect ingredients for a lasting friendship.

From that day on, they became frequent visitors and best friends. I loved spending time with Ele. Her even temperament and gentle sense of fun was a welcome relief from my mounting worries; Rosie was fast approaching twenty-one months of age and her arrested development was becoming increasingly difficult to ignore. It was beginning to dawn on us that our concerns might not be down to our parental shortcomings or lack of a magical mothering formula.

Maybe it wasn't all in our heads after all.

CHAPTER THREE

SWAYING OPINIONS

It was February and I was attempting a mad dash through bitterly cold, torrential rain with bin bags full of washing that I was taking to the launderette. The bracing jolt of a good soaking, paired with the white noise of the raindrops, catapulted my awareness right into the moment and it felt wonderful. For the first time in weeks I was free from my own mind, where fear and hope about Rosie had taken over my senses and declared an inner war. The fear-to-hope ratio was pretty even and in many ways that was where my difficulties lay. I like to have a firm grip on reality so I can be proactive – whatever comes my way – but I just couldn't tell where I stood. So I stood nowhere, in limbo. All I could do was wait. Wait and cling to hope, as the fear of a very different life cast its shadow.

As I approached the launderette I saw a familiar figure, also running, laden like me with washing and similarly soaked. It was at this moment that Bonnie re-entered my life. I say re-entered because we were childhood acquaintances, who'd both lived in red brick terraces on Bisley Road, at the top of Stroud (or 'the top of town,' as we locals say). The top of town was where you'd find your typical 'Stroudie': green-minded, community-oriented, and perhaps, dare I say it, a little bit 'hippy'. Most of the residents on our street (our families included) ate homemade yoghurt and baked their own bread. As a child it felt like a safe and nurturing place to grow up. Bonnie is a couple of years younger than me so we'd never really hung out much back then, but our paths would often cross at our local park, Daisy Banks, or down at the Heavens, a valley of steep rugged fields popular with the local children.

As we reached adulthood we lost touch. Then Bonnie went on to marry Jon, who we'd known through a different circle of friends. Unbeknown to me, she was about to become one of the most important people in my life.

'Hi Bonnie!' I exclaimed as we bundled out of the rain and into the warm, brightly lit launderette.

'Kara!' she answered merrily.

We dumped our bags of washing on the floor and hugged.

'God! How long's it been?' I asked.

'Too bloody long!' said Bonnie, smiling. Then she turned her attention to the washing. 'Look at it all!' she exclaimed. 'This lot would dwarf Kilimanjaro!' We both laughed. 'My God, I just leave it and let it pile up and up and up! It's sick really.'

Our collective mountain of washing did indeed look incalculably large.

'Nah, it's just a sticky, smelly testament to our babies!' I said, trying to make her feel better.

'Yeah, I heard you'd had a baby… Rosie is it?'

'Yes. And you've got a boy? Oli?'

'The Stroud grapevine is working well I see!'

Bonnie filled half the washing machines at great speed before anyone else came in and I quickly monopolised the rest.

'This is what comes of having little ones – and no washing machine,' said Bonnie reaching into her handbag and pulling out her purse.

'Mine bust ages ago,' I replied.

'So did mine. Hard to find the time to come here… Jon's looking after Oli.'

'Yeah, Andy's with Rosie.'

We slotted coins into our machines and switched them on.

'Nice to get some time out, though…' Bonnie said, sitting down with her back against one of the tumble dryers, relaxing into its warmth. She let out a sigh and closed her eyes as if sunbathing.

'It's a rare and beautiful thing!' I joked as I joined her. 'Our little holiday in the launderette.'

Amused, she opened one eye and chuckled.

Our conversation almost immediately focused on our children and I confided my fears about Rosie.

'Oh my God, don't worry!' she said, turning to me with a confident smile. 'She'll get there. Everyone does in the end.'

'I hope so…' I said, my voice trailing away.

It was dusk now and we fell into a comfortable silence and watched as the icy rain slashed down in sheets on the streets and shops outside, running down the hill in busy little rivers. The launderette is always lovely and warm, but the scene of people dashing for cover and cars slowly negotiating the chaos under the light-starved skies made it feel like a toasty paradise.

We chatted easily as we dried and folded our washing, making the most of our temporary freedom.

In the years that followed I came to learn that Bonnie is an amazingly strong woman. She's what you might call a stormy weather friend. Where there is adversity and challenge, Bonnie's light will shine brightly. There are so many people taking refuge under the safety of her wings that it's hard to know how she has time to breathe. Take advantage of Bonnie, however, and she's a woman to be feared. With one eye fixed on the bigger picture, she's a people-helper, not a people-pleaser, so she won't mince her words. The other thing you need to know about Bonnie (or Bons as I like to call her) is that she's a bit of a goddess. She has the kind of creamy voluptuous curves that scream sensuality. It's written in the way she moves, with an assured, gentle grace. Her beautiful photogenic face has a bone structure to die for and she has a voice like liquid chocolate. She could (and should) have a glittering career on Radio 4 and would make Mariella Frostrup sound like a rough old dog on forty fags a day.

Our chance meeting led to numerous coffee dates for us and regular squash games between Andy and Jon. Fate had bonded us over dirty, sticky washing but the future held something unimaginable for us both.

★ ★ ★ ★ ★

Back in Painswick, whenever I spoke of my concerns about Rosie, the reaction was much the same as Bonnie's had been.

'Everything's going to be all right,' said Paul, the proprietor of The Shetland Shop, who I'd bumped into on the way back from a trip to the local Spar shop.

'Look at her! She's adorable! She'll be OK.' He squatted down to her level and stretched out his hand. 'Hello, sweetheart,' he said softly.

Rosie grabbed his index finger, leaned forward and grinned as he bounced it up and down.

'My brother's son didn't speak till he was three and he's fine now,' he said, 'all grown up, wife and kids.' He stood up and looked at me sympathetically. 'Don't worry, love…' He spoke with such sincerity that I instantly felt reassured.

We changed the subject to the tropical fish displayed at the back of his shop and as we spoke I studied his long wild tan-grey hair and barbell earrings. The memory of spotting his wife strolling naked around their garden flashed into my mind and I wondered, *What is the deal with those two?*

Valerie and Paul doted on Rosie, often beckoning us into the shop to let her choose a toy. They were always up for a friendly kerbside chat, making village life pleasant and fun. As months rolled into years their story unfolded. First, they revealed that they went on naturist holidays. We're 'live and let live' types, so we thought, *Cool.* Then one hot May day, Valerie, an amazing botanical artist, popped round with a present for Rosie, a painting of the letter 'R' intricately interwoven with roses. Rich had just popped round for a cuppa (skilfully avoiding work) and we were all sitting in the garden with Rosie happily running up and down the path.

'Wow, Valerie, it's beautiful.' I was overwhelmed. 'That's so kind of you, thank you so much!' We all admired her talent.

'It must have taken you ages,' said Andy.

As she explained her methods, I couldn't help but be impressed with her physique. *She looks great for her age*, I thought. Then, I noticed two ring shapes around her nipples, clearly defined through her tight red dress. *They must be pierced!* I thought, trying not to look surprised. I tried not to look again but my eye kept getting drawn back to them like a magnet.

After she'd left I asked Andy and Rich if they'd noticed anything.

'No,' said Andy, either secretly wishing he had, or telling a well-played white lie.

'Of course I did!' said Rich, smiling broadly. 'They were at eye level.'

'I know! Surely she'd have worn a bra if she didn't want anyone to know!' I replied.

'So what d'ya reckon? Are they into bondage? Are they swingers?'

'They're into fetish and dressing up!' Rich replied with amusement. 'It's pretty much common knowledge.'

'Flipping heck, I love them even more now!' I said, giggling. 'Well, you'd have never thought it driving through this quaint little village! You know, what lies behind closed doors and all that.'

'Each to their own,' added Andy, who was equally amused. 'I knew there was something cool about those guys.'

The following year they invited us to Valerie's sixtieth birthday party. We declined, but it was a nice gesture nonetheless. Apparently there was a male guest wearing leather bottomless trousers. It was the talk of the village! But they didn't care who knew. They were upfront and proud of who they were and I couldn't help but admire them for their openness. They've been our good friends ever since and they remain very much on our Christmas card list.

★ ★ ★ ★ ★

Although people's reassurances about Rosie were well meaning, they inadvertently contributed to my perpetual state of confusion. I hoped upon hope they were right in what they said. I wanted more than anything for my daughter to be able to have a normal childhood, full of fun and friendship and opportunity. I'd have given my life for it. But this hope was becoming my tormentor and my blindfold. The more I clung to the idea of the life I had envisaged for my family, the further it slipped from view.

My balanced, all-embracing mum took me the most seriously. She didn't try to brush off my concerns or reassure me that everything would turn out all right; instead, she listened.

'I just don't want you to worry,' she said gently after one of our long chats. 'Whatever happens, worrying will not change anything about Rosie – but it will consume *you*.' Of course she was right and it felt comforting that there was someone in my corner looking out for my state of mind.

When my dad came over to visit he took another stance.

'You're bein' paranoid,' he said curtly, in his strong Forest of Dean accent.

'No, she really *is* behind, Dad,' I answered, knowing that I had good reason to be concerned.

'No. She's not. She's all right, look at 'er.' I looked up and felt my heart sink. We were sat in the garden. Rosie was stood by the garden wall, babbling to herself and running her fingers over its bumpy surface.

Surely normal kids her age are discovering dolls? I thought. Suddenly my throat felt tight.

'Look,' my dad continued a little more gently, 'you've been mollycoddlin' 'er, that's all. Leave 'er alone. She'll come on soon enough.'

His words, though well meant, stung. It wasn't the first time I'd heard this theory from people we knew and quite honestly it killed me. If Rosie's stalling development lay with my parenting skills then surely I had no right to call myself a good mum! And the frustrating part was that I was giving parenthood my all – Andy too! We read to her, we took her out, we doted on her. We did everything in our power to encourage speech and play skills and fill her world with love. So where on earth were we going wrong? Or were we, like my dad said, being paranoid...

The same day as my dad's visit, a letter arrived. Rosie was due for her two-year review with the health visitor. It requested that I fill out a questionnaire in my Child Health Record book and bring it, with Rosie, to an appointment just before her second birthday.

I dug out her book with its bright red cover and hesitantly flicked through the pages. Inside there was a list of twenty-nine questions like: 'Can she search for a toy you have named? Can she demand a desired object by pointing? Can she build a tower of two bricks?' All I had to do was tick the YES or NO boxes – but I agonised over some of them; I had seen her do almost everything in the book, but in many cases she had done them only once.

'Well, it's not asking me *how many* times she's done them,' I reasoned, 'just *if* she's done them,' so I finally ticked all the YES boxes and hastily shut the book. 'Surely the health visitor will notice if something's wrong.'

But in the days that followed the questions in the book haunted me. I knew in my heart of hearts that something was amiss but I was too busy clinging onto the reassurance I had been given from friends and family to face it.

On the day of the review, Rosie and I arrived at the doctor's surgery in two very different moods. I was nervous. I had planned to be open with her about the concerns I had for Rosie and was afraid to hear her reaction. Rosie on the other hand was excited by a new environment, letting out a little whoop of delight as she headed for the doll's house in the corner of the waiting room. The sunlight streamed through the French doors, backlighting her blonde curls, encircling her head like a halo. She was in her best dress, a white one with huge pink roses printed on it, and she looked utterly adorable. She squatted down, daintily picking up a doll (which reassured me), giving it a little squeeze before throwing it down as a book took her attention. Thumbing the pages she muttered to herself, 'Ah… dog-gen, bug-gen, bog-gen, tg tg tg.' I hoped and prayed there was a picture of a dog on one of those pages but I was never going to find out because the door opened and round popped the head of the health visitor.

'Rosie Morris?'

I got up, took Rosie's hand and together we followed

her down the corridor and into a treatment room at the end.

'So how's things?' she asked casually as I sat down in the patient's chair and Rosie explored the room. 'Have you filled in your red book?'

'Yep, here you go,' I replied, handing it over with a nervous smile. The red cover shone with an air of urgency. It felt to me as though our destiny sizzled within its pages, waiting to burst out and reveal its truth.

She leafed through the pages briefly. 'Any concerns?' she asked, without looking up.

I took a deep breath. I wanted to say, 'Yes, I'm feeling totally desperate! I'm worried out of my mind about Rosie but don't know what to think, I feel like a terrible mother doubting the abilities of my child when everyone else is telling me she's fine. I'm so confused!' but I just couldn't speak the words so I blurted, 'No, everything's fine, she's lovely.'

Rosie was playing in the curtain that pulls around the examination bed. She was all wrapped up in it, shyly peeping round at the health visitor, charming her with a beautiful smile.

'Five, sick, seven,' she whispered.

'Eight, nine…' encouraged the health visitor. There was a little pause. No reply. 'Well, she is lovely… a real credit to you.'

'Thank you,' I replied simply, flashing a smile.

'Everything looks good here but if you have any concerns feel free to ring me.'

'Thanks I will. Come on, sweet one,' I replied, turning to Rosie. 'Take care, see you again.'

We could not have got out of there more quickly.

Over the next few days I was propelled into party preparations. Andy had gone to Glastonbury Festival with his brother Nigel, so it was down to me to give Rosie a proper second birthday celebration. Presents had been bought; balloons had been blown up; a cake was baked; cards and presents had arrived in the post; and by one o'clock in the morning the scene was set with presents piled high in the middle of our tiny living room floor, begging to be opened.

She's going to love this, I thought proudly, heading for bed.

But the next day the penny would finally drop and I would walk the final steps into a world in which I had never planned to be.

★ ★ ★ ★ ★

We woke at 8am.

'Happy Birthday, Rose!' I whispered, scooping her into my arms. 'Wow, you're two! Amazing! Two years old today! Two years of cuteness, two years of loveliness!'

She raised a sleepy coy smile and giggled as I kissed her toes.

'Up!' she said suddenly, grabbing my hand and tugging me out of bed.

'Yes, up! Let's get up! There's a surprise for you downstairs!'

When we reached the living room, Rosie eyed the pile of presents and waddled up to them, her sodden nappy widening the gait of her fat little legs. Then she extended her finger and daintily touched the colourful wrapping paper before turning and walking away. A legendary story flashed into my mind about my sister Emma, who, at two years of age was found sitting beneath the Christmas tree with a triumphant grin on her face having unwrapped every single present. Rosie saw the pile at face value, it never occurred to her that there might be something nice beneath the paper.

Clunk. The penny began to drop.

I tried to put the thoughts out of my mind by preparing a birthday breakfast of croissants and orange juice. Then I changed Rosie into a green linen dress and clipped her hair up to one side. She looked so beautiful but a deep sadness crept in and stole my joy and I wondered how I was going to get through the day. 'Pull yourself together,' I said to myself. 'This is meant to be a happy day!'

I grabbed my camera and began to take some photos. 'Look Rosie! Look at my camera! Smile, sweetheart!' I said, fighting back tears before a knock at the window distracted me.

'Come in!' I called, putting on a brave face.

I heard the familiar click-clack of the passageway door opening and in walked Goldy and Lily.

'Hi guys! Thought it might be you!' I said. 'Perfect timing! Come in, come in, I'll make some coffee.'

Goldy was in her usual garb: short skirt, tight top and biker boots, and Lily was dressed for the party in a floor-length deep turquoise-blue Indian cotton dress. Her blonde curls were tied up in pigtails and her feet were bare. She looked like a fairy from *A Midsummer Night's Dream*.

'Hi Kar,' said Goldy giving me a hug. 'Thought we'd come early seeing as Andy isn't here.'

'Lush. I'm glad,' I smiled, deciding not to tell her how I was feeling. This was Rosie's day and I wanted it to be perfect.

'Happy Birthday, Rosie!' said Goldy, handing her a present. Rosie held it for a moment then set it down to run up and down the room. 'I thought I'd give you a hand to get ready for the party.'

'Thanks, Golds,' I replied. I was grateful. I had a lot to do. Then I turned to Lily. 'Can you help Rosie open her presents, Lils?'

I handed her a present. Lily had blossomed into an adorable toddler. Quiet and observant as a baby, she was now full of smiles and highly inquisitive. She immediately sat down, deftly tearing off the paper to reveal a colouring set. Rosie stopped running from time to time and silently watched as the presents were unwrapped, but as each emerged from its colourful paper she showed little reaction. Lily however, was in her element, delighting at each and every one.

Clunk. The penny dropped a little more.

The anxiety that I'd felt first at her birth, then at the doctor's surgery all those months ago, shot through my heart once again. There was no way out now, no reassurance, nowhere for my fears to hide. A mirage of our future shone before my eyes. Still, I said nothing to Goldy.

We cleared away the paper and I made fresh coffee, which filled the air with its rich, earthy fragrance. We drank and I watched carefully as our little ones played together. Lily was much more determined than Rosie, winning every battle for a preferred toy – Rosie would just let go… not really normal toddler behaviour. Lily was more constructive with her play, more scientific and creative. Rosie would engage more fleetingly with toys, preferring to run up and down the room or examine the details of things.

Click. Down goes the penny.

I began to feel a kind of out-of-body experience as the inner and outer me separated into two functioning entities. I was on autopilot. The 'outer me' carried on talking, smiling, answering congratulatory phone calls and preparing for Rosie's party, but inside I was dying, finally seeing things clearly.

Kerryann popped round with Georgina, who strode confidently into the garden and plonked herself down in the sandpit. Trowel in hand, she set to digging, filling the bucket bit by bit and tipping it out to make a rudimentary sandcastle. Rosie joined her but grabbed handfuls of sand and let it run through her fingers, repeating the action over and over.

Down dropped the penny. Clink, clunk, clink.

As the 'outer me' went off to get juice and biscuits, the 'inner me' screamed: *Something's wrong, something's definitely wrong!*

In the afternoon, Andy's dad and granny arrived. It was all gifts and smiles as we sat in the garden for Rosie's birthday tea. Like the year before, she ignored the cake so Lily and Georgina were asked to blow out the candles.

'Hooray!' everyone cried.

An almost unbearable sense of panic was contained by my smiles. *This isn't right!* I thought. *She should be able to blow out her own candles at age two.*

After tea, the children got down to play and I watched in masked horror as the developmental gap between them became blindingly clear.

'Come and sit on my lap, my love,' Granny called to Rosie as Goldy and I cleared the table.

Absorbed in running between the garden fence and the sandpit, Rosie ignored her request, so I picked her up and placed her gently on Granny's knee. Rosie immediately wriggled off her lap to return to her ritualistic game of running. Disappointment flashed across Granny's face before a smile politely replaced it. My heart sank. Then, to her surprise and delight, Lily toddled over to her, cuddled up and they contentedly sat together for a good few minutes while they talked and sang nursery rhymes. Although it was a lovely scene, it was a hard thing for me to see. Lily had innocently given Granny the intimacy that she craved from Rosie. Watching them interact so happily filled me with an overwhelming sense of grief, as I came to the realisation that the lives of our whole family were about to change forever – and I had no control. Nothing could stop it. It was one of the worst moments of my life and I could share it with no one. It should have been one of the best. My girl was two… I should have been on cloud nine.

The following day, I bundled Rosie into her pushchair and we headed to the phone box opposite the church. I pursed my lips, pushed some money into the slot and dialled the number for the health visitor.

'Hi. I'm Kara Westermann-Childs, mother of Rosie Morris. Do you remember me? We were in the other day, for her two-year review?'

'Yes I do, how are you, what can I do for you?'

My heart thumped loudly as I struggled to find the words but there was no softening it. 'Well, you know I said everything was OK and I had no worries…?'

'Yes,' she replied in a quizzical tone.

'Well… I lied.'

★ ★ ★ ★ ★

Andy came back from Glastonbury to a completely different family to the one he'd left behind and together we spent an agonising week waiting for the health visitor to come and do a more detailed and targeted version of the two-year review.

When the day eventually arrived, she sat in the window seat of our living room, opened her black leather bag and pulled out an array of toys designed to see if she had reached the appropriate milestones for her age. There was a peg board to assess her fine motor skills; a dolly and bed to see if she could demonstrate imaginative play; some small one-inch wooden blocks to measure her balance and precision; and flashcards to see if she could point to pictures and demonstrate what they were.

Rosie flunked most of the tests because she was fixated on a *Noddy* book that she held tightly in her hands. She wasn't so much reading it; it was upside down for a start but she lifted the book to her mouth, flicking the pages against her lips, repeating the ritual over and over. She was engrossed and there was nothing we could do to reach her. She only stopped when the health visitor put the peg board on her lap and called to her. The brightly coloured pegs instantly gained Rosie's attention and she dropped the book and headed across the room to get a closer look.

'Rosie, can you put the peg in the hole?' asked the health visitor, handing her a small shiny red peg. Rosie took it and quickly shoved it in her mouth before looking at her defiantly.

The pegs were chokingly small so I rushed over to intervene.

'Rosie, spit it out!' I demanded cupping my hand under her chin, but she pressed her lips tightly together.

'Come on Rose, just spit it!'

This went on for several tries until I eventually managed to prise it out with my finger. I rubbed it on my top before giving it back to the health visitor all chewed and distorted. She was not impressed. She frowned, put the toys back in her bag and zipped it shut.

Then she gave us the news no parent ever wants to hear.

'Rosie is showing signs that she has some significant learning difficulties. She needs more assessment, so I'm going to refer her to a specialist.'

Even though deep down we knew it was coming, hearing the words, having that last semblance of hope snatched away, was like being hit square in the face by a runaway train.

She carried on talking but I was numb with shock and her words just jumbled about in my mind like muffled echoes. So it was true. My fears were all true! I could hear her jabbering on about special schools, portage and speech therapy – words that tangled with my rush of thoughts. I could feel myself welling up and just wanted her to leave.

Get out! Just leave us alone, I screamed in my head.

But she carried on, explaining how: 'It doesn't matter that Rosie has a disability, as long as she's happy.'

It was a platitude designed to soften the blow and ultimately, I knew that she was right but in that moment all

I could see were the challenges that lay before us all. Our lives would never be the same again.

I glanced at Andy who was holding Rosie protectively and had suddenly stood up to indicate to the health visitor that the meeting was over. He must have been feeling the same way as me – we needed time to digest this. Rosie rested her head on Andy's shoulder, pouted her lips and gently held her eyelashes between her thumb and first finger.

'Ummmmmmm. Ummmmmmm,' she began, in a deep, croaky, guttural hum.

'I think she's tired,' Andy hinted, heading towards the door. Luckily she got the message.

'OK, I'll be in touch soon,' she said, as if there wasn't a care in the world.

The door clicked shut and we looked at one another for a long time, each trying to read the other's mind.

The tears in my eyes distorted his gentle solid gaze. 'She's my girl. My baby girl,' I whispered unsteadily.

'I think… I hope, it's going to be OK,' he whispered back, 'because we're going to give her the most amazing life. We live for her now.'

Rosie was dropping off to sleep nestling peacefully into the warm saltiness of his neck.

'I'm just going into the garden for a bit,' I said softly, as the dam I had been holding back for so long began to break. I ran blindly into the garden shed, and in its privacy slumped against the wall and gave in to my tears. I was catapulted into a kind of sadness and despair that I'd never touched before and I allowed myself to feel the sorrow, the grief, the fear of the unknown. I embraced it all and let it rage through my body unhindered, out into an indifferent universe to meet and mingle with the collective pain of a million others. The life that I'd wanted for Rosie flashed before my eyes; all the dreams I had for her shattered, and in that tear-drenched moment I mourned them all, as they quietly slipped away. Then, quite suddenly, I pulled myself together, wiped my tears and walked back into my life after finding a kind of strength that has stayed with me to this day. Yes, I had plummeted to the abyss of sorrow, but there I found an equal measure of love.

When I walked back into the house, Rosie was asleep on the sofa under a blanket, her red cheeks glowing softly in the dim light of the living room. The soft 'ting' of a teaspoon told me that Andy was in the kitchen making tea.

'Wow, tea! Just what the doctor ordered,' I said as I entered the kitchen. 'Shall we go and drink it in the garden?'

'Yeah, go on then,' he replied, looking a little strained. We tiptoed past Rosie, pausing to watch her sleep, and slipped quietly outside.

It was a beautiful English summer's day and the sun yielded its penetrating heat as we sipped our tea, assessing the intricacies of the meeting.

'Her life is never going to be the same, Andy. Everything looks different now,' I said matter-of-factly.

But Andy sagely got to the truth of the matter.

'No,' he gently replied, 'nothing has actually changed, she's still the same person – our wonderful celebrated daughter – only our *knowledge* about her is different. We can't tarnish her purity with fear and labels.'

Of course he was right.

It was a good place to start.

CHAPTER FOUR

A PREGNANT PAUSE

Perched on the edge of my bath, I waited as two pink lines slowly appeared on a pregnancy test. I checked the instruction leaflet at least three times – it was indisputable, I was pregnant again.

I bounded downstairs to find Andy and break the news.

'Really? Wow! That's fantastic, Kar!' he said, lifting me off the floor and planting a kiss on me.

Next I told Rosie, who was sitting by the fireplace playing with a pile of multicoloured building blocks.

'Hey, Rose, you're going to have a little brother or sister!' I sang happily, kneeling down to her level and smoothing her hair from her face. 'Mummy's having a baby! Baby, baby, bayyybeee!'

She gently took away the wooden block she'd been tapping repetitively on her scarlet lips.

'Baby,' she said softly, the perfect response. I hoped it held meaning rather than just an echo of my words.

'Yes sireee Bob!' I chortled in an American accent,

placing a kiss on her plump little cheek. 'Home grown and beautiful just like you.'

I started showing a bump from day one, but only because the second I discovered our happy news I stopped holding my tummy in. 'Who cares if anyone makes the embarrassing mistake of asking if you're pregnant now,' I reasoned. (It had happened once and kick-started a two-week crash diet that ended in a truly epic fail involving lemon cheesecake.)

At last we had good news to balance a difficult announcement that we were yet to share: our firstborn, precious and adored, has a learning disability. What was once a pestering suspicion had gained reality status and would soon engender its place in people's minds as FACT, never to be dismissed or doubted again.

We'd had a couple of opportunities to tell the family but there never seemed to be a 'right time', so I decided that before I told people who might have an emotional reaction to the news, I'd try telling a stranger on neutral territory. The cashier at the local supermarket was an obvious choice.

Rosie wasn't just a handful in supermarkets – she was chaos. She wanted everything off the shelves and onto the floor. She wanted to run blindly up and down the aisles paying no attention to anyone. She wanted to eat the food and she wanted it NOW. Inevitably, after a few minutes of excitement, she'd get overstimulated and have a huge tantrum. I quickly discovered that the best way to avoid this mayhem was to put her in the trolley, grab a packet of crisps from the snacks aisle and let her munch them while I rushed around like a mad thing and got the shopping done. This strategy worked well until we reached the checkout.

If there was a queue, Rosie was guaranteed to want to get down from the trolley and create mayhem. This was fine if Andy was there as he could take her off, but if I was on my own she'd have to stay put or I'd lose my place in the queue.

On this particular occasion I was alone. There was a big queue at the till and it wasn't long before Rosie was yelling for Britain, having thrown her crisps across the floor, resulting in disapproving frowns from my fellow shoppers. I tried everything to soothe her: a cuddle, more food, pushing the trolley back and forth in the little space I had in the queue, but nothing worked so I swept the crisps under the checkout with my foot and smiled apologetically at the cashier who returned a warm sympathetic smile. By the time our turn came, Rosie was a fireball of rage, flailing about in her trolley seat like a child possessed.

'You've got your hands full there, love,' said the cashier, scanning a bag of apples.

'Yes I have,' I replied, the strain clearly showing on my face. 'You see the thing is, I… I just found out… I've just been told she has special needs. She doesn't understand that she has to wait.'

There. I'd said it. The words that I just couldn't form were finally out.

'Does she? Oh. What a shame.'

'Humm. She's lovely though,' I said, trying to sound optimistic. 'When she's not having a tantrum she's lovely, really she is.'

'Yes, love, I'm sure she is. She's very pretty too,' offered the cashier.

'Thanks.'

'Still, it can't be easy for you...' she continued, 'I couldn't do it. I'm sorry for you, I really am. Not an easy job at all.' She shook her head to herself as she scanned a tin of baked beans.

'It's not easy *right now*!' I joked, reaching into my bag to find a tissue for Rosie whose hot face streamed with angry tears. 'But she's my daughter and I'll love her no matter what.'

'Of course... and I can see you're a lovely mum. You'll be just fine. You'll be more than fine.'

'Thank you,' I said.

Every time I went shopping after that, she'd ask after Rosie and I'd tell her the latest developments, my worries, our little triumphs. In my opinion, supermarket ladies (as well as hairdressers, and shopkeepers) are the listening ear of the community – the unsung heroes of the nation's mental health.

This practice run made telling our families a little easier. Instead of phoning everyone to break the news, we let it spill out organically over time. It felt more natural to tell people face to face when we had Rosie with us. It was the only way to demonstrate the unshakable fact that the idea of having a special needs child sounds scary but the reality was far different... Rosie wasn't just a child with special needs. She was a special child. She was unique, mysterious and magical. We knew the people who loved us would be concerned and that they would worry about the challenges that lay ahead, but we also knew that Rosie's sweet, compelling nature would allay some of their fears and bestow hope. The universal reaction was that of support. Perhaps they put on a brave face for us, keeping any sadness for a more private moment. Perhaps they were unperturbed. I suspect it was a bit of both.

My mum – the oracle of good sense and wisdom – summed it up best: 'Rosie is Rosie. And no matter what anyone says she'll always be Rosie. Everything happens for a reason, and you two are meant for her. You just have to get on with it and not think too hard about the future.'

Everyone, to their eternal credit, treated Rosie exactly the same as always and we did just as my mum had advised; we got on with living day to day and stayed as sanguine as we could. Sometimes we'd have a bad day but the good days far outweighed them. One thing, though, was abundantly clear: this adorable little girl, so unique in her ways, so gently placed upon this earth – had stolen our hearts. We had a flickering hope for a better future and were relieved to have emerged from all the bottled-up worries into a place of growing acceptance and readjustment. As my belly swelled with new life, we had a pregnant pause consisting of calm. A temporary outbreath of hope.

It was the calm before the storm.

★ ★ ★ ★ ★

Within a couple of months of the health visitor's call, we received our first appointment with a paediatrician. I wanted to arrive prepared, so I turned to the information superhighway of the internet to find out more about Rosie's difficulties. This was daunting in itself. I'd never been good with computers. In fact I hated them with a passion because they made me feel stupid. OK, we're talking pre-Facebook days (LOL) – the relative dark ages of the PC, but still, I must confess I was behind the times – even Andy's granny could email!

Andy, however, was born computer literate. You could even say he was a computer geek. In fact let's just call a spade a spade and call him what he is: a Super Geek. Swoon-worthily handsome, kind and funny, but a geek nonetheless.

'Hey, Ands, will you get me on the internet,' I asked, 'I want to google something.'

'Whatever would *you* want to google?' he teased.

'Autism,' I replied cautiously, as we hadn't discussed it before. 'I just want to check Rosie's symptoms before seeing Doctor Thingamajig.'

'Oh, OK,' he replied, suddenly sounding serious. 'But don't freak yourself out.'

He switched on the computer, I typed in 'Autisum', and it asked me helpfully, 'Did you mean autism?'

Not a great start to a now relatively happy virtual relationship.

'Ah, stupid me,' I muttered, clicking on the correct spelling and chuckling under my breath. Then we waited. It was the pre-broadband era so it took a few whirring seconds to respond, before finally listing millions of articles.

'Oh my God, look at them all, Andy! Where do I start?'

'Click on this one… "Top ten autism symptoms". Sounds straightforward.'

Straightforward… The irony of that word was lost on us then. We didn't know how complex autism is, we couldn't imagine the journey it would take us on and we had no idea that this one click of the mouse would start us on what would become months of research.

TOP TEN AUTISM SYMPTOMS:

Failure to respond to their name.
Avoidance of eye contact.
Unresponsiveness.
Obsession with specific objects or things.
Focusing on details and blocking out all else.
Repetitive actions or activities.
Watching the same videos over and over again.
Repetitive movements.
Self-injurious behaviour.
Delayed speech.

We could both recognise several of the symptoms in Rosie, but not others. Notably, she had fairly good eye contact and she was gentle to herself and others, but a lot of the list did ring alarm bells – like the failure to respond to her name, focusing on details and delayed speech.

With a sinking feeling, we ventured onto another website which painted a very gloomy picture of common things that an autistic child *doesn't* do: doesn't point, wave goodbye or use other gestures to communicate; doesn't follow the gesture when you point things out; doesn't make noises to get your attention; doesn't initiate or respond to cuddling; doesn't imitate your movements or facial expressions; doesn't reach out to be picked up; doesn't play with other people or share interest and enjoyment; doesn't ask for help or make other basic requests… doesn't, doesn't, DOESN'T! To varying degrees, every single point could be related directly to Rosie's increasingly bizarre behaviour and they shouted through the pixels at me.

Rubbing my face with my hand I exhaled deeply, 'Is our child autistic?' I said, turning to Andy with wide eyes.

'Bloody hell, I hope not,' said Andy, staring at the screen, still shocked from what he'd read. Autism seemed so foreboding, like a dark cloud sweeping in and possessing a child with potentially devastating consequences. The next website we came across painted an equally bleak prognosis.

'In severe cases, any form of communication is at best rudimentary, at worst non-existent,' read Andy out loud. 'They may need continuous supervision for life and will never recover. With intensive intervention modest gains can be made.'

'Flipping heck, Andy!'

The thought of this becoming Rosie's reality was almost too much to bear.

The non-specific 'special needs' prognosis was more hopeful: 'Communication skills can be better,' he read on, 'and social interaction can be less of an issue. The learning difficulties affecting the child can be tackled with a specialised education programme either in a mainstream or special school, depending on the child's needs.'

This was perhaps a better outcome for Rosie.

'I'll print these pages and we'll take them with us to the appointment,' said Andy after a long silence.

★ ★ ★ ★ ★

Despite our concerns, the paediatrician concluded that the medical profession did not like to give a specific diagnosis any more, but he didn't think she was autistic. His plan of action was to start her on speech therapy and see her again in six months.

Cautiously relieved, we decided to drop into Goldy's house on the way home for a much-needed cup of tea. She was sitting on a low wall in her garden chatting to her mum, Alex, who had come to visit from her home in Australia.

Goldy had been brought up by her mum as a 'global citizen' living all over the world from Sri Lanka to San Francisco. She'd spent her formative years living in a bus during the post 'free love' era of the 1970s and when she was six, she and Alex had walked from Hereford to the Pyrenees in the south of France with a horse and wagon. Alex was anti-establishment and alternative in her views, and even though she didn't trust doctors, we knew both she and Goldy would be anxious for news.

'Well,' said Alex, flicking her hennaed hair behind her turquoise tie-dye top. 'What's the verdict?' They both looked at us intently.

'Well they don't think she has autism…' I replied, in that moment realising deep down that I still suspected she did.

'Yay,' they both congratulated in unison.

'Time to crack open the champagne,' said Alex.

I laughed politely but instinctively knew that this was no time for champagne.

On the way home I approached the subject with Andy.

'Hey, Ands, what did you think of that doctor?'

'Underqualified,' he answered succinctly.

'Humm.'

We drove on in silence for a while, along the winding high-hedged lanes that linked our houses.

'He was only a registrar,' Andy suddenly continued. 'That's a trainee consultant. I don't think he had enough experience to say she's not autistic… And another thing,' he said, the grit of anger rising in his voice, 'if he thinks we're going to just sit back and let him say, "We don't like to give a specific diagnosis," he's got another thing coming. I mean, how can we help her if we don't know what's wrong? When we get home I'm going to phone the doctor and demand to see a specialist consultant.'

★ ★ ★ ★ ★

We quickly realised that having a child with special needs means getting the boxing gloves out and fighting for the right school, the right doctors, therapists and interventions. We were suddenly thrust into a dizzying world of tests and observations, portage, speech therapy and numerous hospital visits. We had to learn new medical and educational language and liaise between the overstretched and often fractured departments within both the NHS and the Local Education Authority to make sure Rosie was getting what she needed. It was a steep learning curve.

On top of all that, as my pregnancy advanced, Rosie began to get more and more frustrated and clingy. She had become obsessed with me sitting in one place, and wanted constant holding. If I got up to do something, like clean the house, wash up or make the dinner, she would cry and wail – and I'm talking flat out, high octane meltdowns – until I sat back down. It was crippling and mentally testing.

I would sit like a prisoner in my chair, Rosie wrapped around my expanding bump, and Andy would run around like a man possessed, getting bottles, nappies, food, toys, books – anything that would help keep her calm and occupied.

How on earth am I going to be able to care for a newborn baby when she won't even let me go for a wee? I would think.

This scene would play out day after unrelenting day in our living room and after a couple of months, we began to worry that there might be a more serious underlying medical problem causing her distress. But the doctors reassured us that she was physically OK. 'It's probably behavioural problems arising from her special needs,' they would say. And as the months rolled on with no progress being made and the crying continuing, 'autism' became a word more commonly bandied around.

Andy and I were tearing our hair out under the strain. The sheer volume and relentless nature of the crying, coupled with lack of sleep, made living in the middle of a quaint little town like Painswick almost impossible.

'Andy,' I said one evening after a particularly fraught day, 'I think we need to move house. If Rosie's going to cry all day long and stay awake all night, we need to get away from people so she can do her thing without us worrying that someone's going to call the social services!'

Andy laughed. 'You've got a point,' he admitted. 'We are a bit hemmed in here, and too far from our old friends. It would be good for us to see them a bit more.'

'Yeah, it'd be fun!' I added. 'And if we lived in the middle of nowhere it would take some of the pressure off…'

'I know. There are loads of tucked-away places around Stroud.'

The choice was obvious. It had to be Stroud. It was time to go home.

★ ★ ★ ★ ★

The rural town of Stroud is *the* quintessential boho-chic place to lay your hat. Aesthetically, it isn't exactly the jewel in the Cotswold crown – not the obvious Cotswold destination for a city slicker to retreat to – so it's evolved into its own secret oasis; a place to settle and live as part of a thriving community that will nurture your soul. Ignore the scattered 1960s concrete monstrosities of the expired Woolworths, the multistorey car park and the police station (please someone knock it down, I beg you!), and you will discover a pretty and flourishing market town nestled in the cleavage, so to speak, of the breathtakingly beautiful Five Valleys that surround it. Individuality is celebrated and encouraged, creating a cultural Mecca of creativity where artists, eccentrics, dropouts and aristocracy live in symbiosis, each contributing positively to the eco-centric micro society at its heart. It boasts the best farmers' market in the country, great art and music festivals and is bursting with locally run health food shops, organic cafés and clothing stores bustling with people from all walks of life.

When I sat down to write about my beloved home town from my current home in Birmingham, I rang Goldy and asked her if she could call me the next time she was in Stroud and let me know what kind of adverts were on the local noticeboards.

'Noticeboards display the personality of a place,' I explained.

'I'm in town now,' she replied. 'Ring me back in five.'

When I rang her back she was giggling down the phone in amusement. 'You're gonna love this,' she said still gleefully. 'There's one here that says, *Channel your inner woodland fairy. Sunday 2–4pm Catswood, Elcombe...* Oh, and here's another good 'un. Listen to this: *Join us for a Rainbow Crystal Meditation, Friday 7:30 at the Painswick Inn.*'

This is Stroud. Every other person is a massage therapist or a yoga teacher, working on a bio dynamic farm or in a folk band. Of course there are a lot of so-called 'normal' people here, but the alternative culture makes the place unique and remarkable. It just wouldn't be the same without the swishing ethnic skirts, the cute woollen-clad toddlers, the make-up free beauty and the myriad of buskers... The shabby fabulosity of the town enchants you; you can't help but fall under its spell. Everyone knows each other and you can't get up the steep pedestrianised high street without bumping into someone or other for a friendly chit-chat. Even if you're not an 'outrageous hippy', most people have good, sound eco-views and practices. Stroud's mayor rides a bike, the rich drive normal cars and the tight-knit socially minded residents feed the café culture.

Nestled among this creative cornucopia are some famous re-settlers from around the UK like Lily Allen, Cath Kidston, Jilly Cooper, Damien Hirst and Philip Treacy, all living comfortable private lives in Stroud's all-embracing spirit. In fact even if you were from the planet Zorg and you visited Stroud, the open-minded folk would sit you down, give you a nice cup of organic soya coffee and listen to your story, because in Stroud you can be yourself. In Stroud you can revolve in a happy universe as if separate from the greed of the rest of the world. This is the town in which I am proud to have been born.

Just a few weeks after realising we needed to move, Andy found the perfect escape. A tiny two-bedroomed bungalow tucked on the edge of a wood at the top of Uplands, situated about a mile up a steep hill from the centre of Stroud. Here we would have the privacy that we craved – we would be in the middle of nowhere, but only a stone's throw from the town.

Our new home, originally a cow barn, was one of four dwellings loosely grouped together on a working farm and livery. You could get to it by driving down a very steep track, flanked by fields allocated for grazing.

We moved in at the beginning of February. It had been snowing for days and the steep track leading to our new abode was like a ski run, so we slipped and slid our borrowed transit van along the bottom track, past the farmhouse, finally taking an icy run-up to our front gate. Dumping down the boxes in the middle of the open-plan kitchen/living room (why does everybody seem to move when pregnant?), we stood and paused for breath.

'Looks just like a holiday home,' Andy said, putting his arms behind his head to stretch his back.

'Right, that's it! We're on holiday from now on,' I stated, putting my arms around his waist, grinning up at him.

In fact it did turn out to be an ex-holiday home, originally rented out during the Cheltenham races. With tacky fixtures and hideous pub-style carpets, it would need a bit of dolling up, but the basic amenities were there, the walls were white and the location was idyllic. There were French doors opening from every room – bedrooms included – onto the lawn that surrounded the cottage, and the views across the hills from the top of the garden inspired the peace and tranquillity we so badly needed. From the living room window you could see horses grazing in the steep fields that rose above us, and on the horizon, the naked branches of windswept trees looked jet black against the winter sky. One tree took on the uncanny form of the Statue of Liberty and I remember joking to Andy that we were living in our very own rural version of Manhattan. Rain would often fall horizontally across the fields, blown north by the insistent wind rushing up the valley to its freedom at the top. This was a truly wonderful place to be and as winter quickly blossomed into an early spring heatwave, we knew we had found our own little slice of heaven.

Rosie settled in well to her new surroundings, but the crying continued. We were desperate for answers so that we could find a way to ease her suffering but the only thing we had to go on was a foggy mixture of blind speculation, contradictory research and weak medical advice. It was like having a jigsaw puzzle but all the pieces were blank; even if we could fit them together, there was no picture to place Rosie in. Questions hung around us like fireflies dancing in an infinite sky, but the answers could never be found. We were completely out of our depth, with no option but to learn to swim and fast!

In July, just after Rosie's third birthday, our second daughter Grace was born in the birthing pool at Stroud maternity hospital. It was a lovely sunny day and after a short and easy labour, she floated up from the pool and straight into my arms like a water baby. She didn't cry but looked straight at me, totally present and alert. It was a gentle arrival – the drug-free birth I had always wanted – and I felt empowered by it.

Because the birth had gone so well, we were back home within an hour and Grace settled into the little wicker crib that I'd prepared in our living room. Andy, too buzzing to sleep, quietly mooched around making tea and writing emails, and I lay down on the sofa to doze, waiting for Rosie to get up. At 6am, she toddled out of her bedroom, rubbing her eyes hazily before climbing onto my lap for a cuddle. I said nothing about Grace's arrival and we sat and read *Charlie and Lola* together in the peaceful first light of the day. Grace stirred and made a little squeaking noise. This prompted Rosie to jump down off my lap and make a beeline for the crib – a small miracle in itself as she rarely took active notice of her surroundings. She leaned over the crib, peeked in, and met her sister for the first time. I sat in open-mouthed amazement, too stunned to speak.

'Aww,' she said, totally appropriately – just like any new sister.

'Rosie… that's the baby from mummy's tummy… she's here!' I said softly.

Rosie ran over to me, touched my belly with both hands, then padded merrily back to the crib for a second look.

'Aww baby,' she said.

I don't think there are any words to explain how miraculous that moment was. Having infrequent, often echolalic speech and no consistent way of showing her understanding of the world, I had no idea if she had any awareness of my pregnancy at all. In this rare and beautiful moment, she had somehow managed to come through her difficulties in the most profound way.

She scrambled back onto my lap and with tears in my eyes, I gave her a kiss and an affectionate squeeze and began the book again: 'I have this little sister Lola and she is small and very funny…'

That moment gives me hope. Even to this day.

★ ★ ★ ★ ★

Though we were going through the mill with Rosie, we were still having very nurturing threads running through our lives that were injecting normality and happiness amongst the emotional chaos. In so many ways we knew we were lucky. We loved where we lived, we had friends whom we adored, we had a beautiful brand-new baby and we had each other. We vowed to continue building our lives and remained positive: Andy started a job with a local furniture-making company; Rosie started a special-needs nursery school in Cheltenham; and I began learning the art of being a mum of two gorgeous little cherubs.

When at home Rosie still hated me moving from the sofa, but because I now had a baby to feed, she quickly adapted to not being able to sit on my lap by climbing onto my shoulders. We'd sit for hours like that, Grace contentedly feeding in my arms and Rosie sitting on my shoulders, playing with my hair. They were some of the happiest hours of my life – with my two girls wrapped around me, I had never felt so peaceful and whole.

Grace was strangely immune to Rosie's crying. She was never upset by it, and it never disturbed her sleep. It was amazing really; it was like she just knew.

The summer passed by quickly. Rich and Ele continued

to be constants in our lives, becoming godparents to Grace. Goldy and Bonnie would often drop round for a coffee. (Well, coffee and far too many chocolate biscuits… and the odd cake… OK *lots* of cake!) It was like our very own private mother-and-toddler group/cake appreciation society. The gossip, the laughter and our children running around us poured easy sunshine into all our lives distracting me from worrying about the seemingly endless stream of appointments that had taken over. There was one appointment that was particularly playing on my mind: a multi-professional meeting to see if Rosie warranted a diagnosis of autism.

The appointment was scheduled for the beginning of November, and when the day finally arrived Andy, Grace, Rosie and I squeezed into a doctor's tiny office with all the professionals that now saw Rosie and had 'the chat'. Rosie was three and a half years old. She fussed her way through the meeting and as they debated her future, I let their voices blur into a bubbling sea of words which blended uncomfortably with Rosie's discontent. I detached myself for a while, I knew where this formality was going and I allowed myself to fall into a numb trance, watching the freezing rain scattering its precious drops on the window, each reflecting a miniscule fish-eye view of the world outside. And in that muted absence of emotions, Rosie got her diagnosis of autism. It was something no parent in the world would want for their child, yet to hear them confirm our long-held suspicion was strangely relieving. Our instinct was right. They believed her autism was mild but warned us that her position on the spectrum might change depending on the speed of her development. This made her prognosis uncertain but at least a firm diagnosis gave us something tangible to work with.

In great British stiff-upper-lip style, we smiled, shook their hands and thanked them profusely for their time. We didn't speak the whole way home in the car. There was nothing worth saying.

Then as we pulled up in the driveway it was Andy who spoke.

'We're gonna do everything we can for that little girl,' he said softly. 'No matter what happens… we're not gonna let her down.' It was a pledge from the deepest part of his soul.

* * * * *

Discovering that your child has autism is a very tender process of adjustment, ending, of course, in acceptance and the celebration of their life as much as any other. It's a question of seeing what *is* rather than mourning what was 'meant' to be. After all, a child, first and foremost, is just that – a child. Then into the mix come their personalities, their quirks, their challenges, their needs. It's the parents that have to adjust their outlook on the future, for the child – innocent to it all – has never changed.

After accepting a new and unexpected life and discovering the surprising delights that this new life brings, there comes the startling realisation that getting something you didn't plan for can be so much more than heartache and hard work – it can also be rather wonderful – and it might just be the making of you.

By the time Rosie got her diagnosis, we could see how lucky we were to have her and what a boon it was to have her in our lives. We never ever said, 'Why us?' because when all was said and done, 'Why not us?' Someone somewhere was going to get this challenge – it's a statistical certainty. We knew we had more than enough love to give to a child needing a little extra care and consideration. To us, Rosie was a gift. Yes, she was challenging. Yes, she was putting us through our paces. Yes, her tantrums drove us round the bend, but she was also funny and captivating and full of life. And as another, blustery, copper-toned autumn surrendered the last of its majesty to a cold, skeletal winter, we muddled on – still together, still a family, still happy.

CHAPTER FIVE

THE CATALYST

People often say that life is a series of lessons. And in the February that followed Rosie's diagnosis of autism, Andy and I were about to learn an especially cruel one: that bad decisions can sometimes come from following good intentions, especially when instinct or reason has been blinded by hope, or swept aside by 'expert' advice.

It had only been three months since the diagnosis and our lives had become taken up with a raft of clinical tests in an attempt to ascertain the cause of her problems. First up was a hearing test. We were told that if a child's speech is not developing properly, then hearing (or lack of it) is often the culprit – so we were given an appointment at a special clinic at Gloucester Royal Hospital where they would conduct a series of play-based aural tests.

When we arrived, we were taken to a playroom where Rosie did a magnificent job of blocking out the world by sitting serenely on her chair, quiet and detached like a transcendent Buddha, while the nurse tried every trick in the book to attract her attention. She rang bells and set off noisy toys but nothing worked. It didn't matter how loud or soft the sound was or where it was positioned, Rosie didn't even twitch let alone turn to see where the sound was coming from. Not even her eyes betrayed a much-hoped-for flicker of registration. Either she was actively and expertly ignoring the nurse and her 'silly' tests, or she was profoundly deaf.

'We have two options,' said the ENT (ear, nose and throat) consultant after analysing the results. 'We either leave her as she is, not knowing whether she can hear properly – which could be affecting her speech and communication – or we give her a hearing test under a general anaesthetic and get some firm answers.'

I frowned at Andy with an almost undetectable shake of the head and he looked back at me with eyes that said 'No way'. We both knew that having a general anaesthetic carried a risk and keeping Rosie safe was our top priority.

'Too risky,' said Andy, turning towards the consultant. 'I say, we don't do it.'

'Yes, but if she is not hearing you, she could be being held back developmentally for a reason we may be able to fix,' the consultant replied.

'I'm pretty sure she *can* hear us, despite her not reacting to your tests,' Andy replied flatly.

'Look, I can understand your reservations,' said the doctor, 'but it's a case of risk versus potential reward. As a doctor I would advise you to allow your daughter to have the test because there's a strong possibility that she has hearing problems. We're only putting her under a light anaesthetic for a short while and the risks are extremely low. Honestly, I wouldn't give it a second thought.'

But we did give it a lot of thought. Mostly because we were pretty sure she could hear us, but in the end we betrayed our first instinct and chose to have the procedure done. It was the logical thing to do. We knew that if she was deaf, her life could be changed dramatically with a hearing aid. Perhaps she would learn to talk. Perhaps she would start to develop normally. It was a dangling carrot of hope we just couldn't resist. We didn't know it then but it was a catastrophically bad decision and one we'd come to bitterly regret.

On the day of the anaesthetic, Rosie was wheeled from her hospital bed in the day unit to the operating theatre in a great mood. Yet it was one of those moments – those 'if only I'd known' moments – that you look back on and wish you could have pressed an emergency STOP button and changed the outcome. If Andy and I could have foreseen the suffering that was about to come, we would have scooped our precious daughter into our arms and run. Instead, filled with hope, we sped along the long corridor towards our fate like lambs to the slaughter.

We were greeted by a smiling nurse, whose uniform was covered in primary-coloured balloons.

'Hello, lovely one,' she said bending down to Rosie's eye level. 'In a little while we'll go down to the Special Theatre, but we need to get ready first, OK? Follow me.'

Rosie blanked her, but the nurse continued smiling anyway and helped push the bed into an enclave just off the corridor where a few other anxious-looking patients lay in their beds waiting for their various operations. Andy decided to take Grace to the hospital café and Rosie, much to my relief, decided to take a nap, so I perched on the bed next to her trying to control my nerves.

After a few minutes the same nurse returned and wheeled Rosie's bed into the shiny sterile environment of the operating theatre where a small team awaited us: another nurse, an anaesthetist, and the surgeon performing the procedure.

'I'm going to put this mask over her face which will make her drift off to sleep,' said the anaesthetist cheerfully. 'As soon as she's asleep you can go back to the ward and wait until we call you.'

'I'd like to be here when she wakes up if that's possible,' I replied purposefully. 'Can you *definitely* call me just before… she might get scared otherwise.'

'Yes of course,' he replied reassuringly. 'I'm going to put the mask on now…'

Still drowsy from sleep, Rosie allowed the mask to be placed on her face and I squatted beside her looking into her eyes with the most gentle and comforting smile I could muster. Holding her hand I began to count very softly, 'One, two, three, four…'

Her eyelids blinked heavily until they finally gave way to the drug.

'OK, love, you go up to the ward and I'll call you soon,' said the nurse touching my shoulder. 'She'll be OK.'

I stood up and headed for the door. 'Thank you, nurse,' I replied, glancing over to Rosie lying as if lifeless on the operating table.

Andy was on the ward reading Grace a picture book when I found them. Grace reached out to me sweetly and I sat in the chair next to the empty space where Rosie's bed had been to breastfeed her. Andy looked pale and pensive.

'She was really good, Andy,' I said as reassuringly as I could. 'She just lay down and fell asleep like a little angel.'

'Aw, bless her,' he replied, a faint smile tweaking the corner of his mouth. 'I bet the test comes back fine.'

'Yeah, Sod's Law,' I agreed, 'and she'd have gone through all this for nothing.'

'Well not for *nothing*... at least we'll know for sure that she can hear properly. Never again though. I hate hospitals. The clinical smell is like... blech!'

I laughed. 'Hope we're allowed home straight away. Rosie's going to be climbing the walls when she wakes up.'

When your child is in hospital under a general anaesthetic, the wait for them to come out of surgery seems like an eternity, but in real time it can't have been more than an hour before a staff nurse came up to tell us she was out of theatre and in recovery. A wave of relief poured over both of us. It was over. All we needed now were the results and permission to go home.

'Thank you, nurse, thank you so much. I'll go down right away,' I said, handing Grace to Andy.

'Give her a kiss from me,' he whispered.

'OK I will. Love you, Ands, I'll see you in a minute.'

'Love you too.'

I raced to the recovery room. There were a few other patients coming out of their induced slumber, some trembling – all looking like death warmed up.

I heard Rosie well before I saw her. The room was filled with her cries. I could tell she was both confused and distressed. As I rushed to her side I instantly felt guilty for what we were putting her through and angry with the nurse for not getting me sooner. We couldn't prepare her for the operation and now she couldn't communicate why she was distressed.

'It's OK, she's just having a little trouble adjusting to coming round from the anaesthetic, it happens from time to time,' said the nurse, putting an oxygen mask on her face which only served to muffle the cries. I felt helpless. All I could do was try to comfort her.

I don't know why, but as we wheeled her back to the children's ward, she began to calm down. Perhaps it was the whirring sound of the wheels as we whizzed along the linoleum-clad corridor, or the repetitive blur of lights above her head, flashing her into woozy submission, but gradually she fell back to sleep and when we arrived back on the ward she was tranquil and dozy.

'My God, did she scream!' I whispered.

'Oh no! Poor thing!' said Andy, handing me a sleeping Grace before rushing over to see her.

'It's all right, she's better now,' I reassured him. 'She'll wake up in a mo and we can go home… I swear I'm never leaving that hillside again!'

He smiled at the thought of our little home haven.

'An episode of *Friends* and a cuppa tea when we get back,' he replied chirpily.

'The "Andy and Kara" antidote to stress!' I joked.

'Anyway,' he continued, getting back to the point, 'are we going to find out if any of this was bloody worth it?'

'The surgeon will come and tell us in a bit,' I replied. 'It's OK, hun, we'll be out of here in an hour, tops.'

'Well, all I can say is thank God the kids are asleep!' Andy joked.

'Too right. Oh the chaos they could be causing if they were awake!'

We fell into silence for a few minutes until the surgeon walked in, still in his scrubs and Crocs.

'Well, good news!' he said loudly, waking up both children at once. 'Rosie's test came back fine. Her hearing is perfect.'

'Great news!' said Andy. 'Sad we had to put her through all that to find out, but a relief to know she's fine.'

'Well that's one more thing to check off the list,' replied the surgeon, before adding: 'How's she doing?'

'Well, only just waking up, but fine I think.'

'Great. Well, when she's woken up properly, had something to eat and drink and found her feet, you can go home.'

Rosie, now wide awake, had spotted a boy in the bed opposite us eating a packet of crisps. Thrilled that she had discovered her favourite snack, she jumped off the bed and darted towards him enthusiastically.

'Watch out, Andy, she's going to go for the cri…' I began, but he was already on her trail, picking her up before she could get within crisp-grabbing distance. She twisted in his arms.

'Uh oh. Here comes a tantrum!' said Andy with a frown.

'Can't you discharge us now?' I pleaded to the surgeon. 'She's going to be impossible to contain in here. Can't we just take her home straight away, she's fine now… look!'

The surgeon smiled. 'Well she's certainly not wobbly on her feet! We'll see what we can do. Why don't you take Rosie down to the playroom and I'll ask the nurse to get your discharge papers.'

The playroom was small, bright and inviting. Toys, books and craft materials sat temptingly on every surface within reaching distance of even the smallest toddler. The minute we arrived, Rosie was set to chaos mode. A green plastic cup full of pencil crayons caught her attention and she ran towards them with a little whoop of excitement. From experience, I knew she wasn't interested in drawing and I wasn't close enough to stop her so I called out, 'Rosie, no!' as she casually grabbed a handful of the crayons, stood purposefully back and opened her hand.

'Woo!' she said in celebration as they clattered onto the floor. Then she did a happy little hop and watched eagerly as they rolled in every direction.

We were not alone in the playroom and a few of the parents sitting quietly with their children looked over at me quizzically as I ran to tidy up.

'Let's put them back,' I said patiently – almost melodically, trying to look calm and nonchalant. Rosie squatted down and grabbed one of the crayons, thrusting it into her mouth.

'Out of your mouth, Rose,' I said, quickly removing it. The thought of all the children coming in here touching the toys and spreading their various illnesses which, frankly, put them in hospital, was not a good one.

'This is a nightmare,' I muttered to Andy, who was playing with Grace.

Luckily, the nurse came in almost immediately with our discharge forms and Andy handed me Grace so that he could sign us out. I watched as Rosie wandered across the room heading for some books. Suddenly, she stopped in her tracks and turned around. Then with a jerk she began to shake and lose her balance. She stumbled back a few paces but it was her face that alarmed me. Her eyes had suddenly become vacant, her face pale. She began to lose consciousness.

'Andy... Andy! Quick...! Rosie!'

Andy instantly dropped the pen and it fell as if in slow motion as he dashed across the room, catching her just before she hit the floor. She twitched uncontrollably in his arms, eyes blank and dribbles spilling out of her mouth.

'OK, let's get some help,' said the nurse. So we ran back to the ward with Rosie limp in Andy's arms, still twitching and beginning to go blue. The nurse led us to a bed and dashed off to get a doctor.

Suddenly she stopped twitching and colour returned to her face.

'Rosie, Rosie!' I called in the same voice I would use to wake her in the morning. No response.

'Kar, she's breathing... don't wake her. Leave her to sleep it off,' Andy interjected. He was stroking her hair, white with fear but still level and composed.

'What the hell was that? Looked like some sort of fit,' I said in a wobbly voice. Unconsciously, I rocked Grace back and forth on my hip as if to soothe her but she was fine, gurgling happily and sucking her fingers.

'Oh my God, that freaked the shit out of me,' he said finally. 'Where the hell is the doctor?'

When the doctor finally arrived we described the incident as clearly as we could.

'OK, has anything like this happened before?' he asked looking unworried.

'No, never. But what happened – it didn't look normal,' I said, pressing him to take us seriously.

'I don't think it will be anything to worry about,' he said dismissively. 'When she wakes up we'll examine her and if she's fit and well, send her home as planned.'

'What!' said Andy when he was out of earshot. 'Nothing to worry about. Jesus! Who are these people…? I just want to get us out of here.'

I nodded with wide eyes.

'Bloody hell, Kar, you look like you just jumped out of the way of a speeding bus! Sit down a minute. Let's try to stay calm.'

I grabbed Grace a rusk from my bag, which was hanging on the arm of the pushchair, and came back to sit. By the time I returned, Andy was hunched over the bed with his head in his hands.

'Hey, you've got to stay calm too!' I said, trying to lighten the mood.

Then out of nowhere, Rosie began to shake and stiffen and go blue. She was making a strange clicking sound with her mouth like a failed swallow.

'Oh – aagh! It's happening again… NURSE! Can we have some help over here? Can somebody help us!' called Andy desperately. There were children in beds all around us and one parent dashed off to get us a nurse who took one look at Rosie and rushed off to find a doctor. A different one returned with her just as Rosie stopped jolting and fell unconscious for a second time. Again we described what had happened.

'Sounds like it could be night terrors,' he said in a tone so dismissive I wanted to scream.

'I'll make a note of it and we'll keep an eye on her, see what happens,' he said walking away.

'That was NOT night terrors!' I said indignantly. 'Something is wrong, Andy, I can feel it.'

'OK. OK, let's not get ahead of ourselves. That might be the end of it, whatever it was.'

We sat as calmly as we could. Grace had picked up on our anxiety and started getting fractious so I let her have a chocolate bar.

'Thank God for junk food!' I said to Andy, with a gentle smile.

We both stared at Rosie for signs of waking up. We both desperately wanted to go home, irrationally believing that escaping back to our normal lives might make it all go away.

Then, like a nightmare, another attack possessed Rosie's body – this time more violently. Again we called for help and this time doctors and nurses swarmed around her and we were asked to get out of the way. Horrified, we stood helpless as oxygen masks were thrust onto her face and IV drips were put back into her arm. She shook and looked grey and a little stream of blood leaked out of the side of the mask trickling down towards her ear. The panic, the dread, the fear, was overwhelming. I thought she was dying and I could tell from the look on the doctors' faces that they were gravely concerned. Voices were urgent, body movements swift, faces deadly serious. Something was injected into her drip and she stopped shaking. Her bed brakes were released and they began to roll her away.

'OK, Mum, we're going to take your daughter up to HDU so we can have someone with her all the time. If you'd like to follow?' said a nurse.

'Um, OK…what's happening to her? Is she OK?' I asked, visibly shaking.

'Well, we don't know yet, but we've managed to get her stable for the moment. We'll get her up to HDU and do some more thorough investigations.'

'What the hell is HDU!' said Andy under his breath as we sped up the ward.

'I think it stands for High Dependency Unit,' I replied. My head was spinning. Grace was still on my hip but I hardly noticed she was there. All I could focus on was Rosie, with an oxygen mask on her face, unconscious.

'Why oh why did we let her have a general?' I fretted. 'I could ki…'

'… ick myself,' Andy finished. 'My God, Kar, what have we done?'

HDU in the children's ward at Gloucester hospital is a small, light-filled room with two beds at opposite ends. It has huge windows down one side taking up a large proportion of the wall. It's a room with a view – across industrial Gloucester – which on this particular day looked grey and devoid of all joy in the grip of winter's steely vice. The only redeeming feature is the outline of Gloucester Cathedral, piercing the monotony of concrete lines with its tall and elegant spire.

The room is pleasant enough. Colour is jovially splashed in primary reds, blues and yellows on clown curtains surrounding the beds, and heart monitors, oxygen masks and drips are the *décor du jour*. It's clean and smells, well, like hospitals – and it's the last place any parent would want to be with their child; when you come into HDU you are entering the scene of your own parental nightmare.

Facing the reality that your child has been placed in one of these rooms is a terrifying ordeal but the staff nurses – who are stationed there 24/7 – become a much-needed lifeline. Always smiling, quiet and reassuring, they are nothing short of amazing with the children, which is a great comfort to helpless and panicking parents of very sick children.

The first thing they did with Rosie was to wire her up to just about every machine available to man. She was put on a saline drip to make sure she had fluids, and wires were attached to little sticky discs and put on her chest, wrists and legs to measure her heart rate and monitor her breathing. She looked like a rag doll on strings.

After this ominous-looking procedure, Rosie experienced her fourth episode, which was looking more and more like some kind of epileptic fit. By the fifth I began to panic that this was never going to end. She seemed unable to wake up. Every time her consciousness surfaced, she'd have another huge fit that would stop her breathing for so long she would go blue. Machines would bleep, oxygen masks would be thrust on her face and doctors would be called. We were petrified.

It suddenly dawned on us that if anything was going to happen to Rosie, family and close friends should know now, so we began to phone people from the reception desk. Poor Ele bawled so loudly that I wasn't quite sure what to say to calm her down. My Christian friend Jo formed a prayer group. We were grateful to have so much love and support around us, and with everyone rooting for Rosie, we felt stronger. Phoning my mum was hardest of all. Somehow it made things real – it validated things. It took the possibility of it all being some kind of bad dream and made it actual. She told me to stay calm and take things one step at a time. And that's exactly what we did. It was all we could do.

After a few hours we were joined by a family with a daughter who had suspected meningitis. She must have been only two or three years old – another parental nightmare playing out vividly before us.

The nurse immediately told us that HDU was no longer a safe environment for Grace.

'Can you not get a babysitter?' she asked, in a soft Irish accent.

'Not at this short notice,' I replied. 'Besides, she hasn't been away from me yet.'

'OK, Mum, I'll see if I can get you some accommodation in the hospital… In the meanwhile, I've got a nice pram you can borrow that will do as a bed for your baby. You could take her to the playroom perhaps, or to the café…'

No. Longer. Safe. The nurse's words rang in my ears and had the effect of making the hospital environment feel like a virus-infested deathtrap. As I took Grace down to the playroom I couldn't help but think about those Dettol adverts where germs become visible cartoon characters that inhabit all our household surfaces and multiply like rabbits. I could almost see them creeping silently away on the walls, the floors, hanging in the air – despite the ward being scrupulously clean. Rosie *had* to be here, I reasoned. If she caught another disease in the process there was nothing we could do. Grace, on the other hand, was only nine months old. She was far too little to deal with threats like meningitis and MRSA. All she wanted to do was crawl around on the floor and innocently shove toys in her mouth. I hated having her with us but neither

Andy nor I could think straight enough to come up with an alternative.

During the day we split our time between the playroom, the café and the hospital shop, and every three hours Andy and I would swap duties. At night they gave us accommodation in the bowels of the hospital, where throat-drying air-conditioning meets shock and partial sleep in timeless limbo. At changeover time, the one who was with Grace would push the pram down a maze of dimly lit, silent corridors back to the children's ward. We'd whisper updates at the doors of the HDU and briefly embrace before parting to continue our nightmare alone.

★ ★ ★ ★ ★

Dawn brought new hope. Rosie had stopped fitting for at least two hours. She was finally responsive and drinking. By breakfast she was sitting up in bed and eating toast, still wired up to the nines – but we had real hope that her ordeal was over. Things still looked good by the doctors' rounds at 9am and we were discharged by three o'clock in the afternoon. Despite having overheard one doctor conceding to a colleague that he had seen 'one other case like this following a general anaesthetic', the medical staff insisted that what had happened was in no way related to any kind of bad reaction. Instead, they insisted the whole incident was a coincidence.

'So, you're saying to me that if we hadn't brought her into hospital for an anaesthetic she'd have had all these episodes anyway,' said a furious Andy.

'Yes,' said the doctor emphatically, 'pure coincidence.'

We were incensed by this. The probability of them being right was infinitesimally small, but what power did we have over the word of a qualified doctor?

If he had said to us, 'I have seen one other case in my career and I'm sorry, but a very rare complication to having a general anaesthetic appears to have triggered seizures in Rosie,' we would have felt more at peace. But to be told there was no link whatsoever exasperated and confused us beyond measure. Perhaps they were just covering their backs. People sue for practically anything these days.

We went home feeling shell-shocked and angry – but at least we were home – our little isolated nook, on a rolling limestone hill of grass and winter mud. The nightmare had abated but by the weekend we were back in hospital with more of what the doctors now believed to be epileptic fits. The doctors discussed anti-epilepsy drugs but we were reluctant. We wanted to be sure that this wasn't just the tail end of a toxic reaction to the anaesthetic before putting her on medication for the rest of her life. Besides, after the big denial over the anaesthetic, we didn't exactly trust them. The doctors agreed, and discharged her on condition that we commence treatment if she had any more seizures.

A week passed by, then another, and we both cautiously supposed that Rosie was getting better. She was very tired and withdrawn but she was growing stronger every day so we tentatively began to get on with our lives again, building back to our usual routine. Whilst all this was going on Grace was beginning to talk, point, wave and play constructively. We were relieved to see she was developing normally and delighted in every new development. Her rude health was a boon to us, bringing a sense of balance in a very turbulent time and her sunny nature brought smiles to us all – Rosie included.

By the Sunday Rosie had caught a sickness bug and our day was taken up with keeping on top of the chaos that ensued.

'Oh isn't life a peach!' Andy quipped, as he handed me a sick bowl. He had the wonderful quality of finding comedy in almost anything.

'Let joy be unconfined!' I replied, smiling broadly.

'Hey, Kar, we've run out of nappies,' he said, in a more serious tone. He hadn't left me home alone with Rosie since her last fit. 'I reckon things are OK enough now for me to just nip down the shop… I'll be back in, like, half an hour.'

'Yeah, go for it,' I replied, trying to sound upbeat. 'We'll be fine. I think we're out of the woods now anyway.'

The phone rang.

'OK, so I'll see you in a bit, yeah?' he said, waiting for my nod, before rushing to answer it.

The sun streamed through the window warming the back of my head and despite the threat of snow on the weather forecast, winter was momentarily chased into an early retreat. As I listened to the babble of Andy's voice on the phone, the jangle of car keys and the front door click shut, I gathered my steel, closing my eyes for a second. 'I can do this. We'll be fine,' I said out loud.

'Book!' declared Grace, who was sitting on the carpet, merrily turning the pages and pointing to the pictures inside. Rosie was snuggled into me on the sofa, smelling faintly of vomit, delicately holding her eyelashes with the tips of her fingers, humming.

Suddenly and without warning, she exhaled a strange shouting noise and began to shake. 'Oh my God, oh my God…' I said, springing to my feet in a panic. She was fitting again. I lay her on her side on the sofa.

'Oh no! It's OK darling… Mummy's here,' I said, feeling at once the pointlessness of my reassurance. Blue and jerking, a little pool of blood gathered on the sofa cushion. I wiped her mouth with my sleeve.

'Come on, Rosie, breathe… just breathe,' I chanted under my breath.

'Book!' declared Grace again, oblivious to the unfolding crisis.

'That's right, sweetie! Book!' I replied, in a state of autopilot. 'OK I need the phone…' I muttered to myself, looking to see if Andy had left it within arm's length. 'Ambulance… I need an ambulance.'

I couldn't see the phone but I couldn't leave Rosie during a fit and I was beginning to panic as the length of the fit extended from one minute, to two. Finally, she began to breathe normally and fell into a snoring sleep. Red-faced and heart pounding I ran to find the phone, but it was nowhere! Frantically, I tore the house apart, clothes and cushions flying in all directions.

'No phone, no fucking phone…' I said to myself, too frantic to care about the 'don't swear in front of the kids' rule.

'OK, Kar, take a breath… it must be somewhere…'

Then it dawned on me… Andy was on the phone to someone or other before he went out. My heart almost stopped.

'It's in his pocket,' I whispered to myself in horrified revelation. 'It's in his sodding pocket!'

Rosie needed an ambulance and there was no way I could contact the outside world. This is where I can safely say I went into irrational mode. Cogent thought utterly deserted me. Some people keep it together really well in a crisis and I'd done OK during past tribulations, but on this occasion, I have to confess, I failed quite spectacularly. Of course, I didn't want to leave Rosie in case she had another fit, but we needed medical help – and fast.

'If I run,' I thought to myself, 'I'll get to the neighbour's house in about one minute.' I grabbed Grace and ran outside to the front gate. Then I stalled, running back in to see if Rosie was OK. I ran out of the house again, this time reaching halfway across the road before returning. I just couldn't leave her. What if she choked on her own vomit? Seconds after getting back into the house she had another fit.

'Come on, Andy, come home!' I said, hoping that somehow he could telepathically hear me.

'OK, OK, think, think, THINK…! Right, email!' I yelled to myself after the fit had subsided. I ran back and forth from Rosie to the computer like a headless chicken and mumbled to myself like a madwoman as I tried – for the first time in my life – to send an email.

After several frenzied attempts, I managed to work out how to get to the 'Compose' box, so I typed a desperate message: 'If anyone gets this message can they please phone for an ambulance straight away. Rosie has had another fit.' I typed a few names in the 'To' box: Mum, Goldy, Andy and pressed 'Send'. It didn't work of course and brought up a yellow box saying there was a problem with the email addresses.

'Shit… fuck… come on!' I said, frantically pressing 'Send' over and over again.

Then I heard the rumble of an engine and the rasping noise of a handbrake.

'Thank God!' I sighed, as I heard Andy's feet crunching over the gravel towards the front door. He breezed into the kitchen holding several bags of shopping.

'Flipping heck, Kar, what's happened?!' he said, looking round at the contents of our house strewn across the floor. He smiled questioningly at first, then he saw my face and his smile dropped.

'I… I… couldn't find the…' I stuttered, 'Rosie. She's had a fit. I was looking for the phone… We need to call an ambulance. Now! You see I couldn't find…'

Andy closed his eyes and cringed as he slowly pulled the phone out of his pocket.

'I must have put it in my pocket without thinking. Idiot!' He slapped his head with the palm of his hand then walked towards Rosie who was sleeping on the sofa, pale and twitchy.

'OK. Let's not wait for an ambulance, let's take her in the car.'

'Have you got stuff for the freezer in these bags?' I replied – clearly still in shock.

'Sod the bags, we're going now! You grab Grace.'

When we arrived at Stroud Hospital, Rosie was thankfully rushed in and assessed. We explained what had happened: the anaesthetic, the multiple fits, the sickness bug. Torches were shone in her eyes and to our dismay we were sent home!

'I don't think she'll have any more,' declared a rotund nurse in her matronly tone.

'Look, I'm not being funny, nurse, but she could well fit again... and if she does, it could be dangerous.'

'Well, if she does, then she needs to go to Gloucester hospital.'

'Bu...'

'It's OK, Kar. Let's take her home and see what happens,' Andy conceded.

I breathed out a sigh of defeat and we prepared to leave but I instinctively knew where this was going...

Of course, we didn't get out of the hospital before Rosie fitted again and we were transferred from there, by ambulance, to Gloucester hospital – me in with Rosie and Andy following with Grace in the car.

The fits continued in the ambulance, which had to stop intermittently to administer diazepam and give her oxygen. With each seizure, Rosie's condition deteriorated so we wove through the traffic with the lights flashing and siren wailing. It all felt so surreal – I couldn't quite believe what was happening.

The next twenty-four hours were a blur of sixteen full-blown tonic-clonic seizures, which the doctors could not get under control. We were back in HDU and Rosie was so poorly that she couldn't hold her bottle, let alone figure out how to suck from it. When she opened her eyes there was no recognition in them. As well as the big tonic-clonic fits, where she would jerk around and foam at the mouth, she also had little partial seizures that she'd tragically try to fight before they consumed her. There was also one curious little fit where just one pupil rapidly expanded and contracted. That little one scared me the most. We were told to look out for one pupil being bigger than the other because it could be a sign of brain damage. Terrified, I told the nurse, but she dismissed it. I don't think anyone was catching onto the seriousness of the situation. We were even moved out of HDU as the fits continued! I had never felt so helpless and desperate in all my life.

On the first night, Goldy, like an angel, came and got Grace so we could both concentrate fully on Rosie, then in the morning she brought her back for a feed. (I was still breastfeeding and by the time she arrived my boobs were like agonising blocks of concrete!) In the days that followed, I lived for those visits. Grace was a ray of sunshine, a vivid, smiling connection to normality.

On the second night, Andy went home to look after Grace. Now alone, my feelings amplified. I was swimming in a sea of terror and love. The terror I expected, but the love took me completely by surprise. I found myself sitting deep into the night with this silent, raging, desperate, endless, exquisitely painful vigil of love that would burn for Rosie's well-being as I watched her sleep. To take my mind off things, I'd flick through the pages of the only reading material in the room: *Hello!* magazine and the *Holy Bible*. The heady combination of stress, worry, seizures and lack of sleep, coupled with updates on the Royal Family, details of Madonna's latest plastic surgery and promises of God's holy salvation, made me feel like I was slowly going mad.

At night, the ward was hollow and quiet but for the occasional patter of footsteps and the buzz of the doorbell. Occasionally a nurse would slip into the room, lift one of Rosie's eyelids and shine a torch in her eye. Rosie never reacted to the light; it was as if she wasn't there any more.

I couldn't sleep so I turned my chair a little towards the window and drawing my knees up to my chin, sat in the dark looking out over the city. The weather had turned cold again and a couple of inches of snow covered the rooftops. The city looked cleansed, quiet – ethereal even – as if the snow had brought it peace.

The sound of the door opening caught my attention and I was surprised to see Goldy walk in.

'Hi Kar,' she said quietly.

'Goldy! What on earth are you doing here? It's two o'clock in the morning!'

'Yeah, I know, I couldn't sleep. Thought I'd pay you a visit.'

I rose to give her a hug.

'I can't believe this! You're amazing, Golds... I've been going a bit stir-crazy,' I whispered, almost falling into her arms. 'You're a nutter coming all this way... and in the snow!'

'Don't be silly,' she whispered back, giving me one of her ample Goldy hugs. It was so comforting that for a second I escaped my world.

She sat with me in the dark as I relayed the events of the day, then got up and stood pensively at the window, remaining there for a long time after I'd fallen silent. Outside, plump flakes of snow floated silently in random directions through the still air.

'She's lucky to have you, Kar,' Goldy said at last. 'You and Andy are going to get through all this.' She turned to me and smiled warmly before adding, 'With a little help from your friends.'

'It's times like these when you see who your true friends are,' I replied, smiling back and standing up to join her.

I could see the maternity hospital beyond the car park below us and counted along the windows locating the exact room where Rosie had been born. Memories of Rosie's birth flashed into mind: how happy we'd felt, the elation on Andy's face when he became a father for the first time and my first moments of holding Rosie, looking at her perfect little fingers and toes and tucking them snugly back into her blanket. They all seemed so poignant now. I looked back at Rosie, sleeping in the half-light, wired up to monitors and a drip.

'Three and a half years ago, I was in that room over there giving birth!' I said gesturing towards the building.

'No!' Goldy replied, leaning forward and placing her hands on the windowsill. 'Is that the maternity hospital?'

'Yeah! That's the exact window, Golds… the third one in… see it? I would never have imagined then that we'd be up here now, going through all this.'

She turned to me, 'Me neither. Now, Kar,' she said, changing the tone 'I've gotta tell ya, please don't be offended, but you look like shit!'

'Thanks!'

'Well, I'm your friend – and you do. You don't smell too clever either. When's the last time you ate? Or had a shower, or brushed your teeth?'

'God only knows.'

'Well you've got to sort yourself out. You'll fall apart otherwise.'

She was right. I didn't really care about me any more. I had greasy hair and had been living on chocolate bars.

'Well, listen, Miss Skuzzy, go have a shower and get something to eat. I'll watch Rose.'

It was the nicest thing a friend could have offered.

★ ★ ★ ★ ★

On the third night, after another day of unrelenting seizures that baffled the doctors, Andy sent me home to get some clean clothes and have some time out.

'I'll be back before you know it,' I promised.

'Take as long as you need. Have a nap! Kick back for a couple of hours,' Andy replied sweetly. He settled in the chair next to Rosie and I left them reluctantly. Outside, the hospital car park was empty and dark and the sound of a city fox crying in the distance made me jump so I hurried to the car. But the further away I walked from the hospital doors, the more I wanted to go back. Driving away was one of the hardest things I've ever done. *If something happens to her when I'm not there I'll never forgive myself*, I thought.

It was a half-hour drive home so I pulled into the nearest garage to buy some petrol and grab a snack. At the till I was suddenly overtaken with the urge to buy cigarettes so I asked for a packet of Golden Virginia and some blue Rizla.

I hadn't smoked for years but the skill of making roll-ups came back to me as easily as riding a bike. As I pulled out of the station I lit up and inhaled deeply. Then I coughed. Then laughed. Then cried. I was terrified that this whole episode was going to end with Rosie either severely brain-damaged or worse. I knew from what the doctors were telling us that Rosie wasn't recovering. It felt like we were losing her. She no longer recognised me, or reacted to her surroundings. 'What's going on? Why's this happening?' I asked myself. Then I began to feel angry. How could someone so small and innocent be subjected to something so cruel? I had always believed in some kind of higher entity, but if there was one, I was sure that he or she had certainly abandoned us. It was the first time in my life I had lost my faith and suddenly I felt truly alone. I bawled and sobbed and smoked all the way home.

★ ★ ★ ★ ★

The next morning, a very switched-on doctor finally came onto the ward and seemed to know exactly what Rosie's problem was and how to deal with it.

'Your daughter has non-convulsive status epilepsy with breakthrough seizures,' he said, in a businesslike manner. 'We're going to try her on some new drugs. We have to break her out of it as soon as possible.'

'Pardon my French but what the hell does status mean?' Epilepsy sounded bad but *status* epilepsy sounded horrendous.

'Status is where the brain is constantly fitting and can't break out of it. Your daughter is in a serious situation. If she is not out of this cycle in four hours from now we're going to have to transfer her to Frenchay Hospital in Bristol and have her put into an induced coma under deep anaesthesia. A ventilator will control her breathing, it's the best we can do.'

Horror doesn't cover how we felt. It was now clear that Rosie wasn't just fighting against her epilepsy – she was on the verge of fighting for her life.

The doctor ordered Rosie back to the HDU and despite the shock of her prognosis, we were relieved that someone finally had a handle on things.

Over the course of the day Rosie was given a bucketload of new medications and an EEG (electroencephalogram) test confirmed that she was finally out of status. We couldn't have been more relieved.

The fits under control, we spent a few more days in hospital for observations and Rosie started a heavy regime of anti-epilepsy medication. During the day I'd carry her round the hospital ward to give her a change of scenery but I could see from her expression that she barely noticed. I imagined that her unfocused eyes would see little more than a blurred trace of colour and shape as we paced the corridors. I wondered if she was ever going to be the same again.

Rosie improved a little every day and after ten days we were finally sent home.

If it had felt surreal going to the hospital in an ambulance; it felt more surreal bundling Rosie into our car and taking her home. It felt like we'd been away for an eternity, and we were returning, battered by the cards life had dealt us. So when we walked through our front door and into a spotlessly tidy house we were overwhelmed! Goldy and our good friend Rowan had cleaned it from top to bottom and Bonnie had baked a quiche and stocked the fridge with milk, salad and fruit. We were overwhelmed by their kindness. To have support like this from our friends made us feel like we could survive and move forward.

We were in and out of hospital almost weekly from then on and over time a pattern to Rosie's fits emerged. They appeared to be triggered by common viruses like a stomach bug or cold. She'd fallen into a vicious cycle of catching a bug, having a cluster of fits, going back to hospital, recovering, and then going back to her nursery school where she would pick up a new virus. What's more, she was appearing to regress. We hadn't heard her speak in weeks. The few words she'd had in her repertoire were now replaced by repetitive guttural sounds. We believed that this was down to her never having enough time to recover between seizures. It was heartbreaking to witness and we knew that something had to change. But what?

The pressure, the lack of sleep and Rosie's constant meltdowns and seizures sometimes got too much and Andy and I began to have explosive rows. Memories of slamming doors and speeding up the lane in the car to God knows where (only to ring and apologise from the phone box down the road) remind me of how much we were drowning.

I finally hit rock bottom one afternoon in April when I ended up sitting on the front step of our house, crying hysterically. I can't remember the trigger but there must have been a catalyst that had made me snap, like an argument or a seizure or something small like stubbing my toe… Anyway, all I can remember is wondering how I was going to find the strength to carry on and leafing through the phone book to find the number for the Samaritans. I wasn't suicidal but I just couldn't see how to go forward. In that moment I couldn't see a single chink of light at the end of what felt like a very dark tunnel. Then a thought struck me and I decided not to dial. It was a very simple one but it changed everything: 'You may feel like you're drowning right now but one day all this is going to be in the past. Just hold on, have patience, and let time change things.'

I thought about the summer and the changing seasons and made a mental note to come and sit in the same spot in

September and see what had changed. 'For better or worse, things will be different then,' I told myself.

I couldn't have guessed what those differences would be if I'd lived a thousand lifetimes… And if a fortune teller had told me that in just three months' time I'd be standing with my four best friends, on a stage in front of a screaming crowd, naked as the day I was born… I'd have told them they were crazy and asked for my money back!

CHAPTER SIX

BARE NECESSITY

It's hard to talk about friendship without sounding clichéd. It's the same with love. Talk about love and there is the danger that you will come across like a long-haired hippy who is lost in ideals that no longer have top priority in this hard, competitive world. Well, dear reader, I'm going to go out on a limb; I believe in love and I am lucky enough to know the meaning of true friendship and the power of a good community. All this, I can say without a single doubt, I owe to Rosie. No, I haven't been smoking wacky baccy, or suffered a nervous breakdown after writing the last chapter (it was close), I'm stating my case because without the support of my extraordinary friends and the backing of my community I would never have been able to achieve everything I've set out to do for my daughter. I believe now, but I didn't then. Back then we were still reeling in the aftermath of the onset of Rosie's epilepsy, wishing it had all been a bad dream.

'Acceptance, like forgiveness, can be one of the hardest things in the world,' Bonnie said to me after we'd got back from one of our hospital stays.

'OK,' I replied slowly, wondering what she was getting at.

'It's like, you have to take what life throws you because it's tangible and absolute. The act of *acceptance*, on the other hand, like forgiveness, is a choice.'

'Hummm. What are you trying to say, oh wise one?' I joked.

Bonnie didn't find it funny. 'Look, hun, you and Andy haven't had it easy lately and we're all worried that if you can't come to terms wi—'

'No, no,' I interrupted, putting my hand on her arm. 'Compared to what some people have to deal with, it's OK. *We're* OK. Well, we're not… we couldn't be more tired and drained and falling apart at the seams – but you know what I mean! We have no right to stew in our own misery. Not really.'

Bonnie laughed. 'No. That's not *acceptance*! You're contextualizing it!'

An image flashed into my mind of my wispy-haired angelic toddler possessed by a seizure, and hatred for the condition instantly filled my heart. I couldn't deny it, I loathed everything about epilepsy and I resented it imposing itself in our lives. It gave nothing but pointless suffering in its arresting paroxysmal grip.

'Autism I can deal with,' I said, thinking about Rosie's quirky, selfless, feisty personality. 'It's part of who Rosie is. There is something amazing shining out of her that she owes to being autistic.'

'And she changes everyone she meets,' Bonnie added smiling.

'Yes she does. But the epilepsy, Bons,' I continued, with

agitation creeping into my voice. 'There's nothing positive about it, if you know what I mean. I'm sorry, but I hate it. I never really knew hatred before this.'

'Well, you've got to drop it and fast, because thinking like that will destroy you,' she insisted. 'OK. Look at it this way. You have no power or control over the fits. Love it or hate it, epilepsy is in your life now. But if you look at it like an enemy it's going to eat you up. Acceptance is your only option if you want to stay sane – and you have to stay sane – your family needs you.'

Of course, she was right. If we were to obtain a smidgen of sanity, we had to deal with the epilepsy with acceptance, hope the medication would eventually ease her symptoms, and forgive ourselves for making the choices that had led us here.

★ ★ ★ ★ ★

The fallout from the sudden and severe onset of her epilepsy was mammoth. A squalling torrent of clinical and genetic tests engulfed our days and haunted our nights. Rosie was poked, prodded, scanned and jabbed like a pincushion for a wealth of diseases and syndromes from fragile X syndrome to cancer. Clinicians dispassionately debated and defined our daughter's potential prospects until we wanted to scream. She was under the care of a paediatrician, a neurologist, a geneticist, an educational psychologist and a speech therapist, who often contradicted each other's opinions and sent us into a tailspin of confusion. We had no choice but to learn to live with the worries and uncertainty of Rosie's potential prognosis and develop the skills to see all the good in each day. Needless to say, we didn't always succeed.

Funnily enough, though, the antidote to the stress about Rosie was Rosie herself. She would still cry several times a day (which, let's be honest, is never easy) but when she was calm, she was charming and fascinating. The way she looked at the world often had me transfixed. She didn't have the same priorities as everyone else or the same interests. For example, she loved the stones on our driveway and would sit for hours scooping up handfuls, lifting them skyward and letting them tumble from her hands; she loved bending forward and running across the garden with her hands stretched behind her back like wings; she was fascinated by leaves and would watch them, spellbound, as they shimmered in the breeze; and she would sit on my lap and look so deeply into my eyes that I felt as though she could read my soul. It was easy to be in awe of her and the unfiltered way she approached her life. I recall a day when we had what I call 'tropical rain', huge raindrops of great volume, surrendered by heavy cloud. Rosie was standing looking through the patio doors, transported by the drama of the moment, so I opened the door – just to see what she'd do. She stepped outside without hesitation, turned her palms upward and stood perfectly still as if drinking in all that the rain had to offer her senses. Then, she walked to the front gate and watched in wonderment as our steep driveway transformed into a river, carrying with it stones, leaves and mud. She saw the magic of the moment and revelled in it whilst the rest of the world rushed on and I remember thinking how exceptional that was. These were the moments that filled our lives and our hearts, and we made the best of every day, never venturing much past the fields that surrounded us and living simply.

As we settled into our new lives, it became clear that accepting a situation didn't mean inaction or giving up. As far as we could see we had problem-solving to do that involved a good deal of forward-thinking. Our days were spent working out new ways of approaching our situation, and our evenings in front of the TV were replaced by hours of squinting at articles on the computer, until in the wee, small hours, our eyes watered too much to see the screen and our bodies hungered for sleep.

Slowly but surely we began to hatch a plan.

To try and gain some control over Rosie's seizures, we decided to actively avoid the viruses that were triggering them, so we made the radical decision to take her out of nursery school. Though fallible, the plan worked quite well; if people had colds or tummy bugs, they just didn't visit us. Of course, she still got the odd illness but we found that we were spending a lot less time in hospital, which was life-changing for us all.

Now that school was out of the mix, education became a big issue so we turned our research to home education programmes specifically designed for children with autism. There were two stand-out methods: Applied Behaviour Analysis (ABA), and Son-Rise. Both methods advocate one-to-one teaching and both claimed to have transformed the lives of autistic children. They offered tailor-made programmes of education built around the abilities and challenges of each individual child. We loved different aspects of both methods and were thrilled when we found a facility, called Growing Minds, that combined the two. We knew that giving Rosie this opportunity would be her best chance to thrive but there were two obstacles that made this dream almost impossible to achieve: the Growing Minds facility was in America and to implement it would cost upwards of £17,000 per year to run. We knew we had to find the money from somewhere, but how? We had no savings, we rented our house, our car was worthless…

Basically, we were skint.

Days passed and Andy and I could think of nothing short of robbing a bank that would magic that kind of wedge, so I invited Bonnie and Goldy round for a morning of brainstorming and coffee. They agreed to come over the following day.

It was mid-June and the morning had brought with it sun. The girls arrived at eleven, children in tow, so I opened the double doors to the garden to increase their play area and let in the scented summer air. Grace and Ronan (Bonnie's second child who is the same age as Grace) speed-crawled round the living room together like two peas in a pod, and Lily (now three) mothered them both by giving them toys and leading them round the house pretending they were dogs. Oli, Ronan's two-year-old brother, joined in by saying, 'Mine!' taking the toys from the little ones and running off into the garden to hide them. It was a typical toddlers' scene of early interaction.

Rosie, however, was seated on the living room carpet, oblivious to it all. She had some Duplo and was taking them out of their box, one at a time, before patting the pieces on her mouth and discarding them. She was happy. Lost in her own little world.

I made coffee and we settled near Rosie on the sofa. Then, in detail, I explained our situation to my two best friends.

'Well, there's nothing for it, Kar, we're just going to have to raise the money somehow,' said Bonnie in her deliciously creamy voice.

'Yes, but how?' I replied a little desperately.

'Well, we could have some coffee mornings…'

'Yes, but imagine how many coffee mornings we'd have to do to raise £17,000… How about I jump out of an aeroplane, or do a sponsored fast or something?'

'You'd need a hell of a lot of sponsors, but *I'd* support you!' said Goldy sweetly.

'Ah, thanks Golds, but you're right – I'd never get enough sponsors. Trouble is, there are about a million other worthy causes and I need mine to stand out somehow… I've got to do something *so* brave and *so* crazy, people will want to part with their cash.'

'Climb Mount Everest?' suggested Bonnie.

'Go on the game?' teased Goldy.

'With this body! No one would have me!' I quipped, grabbing my wobbly belly and giving it a shake. We all laughed and took a simultaneous sip of coffee before falling silent for a while, searching for that genius idea.

'I know,' said Goldy at last, 'I'll ride a horse down Stroud High Street, naked like Lady Godiva!'

'That is *soooo* Goldy!' laughed Bonnie.

I could picture it perfectly: Goldy, embellished with body glitter, riding side-saddle on a dapple grey, a look of liberation on her face. Then I realised that as Rosie is *my* daughter, *I'd* have to do the riding.

'Well, I couldn't expect you to do it, Golds, and to be honest I haven't got the bottle…'

'Well, I have. And don't be silly… of course I'd do that for Rosie.'

'Maybe we should *all* do it!' Bonnie joked, but there was a hint of conviction in her voice. 'We'd be the talk of the town!'

'Yes we would!' I added. 'I can see the headline: "Big mamas on horseback bare all for Rosie!"'

'Oh, *I* know,' said Goldy, clearly on a roll. 'Let's do a striptease. Like on that film *The Full Monty*!'

'Oh no. Absolutely not!' I said almost spitting out my mouthful of coffee. 'We're girls for a start. Besides, I'd rather jump out of an aeroplane five times over than get naked in front of people – and that's saying something 'cos I'm terrified of heights. I'm not like you, Golds… you put the "sex" in "sexy". I'm about as sexy as a bag of peas!'

'No you're not, sexy mama,' said Bonnie in an American accent. 'You've just gotta work it, girlfriend!' She clicked her fingers like a diva, much to the amusement of Lily who had come to see what all the excitement was about. She copied Bonnie's actions to a tee, blonde ringlets swaying as she shook her head.

'Work it, girlfriend!' she echoed.

'Go Lily, go Lily,' sang Bonnie encouragingly. Lily trotted round in a circle, arms waving and squeaking with excitement, her white cotton dress puffing out with the motion.

'See? If Lils can work it, so can you!' continued Bonnie.

'No I can't! Have you not *seen* me? I can't pull a sexy face to save my life!' I attempted one of those faces where a woman with lustful eyes looks a man up and down – and ended up looking like I had something in my eye. We all fell about laughing.

'Seriously, Kar, I think we're on to something here,' said Bonnie. 'I'm up for it, Golds is up for it… C'mon. What do you say? We could get all fit and healthy. I bet everyone in town would come and see our show.'

I looked at Rosie sitting on the floor tapping yet another piece of Duplo on her face and realised that this was one of those pivotal life decisions where everything can either change in a heartbeat or stay the same forever. It was a no-brainer. It was time to put my prudishness to one side and take the plunge.

'OK, I'll do it!'

'Great!' said Goldy. 'But we need more people. Five girls would look better than four and we definitely need more than three…'

'What about Ele?' Bonnie suggested. 'She's your other closest friend, Kar, she might be up for it.'

'Yes,' I agreed enthusiastically. 'Plus she is HOT! Shall I ring her?'

'Yes! Do it *now*!' said Goldy, almost hopping with excitement.

I ran to get the phone and called her at work.

'Hamptons International?' resounded a voice so posh and so clear I knew it must be Ele.

'Els! Sorry to call you at work…'

I explained everything as succinctly as I could: the education programme, the fundraising, the idea of stripping for charity… 'So we were wondering if you would join us. We need five girls.'

'Of course!' she said without hesitation. 'I'd do anything to help Rosie.'

'You're a total angel, Ele. Thank you!'

'All right, darling, I'll call you later,' she said, as if her boss was listening.

'She's in!' I cried as I put the phone down. We were jumping up and down in our seats now. Three women with a mission that could change everything.

'Brilliant. Ele is sizzling hot – great eye candy,' said Bonnie. 'Now all we need is to find one more girl – The Fifth Element.'

We all had some girlfriends in mind.

'Oh my God, I'm scared now. This is really happening, isn't it?' I said with my hands over my mouth. We all looked at each other in stunned excitement. It was beginning to dawn on us what this was going to entail.

'This isn't going to be a picnic in the park, you know,' I warned, offering a final get-out clause.

'No. It's going to be the biggest and most exciting challenge of our lives,' replied Bonnie with gleaming eyes.

'Huge,' agreed Goldy, a cheeky smile spreading across her face. 'Tell you what, come round to mine tonight and we'll have a go.'

'OK. I guess if we can't do it in front of each other, we can't do it at all!' I replied with rising nerves.

'Well, I can't tonight,' said Bonnie, 'but you two go ahead. And tell me what happens. I can't wait!'

She stood to put her coffee cup in the sink, then, sporting a mischievous smile, sauntered back towards us, giving us a naughty wink as she pulled the neckline of her top to one side exposing her shoulder.

Goldy wolf-whistled. 'Get you, you saucy little minx,' she said encouragingly.

Secretly I was FREAKING OUT! Years later I found out that we all were. Could we do this? Were we mad?

'OK, Golds,' I said with a degree of reservation. 'I'll come round after I've put the kids to bed.'

'Cool. I'll charge up the video camera so we can play it back and see how we look.'

★ ★ ★ ★ ★

That evening, I couldn't contain the broad grin that kept spreading across my face as I trundled our trusty old car along the narrow leafy lanes towards Goldy's house. 'I'll wiggle my hips, swing my clothes around my head and smile a lot,' I thought as I drove, casting my mind to an image of a 'girl who wants to have fun', rather than a 'pole dancer in a strip club who wants you to put ten-pound notes in her knickers'.

I didn't want to be that girl and I wasn't capable of it. Not in a million years.

The closer I got to Goldy's house, the more the nerves, excitement and anticipation overtook me. If we couldn't perform a half-decent striptease in front of one another, the plan for Rosie's education was doomed. A lot was riding on the next couple of hours, so there was a fair amount of pressure to sizzle.

As best buddies we were close, but stripping naked in front of each other (you might be glad to hear) was not our average girlie get-together. Besides I didn't really do 'sexy'. I knew Goldy could pull it off though. She oozed sex appeal and lived through it. From her ample cleavage to her voluptuous curves, she strutted the streets of Stroud like it was a Mecca of opportunity.

I, on the other hand, was not having a very 'sexy' time. I was about as out of touch with 'hot and horny' as a girl could get. Sleepless nights, tantrums, seizures and endless worrying were not the recipe for channelling one's inner goddess. Sizzling, in my case, was a little unrealistic.

Goldy greeted me in the kitchen by swiftly placing a glass of red wine in my hand.

'Dutch courage, love!' she said with a twinkling smile.

'Have you charged up the video camera?' I asked, after taking what could only be described as a desperately large sip.

'Charged up and ready to go!'

'Well, there's nothing for it then…'

'Nope!'

Our eyes met and we both tittered a little nervously. I reached into my pocket and pulled out my tobacco.

'Pre-strip roll-up?' I asked, waving them temptingly.

'Absa-friggin-lutely!' she replied, heading towards the front door.

We sat on her front step.

'I'm going to give these bad boys up when this is all over,' I announced as I rolled mine.

'Yeah, yeah,' Goldy teased, lighting up hers with amusement.

'You'll see!' I protested, reaching for the lighter.

We sat in silence for a while, smoking our cigarettes, drinking our wine and feeling braver with each sip.

'Right then,' said Goldy, rubbing her hands together. 'Let's pick out some music and get down to business!'

We spent the next half an hour or so gradually loosening up by listening to snippets of music from the internet and dancing around the computer. We decided to stay away from the overtly sleazy tunes of a strip club and go for a fun, funky, slinky tone. Destiny's Child, Boney M, Madonna and Ella Fitzgerald all got an airing before we finally settled on *You Sexy Thing* by Hot Chocolate.

I volunteered myself to go first. Rosie was my daughter, so it was only right for me to step up and strip down. As I took my position, facing away from my singular audience, Goldy ran to the computer, pressed play, and made a dash for the camcorder. I could hear squeaks of excitement behind me as she dived onto the sofa before the introduction of the song kicked in.

I tapped my left foot to the beat, waiting for the lyrics and trying to create an element of suspense, before spinning round as dramatically as I could on the words, 'I believe in miracles, where you from, you sexy thing.' I winked at the camera and peeled off my decidedly unsexy woolly cardigan, swinging it round my head, hips swaying from side to side. I felt just about as frumpy and clunky and awkward as a baboon at a debutantes' ball. *Right! Props… I need props!* I thought, spinning round again to scan the room. I spied a trilby hat and headed – as sexily as I could – to grab it, twirling… and dropping it, before putting it on with a little and very un-stripper-like half curtsy. This is when I noticed the camcorder in Goldy's hand shaking – she was almost crying with laughter.

'You want laughs? I'll give you laughs!' I joked, flinging off the hat again and (I have to use this term loosely) 'performing' my best moves with comic exaggeration, driven by the desire to keep her laughing. It was a last-ditch attempt of masking my self-consciousness. I unbuttoned my trousers wiggling them 'seductively' down to the floor, kicking them off like someone who'd just discovered there was a bee inside them. Then I got down on my hands and knees and gyrated about a bit to uncontrollable hoots of laughter from Goldy.

In short, I was about as sexy as a soya bean.

Suddenly, half of the song had passed, so I decided to jump to my feet (like a sex bomb, of course) and whip off the rest of my clothes at top speed, so by the end of the song I'd end up starkers. By the time I was flinging my ample pants across the living room, however (and wishing Goldy had shut her curtains), I was pretty sure she couldn't really see me anyway from the tears of laughter that were streaming down her face. But I'd done it. Strip one was complete.

Goldy did a better job of course, grabbing the broom from the kitchen and circling it seductively as I giggled behind the camcorder and watched aghast through the slotted fingers of one hand as she peeled off her clothes one by one. I'd like to say she learned from my master performance – then improved and embellished it – but that would be stretching it. She had the sexuality to pull off a few half-decent moves and look quite seductive to boot. She was still funny, though, and by the time she was naked, her modesty was shielded by *my* wall of tears. The hilarity of the whole situation couldn't be ignored, but at least we'd completed what we'd set out to do.

'I haven't laughed like this in what feels like forever!' I said, wiping my eyes.

'Well, we may have murdered the art of stripping, but we did it,' said Goldy with a smile that said, 'It's game on.'

Somewhere, tucked away in my cupboard, that video tape still exists, along with a stack of baby videos. Trouble is, I didn't label them all properly and weeding it out always seems to stay on the bottom of my to-do list.

So one day, forty years from now, I bet I'm going to be sitting with my grown-up children and grandchildren one snowy Christmas and someone's going to say: 'Granny, can we look at Mum's baby videos?'

I (now all doddery and forgetful) will say in my sweet old granny's voice, 'Yes dear, of course you can.'

Then the tape of me and Goldy stripping and crying with laughter will flash up on the screen – probably in 3D by then – and I'll break a hip trying to wrestle back the remote control.

Ele, Bonnie, Goldy and I spent the next few days phoning our girlfriends in search of a fifth member. A few said, 'I'd love to, but I just haven't got the bottle,' but the most common answer was, 'I'd love to, but my boyfriend/husband won't let me.' After a fair few 'noes', it began to dawn on me that my triumvirate of best friends were either fiercely independent or they had very understanding men in their corner.

Andy didn't bat an eyelid when I told him our plan. He instantly sensed the spirit of the idea and the weight of the challenges that lay ahead. He knew how hard we'd have to work to achieve our vision and admired our bravery. I couldn't have wished for a better reaction.

One of the biggest challenges we faced was body confidence. Goldy, Bonnie and myself were normal, everyday women who'd had a couple of children each and bore the stretch marks to prove it. For whatever reason, we'd never shed the baby weight gained as we'd become mothers. We weren't supermodels or actresses who make a living from their slender forms, and our partners loved our wobbly bits, so there was no real pressure to snap back into shape. We just embraced (and sometimes hated) our new bodies like a million other mothers out there whose focus has shifted to their offspring.

I think it could be said that I had embraced the frumpy mama mindset a bit too much: bad hair, tummy like rising dough at a baker's shop, bags under my eyes. I was a shell of a woman, one who'd been to hell and back and it showed. I hadn't seen a shaver in months, I had bushy eyebrows and hated my body so much that I was embarrassed to let even Andy see me naked – except in *very* favourable lighting. In short, I'd lost all pride in my appearance and had let myself go. In my case, the feeling of being a 'sex bomb' was a whispering memory belonging to my early twenties and up until now the probability of seeking to regain it was about as unlikely to happen as Tom Jones calling round for a cup of tea. (Although, Tom, if you're reading this, do come round, you're very welcome.) To recoup enough inner confidence to embrace my body even just for me would take a massive leap of faith – so the thought of finding the confidence to work my booty, naked, in front of hundreds of people was terrifying.

For Goldy, becoming a charitable stripper was just the tonic she needed because she was in the throes of splitting up with Nige, her boyfriend of ten years. Although it was her decision to end the relationship she was still sad, especially for their children. The break-up had inevitably knocked some of the wind out of her sails, robbing her of her usual Goldy bravado. Years later she told me that the minute we'd hatched the idea to strip, her life became vibrant again, full of excitement and possibility. All she needed to do was to recapture her usual 'va va voom' and the rest would fall into place.

Bonnie had her Italian Stallion husband, Jon, to contend with. Even though I got the impression he wasn't at all sure about the whole thing, as the strong and silent type, he didn't say much to Bonnie about the commitment she had suddenly thrown herself into. He liked Bonnie at home bringing up the boys. He liked her role as a lamb in the kitchen, tiger in the bedroom. He liked to come home from his day's work as a blacksmith to a hearty home-cooked meal accompanied by a nice glass of *vino rosso*. Jon was all man, and it wouldn't be easy for him to see his wife up on the stage, naked for all to see. But he was also a moral man and was devastated to see Rosie going in and out of hospital all the time. He loved Rosie, who always made a beeline for him when he came round to visit. She liked Jon's calm steadiness. He wanted her to have the chance of a better life as much as Bonnie, hence the silence, but I was well aware that it was a big ask to let his wife become a charity stripper. Not that she asked… He could have thrown an outsized, hot-headed Italian rage and it wouldn't have stopped her.

Ele was as strong-minded as Bonnie and didn't consult her boyfriend Rich before committing herself to the group.

'Predictable,' she said, when I asked her what his reaction was. 'He got very rambunctious and chased me round the kitchen.'

Ele was the only one with performance training and if she was nervous she never showed it. She had an incredible body – slim but shapely, not unlike Dita Von Teese – and she had no post-baby body issues to overcome. Eight years younger than us, she was eight years smoother. She had perfect pins (without a single ripple of cellulite), glossy hair, great skin and a slim waist with a perfectly flat stomach.

'Don't worry, Kar,' joked Goldy during a late night 'fear of nudity' phone call. 'She'll be the "go to" body when we're all finally naked. Her perfect bod will just draw their eye and stun them.'

A few days after we'd formed the group, we all got together at Mills Café in Stroud for our first meeting. Rosie had kept me up most of the night and she'd spent most of the morning in tantrum mode, so Andy ordered me to go.

'Have a little time out with your friends,' he'd said.

Goldy and Bonnie didn't know Ele very well but they instantly clicked and within minutes they were laughing together, swapping stories and discussing their reservations. I could see a kind of electricity building, a sense of chemistry and camaraderie. We had a mission in common that had now bound us in adventure, excitement and trepidation. And as I sat back in my chair, sipped my latte and watched them giggling at the thought of what was to come, I could only savour the wonderful joyous feeling of what it was to have a friend. A true friend that would go to the ends of the earth for you – one that would help you find the strength to accept everything that life brings and strive to make a difference.

CHAPTER SEVEN

PRACTICE MAKES PERFECT

From the moment we'd committed to becoming charity strippers, the idea took on its own impetus and momentum, propelling us into territory we had never imagined we'd tread. I had taken on the task of planning the event and was swept straight into action, but it didn't take long for me to realise the scale of the task ahead and the impact it was going to have on my family. A venue needed to be located and hired for the show. Once the fifth member had been found, there would be five costumes to make; five girls with busy schedules to juggle for rehearsal time; there were photographers to find; posters to make; and advertising to organise. An ever-growing to-do list vied for attention amongst the dinner-cooking, nappy-changing, breastfeeding, house-tidying, shopping and nurturing that being a mother entails. Add to that lack of sleep, tantrums, epilepsy, autism, communication difficulties and hospital dashes and you have a pretty good idea of what I was up against. Luckily for me, Goldy quickly became my 'partner in crime' which was a huge relief. We both knew we'd taken on a crippling amount of work but in many ways that was the magic and excitement of it; we were rising up and fighting to make a difference – and together we felt like we could take on the world.

If we were going to achieve our goal and raise the money Rosie so badly needed, we knew we'd have to captivate the imagination of the whole town.

'All we need to do,' Goldy said, 'is tell all our friends and see if it snowballs. If we can show people we mean business and we've actually got the bottle to do this thing, people will hopefully get behind us. If we can't get support from the locals we're finished.'

She had a good point. At the end of the day this was a money-making operation and generating a buzz would be paramount to our success in regard to selling tickets to our show. Luckily, we had a touch of scandal on our side (we were getting publically naked after all) so we hoped to get tongues wagging just on the strength of that. But would people get behind us? It didn't take long for us to find out.

Before we knew it news of our Full Monty antics began to spread beyond our circle of friends and into the wider community. To our delight people were entering into the spirit of what we were trying to do for Rosie. The mix of adversity, bravery and titillation proved to be a winning formula and we couldn't have been more thrilled, or more relieved, by the feedback. Now we could be a little more certain that our venture was viable.

Most pressing on the agenda – even before recruiting the fifth girl – was the need to think up a name for our budding striptease ensemble.

'What we need is a simple name that will encapsulate everything that we stand for,' I said to Goldy when we'd got together to brainstorm.

'It has to say fun, frivolity and brazen bravery,' she agreed, lifting her arm and signwriting the qualities in the air as she spoke.

'The Montettes?' I volunteered.

'No, there's nothing remotely "ette" about us.'

'The Boutalicious Babes?'

'Nah.'

'Rosie's Angels?'

'No, sounds too much like *Charlie's Angels*… What about The Booty Girls?

'A bit call girl-ish.'

'Big Mamas Go Wild?' Goldy suggested with a cheeky grin on her face.

'My God, yes!' I replied, playing along.

'I can see paddling pools full of foam and naked mud-wrestling…'

'Maybe not!'

'Hummm. Might bring in the wrong clientele…'

Finally, after another stream of rejects, in a eureka moment, it hit us.

We rang Bonnie to break the news.

'It couldn't be more succinct,' she said. 'It says we're willing to do anything to help Rosie and it says we're going to get naked to achieve it. Perfect!'

And just like that, the Full Monty Girls were born.

★ ★ ★ ★ ★

From the get-go we decided to set the bar high. The last thing we wanted to do was draw in a ticket-paying audience then fumble our way red-faced through a striptease that would have them all cringing. We wanted our performance to be professional enough to leave our audience inspired and wanting more, but like a phoenix rising from the flames, if we were to get anywhere near to achieving this, we would have to make something amazing rise out of next to nothing.

Before we even started on the rehearsals, Goldy would come round to my house every day without fail (as long as we weren't in hospital with Rosie) and we would spend hours working out a master plan. By day we'd listen to music, looking for a perfect collection of songs that we could blend into a kind of stripping mega-mix, and by night we'd speak on the phone whilst watching stripteases on YouTube. It wasn't long before we found ourselves drawn into the sumptuous world of burlesque. Legendary burlesque divas like Dita Von Teese and Gypsy Rose Lee captivated our imaginations and fuelled our ideas. They made the removal of clothes an expression of femininity itself, emphasizing the 'tease' in 'striptease'. There was nothing sleazy about their performances – it was like watching art.

Burlesque is a flamboyant world of peek-a-boo. Feathers, frills, frivolity, fabulosity and, of course, flesh make each performance an indulgent celebration of the buttery and oh-so-dreamy curves of the female form. Sumptuous costumes and lavish props make burlesque a feast for the senses – one that appeals not only to men but is also inspirational for women because burlesque performers can be curvy and voluptuous as well as slim. In fact, whatever your size – big, small, slender or bootylicious – burlesque embraces all as a celebration of womankind. Because in burlesque, it's not what you've got, it's how you use it.

For us the discovery of burlesque was a revelation. Though Goldy was curvy and body-confident, neither of us realised the full power of a woman's curves until we clapped our eyes on those YouTube videos. We hoped we would be able to harness the tongue-in-cheek humour and vintage flair of the burlesque artiste and give it our own unique twist. We would have one thing in common with the Playboy bunny-type stripper though – we were going to be completely naked by the end of the dance. Only for a second – before the stage lights went down and darkness concealed us – but naked nonetheless. Most burlesque performers don't get fully naked, flirtatiously stopping at nipple tassels and frilly knickers, but for us, ending up in the buff was part of our message. It shouted: 'We dare to bare for the good of another!' It was a cheeky act of bravery that would hopefully inspire people to support our cause. It was also the moment in the dance that we feared the most. The titillating act of stripping would be fun but the moment of undress was a petrifying prospect – not least because we weren't twenty-one any more. Our audience would not see a line-up of neat gym-honed honeys; they would see a group of ordinary women with all their imperfections on show. Stretch marks, cellulite, the lot.

A few days before our first rehearsal, I took the infamous video of our first strip to my friend Jo, who had worked as a professional dancer for the band Hawkwind.

She was originally from Yeovil, but had moved into the area to live with her boyfriend in a top-floor housing-association flat overlooking Stroud High Street. I called in mid morning. The sun streamed hot through the big sash windows into her immaculate living room, amplifying the smell of washing, which was drying over a clothes horse in the corner.

'Coffee, love?' she said, heading into the kitchen.

'Yes please, I'm dying for one this morning,' I replied, following her. 'Rosie hardly slept a wink last night.'

She eyed me sympathetically. 'Well, now's the time to have a little R&R,' she soothed before putting the kettle on and leaning out of the window to light a cigarette. 'Ah, that's better,' she said, in her rolling West Country accent. 'Apart from no sleep, what's going on with you, Kar? It's been ages since we had a good ol' gossip.'

'Well, you're not going to believe this…' I began.

Jo is like a fake-tanned, perfectly made-up, fashion-forward version of Alice Tinker, the verger character in Dawn French's *The Vicar of Dibley*. They share the same blonde hair, thin face, come-to-bed eyes, and innocent sauciness.

From the second we'd met, our yin and yang personalities united in laughter and I'd often drop round for a chinwag. Jo is naturally funny and big-hearted, and like Andy has a wonderful ability of finding comedy in every little thing, making her easy company. Our sense of humour is perfectly matched and as we're both romantics at heart we'd spend hours either laughing at the silly little details of life or wondering why the people of the world wouldn't just cheer up, love each other and live in peace.

When I explained to her about the Full Monty Girls and showed her the video her reaction was a fit of giggles followed by serious deliberation.

'Oh my giddy aunt,' she said after viewing it. 'If you lot are going to get naked and keep a bit of the ol' dignity, you're gonna need the help of a choreographer!'

'I know... and that's why I'm here,' I replied, not beating around the bush.

'I kind of figured that!' she laughed. 'Look, what you've done so far is a beautiful mess... but yes, I think I can sort you all out. I mean I've never done anything like this before, but I'd to like help. Plus...' she chuckled, 'I'm free of charge!'

'Oh thank you, Jo!' I replied, putting my arms around her. 'I thought you'd be up for it.'

'And I am,' Jo said, growing more serious. 'But I'll tell you this... there's a lot of work to do and if you want me you're going to have to work hard and I mean *really* hard to get it right.'

From day one she was chomping at the bit to get us into a rehearsal because she, more than anyone, knew the hard work that lay ahead of us. As far as Jo was concerned, if she was going to be our choreographer, failure was *not* an option and she was going to work us like a dance teacher from an episode of *Fame* to make us reach our full potential – whatever it took.

Goldy and I began looking for a cheap dance studio of some sort. We explained our situation and what we were trying to do for Rosie and it wasn't long before we found a scruffy little whitewashed dance studio in the centre of Stroud at a reduced rate. It smelled of dusky incense, had an old piano in the corner and its wooden floor was smoothed brown-black by years of yoga classes and play rehearsals.

As the girls arrived one by one to our first rehearsal I was overawed by their dedication to Rosie. They all wore the same exultant expression – that of a woman on a mission – and they had the light of a generous heart sparkling in their eyes.

I had brought a CD player, four red feather boas, three poles (that Goldy and I had unscrewed from two brooms and a mop) and one golf umbrella (because between us we didn't have another mop and it was the only other pole-like object around the house). The atmosphere was a mixture of anticipation, adventure and electricity, which filled the room and rippled between us with hugs, greetings and nervous chatter.

When Jo arrived we could tell she meant business. She was dressed for the part in leggings, complete with pink legwarmers and a long-sleeved hoody with 'Just Do It' printed on the front. We automatically hushed as she crossed the room, then she faced us and put her hands on her hips, instantly asserting her authority.

'Was it something I said?' she asked, laughing.

'No, no! But look at you… wow, Jo! You look like a *real* dance teacher!' I said, stunned by her appearance. Then I turned to the group. 'Everybody… this is Jo!'

'Just call me *Miss*,' said Jo, erupting with laughter again, clearly loving her new role. 'Well I know you, Goldy, but this must be Ele… and you must be Bonnie.'

She greeted them warmly before walking back to the centre of the room and spinning round to face us.

'OK you lot!' she said with a firm-but-fun tone. 'We've got a lot of work to do, and if we want to make this show blow peoples' socks off, it's got to be good. Correction! It's got to be blinding!' She was pacing her end of the room now, like a lecturer fired up to motivate her students. 'For us to produce a show worth anything at all,' she added, 'I need 100% commitment from *all* of you. When we're here, we're here to work!'

I glanced at Goldy and we exchanged excited grins. We were at the starting block of a journey so unexpected that it felt unreal – like being in a film, or watching somebody else's life.

Without hesitation Jo made a beeline for the CD player and thrust in a disc. 'I've brought some music for a warm-up. Does anybody have any dancing experience?' she asked.

'I did ballet when I was five,' I volunteered, 'but I was too knock-kneed to get into first position!'

This produced a ripple of giggles from the girls.

'Oh dear,' said Jo, scanning the others as if to say, *Someone throw me a bone here*.

'I go to belly-dancing and salsa classes,' said Goldy, primly.

'*You* should be fine then, Goldy,' smiled Jo. 'What about the rest of you?'

Bonnie shook her head and looked at Ele who said, 'Well, I've just finished a degree in theatre studies.'

'Get you!' said Jo, teasingly. 'You won't have a problem either as long as you've got a bit of rhythm.'

'My main worry is that I won't remember the routine – I can't even remember my own name half the time,' I confided. I'd been worrying about it for days; the last thing

I wanted to do was let the side down. All the tiredness and stress at home had taken their toll on my ability to think straight. 'Oh, and I can't tell my left from my right...' I added quickly.

'No hope for you then, Kar!' said Jo with a grin.

'Or me!' said Bonnie. 'I've never been to a dance class in my life!'

'Don't worry, folks, it'll be all right on the night as long as we put the work in,' said Jo. 'So let's get started! We'll just have to take the plunge and see how we go.'

She bent down and pressed play on the stereo and as we stood waiting for the beats to start I had a flashback to being fourteen years old at a local disco where everyone was standing around the edge of the room, too inhibited to dance. I suspected that in the case of the fledgling Full Monty Girls, if we hadn't had a choreographer to take charge we could have easily done the same. I could see how valuable Jo was to our motivation – and ultimately our success.

'Right, you lot. This is the moment of truth!' she shouted, as the introduction of the song kicked in. 'Get into line and copy me!'

DJ Casper's *Cha Cha Slide* was the emerging tune, which raps instructions like: 'Slide to the left... Slide to the right... Take it back now ya'll... One hop this time... CRISS CROSS!' – all set to a funky beat.

It goes without saying that we made a total pig's ear of it at first, bumping and crashing into each other whilst trying to keep up with Jo, who of course, had the moves down to a tee. It was like a bad aerobics class on Prozac, but at least we'd broken the ice.

'Excellent!' said Jo, chuckling to herself as she paused the CD. 'Now Kar, you and Goldy have been looking for music, so spill the beans… what have you got so far?'

I hastened over to my bag and grabbed a disc. 'Well, these are our six favourites,' I said heading towards the CD player.

Everyone gathered round and we sat on the floor to listen.

'It took us hours to whittle it down, so we hope you all like what we've come up with,' added Goldy. 'We thought we'd make the final cut together as a group. Me and Kar will go and see our mate Chas on Monday and get it blended into a mega-mix.'

The song choices were: Prince, *Kiss*; Kylie Minogue, *Slow*; Peggy Lee, *Fever*; Shirley Bassey, *Big Spender*; Nancy Sinatra, *These Boots were Made for Walking*; and a burlesque classic – the 1957 brass-band ensemble entitled *The Stripper* by David Rose. Luckily, the girls loved most of them and after much deliberation we settled on a blend of *Kiss*, followed by *Fever*, ending with *The Stripper* for the finale.

'All in all, that gives us about fifteen minutes to get from suited and sexy to gloriously naked,' I calculated.

'It's going to be scintillating,' said Bonnie confidently.

'It's going to have to be,' said Goldy with a deadpan expression.

'Ever the realist!' I said, poking her with a broom handle.

'OK let's take a break,' said Jo, 'then we can make a start on the first song.'

We pushed open the fire escape and ventured onto a wooden balcony for a cigarette. Of course Ele was far too disciplined and sensible to smoke, but she came out anyway and we leaned over the railings, chatting fervently like a group of fag hags having a good old gossip over the garden fence. But the subject, of course, was all Full Monty.

'Who's going to be the fifth girl? How are we going to get people to turn up to the show? What will we wear? What props should we use? What will be our unique style?' Every topic was injected with a torrent of ideas. This constructive banter was balanced by the not-so-secret desire to emigrate to the other side of the world and escape our fate. 'How scared are you? What are you eating? How are you getting fit? Who have you told? What did they say?' Everyone had different views, but as we hashed out the details, one phrase united us all: 'I can't believe we're *actually* doing this!'

'I was at mother-and-toddlers today,' said Bonnie, 'and we were talking about jobs and I said, "Actually, I'm doing the Full Monty to raise money for a little autistic girl…" I just said it! Then I went bright red!'

'That was brave. What did they say?' I asked, imagining a scene of wholesome Stroud mothers spitting out their sips of herbal tea as Bonnie dropped the bombshell.

'Well,' she replied with a cheeky grin, 'they were fascinated and suddenly everyone was chatting and laughing – it all got a bit rowdy, it brought the room to life!' She paused for effect and looked at our open-mouthed reactions. 'Anyway,' she continued, 'one of the mothers, who is now a born-again Christian, said to me, "You're never going to believe me but, before I found Jesus, I was a stripper in a strip joint in London!" She just came out with it! I mean you'd never have thought it in a million years!'

'That is *brilliant*! Th—' began Ele.

'Hang on, hang on, it gets better!' Bonnie interrupted. 'She's offered to come to next week's rehearsal and give us some tips and a demonstration!'

'Yes, yes! Invite her!' we all said, in an excited scrabble. Then I glanced at Jo who looked like her nose had been put a little out of joint.

'As long as she doesn't have anything to do with the choreography,' I interjected quickly. I caught her eye, she smiled and I gave her a little reassuring wink.

Our collective banter continued but after a couple of minutes Jo took the lead and literally shovelled us back into the dance studio again.

'No use talking and not doing,' she said in a pretend Yorkshire accent. She was right, so we grabbed our feather boas and poles and stood in a line waiting for Jo's direction.

'Lose the boas, I reckon. Keep them for the end,' said Jo. 'We need to start the dance slick and modern, but with a cabaret twist.'

'I'm thinking suits and top hats…' said Goldy.

'No! A Fedora hat, like the blues brothers. And sequins!' added Bonnie.

'… and umbrellas.' said Ele, experimenting with the golfing umbrella by opening it and putting it over her shoulder before twirling it suggestively.

'Excellent! We're getting there!' said Jo. 'Now let's put the music on and have a little play.'

'Jo, can you show us some moves first?' I said, heading for the CD player.

'OK, but don't judge me,' she replied a little sheepishly.

I handed her my pole and she got into position, standing straight, legs hip-width apart, head down, upright broom handle front and centre. She shrugged out a bit of tension and waited in the silence.

'Dancing to take her clothes off…' I announced, like the compere from *Strictly Come Dancing*, 'to the Prince classic *Kiss*… Please welcome onto the floor… JO SMITH!'

Bonnie, Ele, Goldy and I couldn't help but applaud and let out a whoop as she lifted her head on the thud of the first big beat. She gave us direct and penetrating eye contact, maintaining it as she circled round the pole with a knowing smile.

'Ooo, this is so thrilling!' blurted Bonnie squeakily, as Jo glided the pole along the back of her shoulders, letting it slide down her arm and drop perfectly into her hand as it hit the floor. Clearly we were in the presence of a pro. Jo continued to make our jaws drop with a blend of funky Beyoncé-esque moves and Fred Astaire-like foot work. She embodied the slinky prowess of a seductress teasing her lover into a frenzy of desire.

By the end of the demo, we were jumping up and down and cheering like groupies. It was clear that she had what it took to produce a fantastic show. The problem was, *she* was not performing and *we*, as amateurs, would need more than a soupçon of her talent and charisma to pull off a dance of that calibre. In that moment it became crystal clear to me that with all the goodwill in the world, we might not be able to make it work. I said nothing though; Rosie was counting on us. Instead, nerves spread through my body and tightened in my throat as we took our positions.

We decided to emulate the beginning of Jo's dance, heads down with the upright broom handle front and centre. I had never felt so body-awkward and stiff; we were a group now, but frankly I was feeling a bit shy. For me, dancing usually occurred under the influence of at least two gin and tonics. Still, as Jo put the music on and counted us in, adrenalin kicked us all into gear.

'Five, six, seven, eight, now *lift your head!*' she shouted.

We all looked up at different times.

Jo stopped the CD.

'OK… let's start that again and lift our heads at the *same time*,' she said patiently. 'The intro goes: 'Da da da da da da da da da…' and when Prince sings, 'Ah uh' suddenly lift your heads, *all together*.' Then she gave a wry smile and said, 'Timing ladies, is everything!'

She was in her element.

We dropped our heads and tried again… then again. This was going to be a long process.

By the end of the first rehearsal we had perfected our first four moves: Head up (all at the same time, of course); bend the knees and hip-flick to the left, then right; circle our stationary pole in four steps; and finally, stand still and move the pole in a figure of eight, bringing it back to centre. I can still hear it in my head now when I recall the mechanics of the dance. We'd chant: 'Up… Dowwwn left, dowwwn right… Rouuuuunnnnnnd… Figure of eight.' Four simple moves. It sounds so easy. But to perform them seamlessly as a group was a feat of engineering to say the least. We'd miss a beat, drop our poles and get the giggles. Gradually, however, through concentration and repetitive practice, we began to feel a hint of what it was like to be a Full Monty Girl. As we banished our nerves and inhibitions, the inkling of something new – something remotely sexy even – began to emerge and we left that first rehearsal on a high.

With a clearer idea of the work that lay ahead and the determination needed to succeed, we decided to meet up three times a week – a big commitment for a bunch of busy mums and an estate agent.

* * * * *

The Christian stripper astonished us with her performance at the next rehearsal. Now a mum of two, she had become all curvy and soft and was dressed conservatively. As Bonnie had said previously, never in a million years would you have suspected she'd once been a stripper. As she spoke about her past, images of her once-toned body dancing seductively on a crimson-lit stage, in a tiny gold G-string, sang vividly in our minds. She explained that she was helping us now because it was a good cause – it was the Christian thing to do.

'Facial expression is the most important thing to get right,' she said smiling. 'Believe it or not, your audience will focus on your face the most whilst you perform, so practice facial expressions in the mirror and make sure you connect with your audience. Eye contact is very seductive.'

We all nodded in unison, captivated by her advice.

'Making shapes with your body is important too and props can be great fun – like this chair for example! Put some music on and I'll show you.'

She showed us the versatility of the chair by twirling it, circling it, and swinging her leg over the back of it, placing her foot on the seat. Then she sat on the chair and performed a dazzling array of eye-popping moves, all delivered with the salacious allure of the seasoned stripper. She made beautiful and, it has to be said, unashamedly suggestive shapes with her body, flirtation dancing in her eyes as she made eye contact with each and every one of us. We cheered and gasped, and hid our eyes not quite knowing where to look! She must have been a master of her craft in her day and we were inspired.

As she left, I wondered if that would be her last performance… not much call for the talents of a stripper in the Christian church. I couldn't help but admire her bravery for coming out and revisiting a part of her life long buried in the past. It truly was a selfless act of kindness.

'What an amazing way for her to express her faith,' Bonnie said as I locked up the hall that night.

'They do say that the Lord works in mysterious ways,' I conceded, half joking.

'Well maybe that performance was like a little blessing to say we're going in the right direction.'

★ ★ ★ ★ ★

The rehearsals continued and every time we met, a little more of the dance was created and perfected. Slowly, as our show began to take form, we began to get fitter and more toned and our confidence began to build.

Years later, Bonnie told me that after eons of being immersed in the job of being a mum, where washing, cleaning and wiping bottoms ruled the day, she'd look forward to rehearsals – even crave them. There was a certain delight in getting the children ready for bed, pouring oodles of gratitude onto hubby and then slipping outside and into the beckoning twilight. As the door clicked shut behind her she'd lean against it and breathe a sigh of sweet release. She was escaping mama-land to do something that was just for her. Grinning from ear to ear she'd negotiate the lanes to Stroud, filled with the exhilaration of being temporarily free. For the first time in her life, she was putting aside her everyday Bonnieness and connecting with a part of herself which, until that moment, had remained a hidden seed.

The rest of us felt the same. Nothing compared to the thrill and liberation of being released from the humdrum of daily life for a few hours where there was just friendship, fantasy and dance. It was the ultimate escape. We were each discovering a whole new persona that we didn't know existed, where our bodies, hidden by years of hang-ups and non-acceptance, could transform, with a wink and a saucy smile, into comely curvaceous vessels, oozing with confidence and smouldering with seductive allure. Well, that was what we were aiming for anyway. By the time we stepped out onto the stage, *that* was how we wanted to be perceived.

★ ★ ★ ★ ★

Meanwhile, in the search for our fifth member, we were fast discovering that strip-ready Stroudies were hard to come by. We'd asked everyone and their granny to join us and found numerous girls who'd initially loved the idea but bailed at the eleventh hour. So we were thrilled when Alix stepped up to the post on the back of a phone conversation with Goldy. But there was a catch: she lived in Brighton.

The lovely Alix 'girl' (so called because of our Painswickian friend Alex) looks like a Disney interpretation of Snow White but with a hippy twist. Tall, brunette and naturally pale, she was the picture of health with her rosy cheeks and dark red lips. Taller and leaner than the rest of us and perfectly toned (due to her being a gardener *and* aerobics fanatic), like Ele, she was the perfect stripping candidate.

'One for the boys,' Bonnie, Goldy and I would joke.

Were we jealous? Truth be told… definitely a tad.

Brighton is 155 miles away from Stroud, so we decided that the rest of us would choreograph the dance and she'd do intensive rehearsals when she could make it up to visit.

★ ★ ★ ★ ★

It rained for the whole of July and when it finally relented at the beginning of August the countryside, bursting with rampant growth, displayed its natural beauty in hues of lush, vibrant green. It was British summertime at its best. The melodic twitter of birdsong mingled dreamily with the scent of wild herbs and flowers whose blooms bobbed and swayed in the fields that surrounded the Stroud valleys. Us Brits know that sunshine is a precious commodity and for a good few days after the clouds had parted, the mood of the nation lifted. People walked around pink with sunburn and at the weekend the air hung heavy with the smell of barbecues and the sounds of lawnmowers and children at play.

It was against this sunny backdrop that Goldy and I cooked up the idea of organising a photo shoot so we could make eye-catching posters and flyers to advertise the show.

'All it took was a couple of phone calls and it was sorted!' I said to Goldy when I saw her later that day. 'Ele knows a professional photographer in London who happens to be in Stroud the exact same weekend as Alix. Plus she's willing to do the shoot for free!'

'Good work, Kar.'

'Lucky, eh? And as luck would have it, Alix knows the perfect venue – also for free – at an art studio belonging to Candida, one of her gardening clients.'

'Yeah, I know who you mean. Perfect! Now we need to get hold of some costumes so we'll look like a proper group.'

So, in the week that followed we scoured the charity shops in Stroud and picked up five mismatched black suits. Then we headed to Gloucester where we found five fedora hats coming in at a tenner a piece. To go under our suits, we decided to purchase black and red basques (which would sculpt our bodies in all the right places) and we also bought black French knickers, an asset-boosting bra and long black satin gloves.

When the day of the photo shoot arrived, Rosie was not in a good way. She'd been fractious all morning and when the time came for me to leave she was still having a meltdown.

'Shall I call it off?' I called to Andy over Rosie's screams. 'I'm worried that I'm leaving you on the brink of mayhem!'

'No,' he replied sweetly. 'Alix is here and we need those photos. Just go. We'll be OK, I promise.'

I got into my car and took a deep breath. I was torn between my family's needs and the bigger picture. 'Just keep going forward,' I said to myself, putting the radio on and trying to shake off the feeling of guilt as I drove away.

When I arrived at Candida's house, Goldy, Ele, Bonnie and Alix were waiting for me by their cars, chatting feverishly. They were in a buoyant mood; this was the first time all five of us would be together and I couldn't help but grin to myself as I parked my car.

Candida lives in a beautiful old mill cottage with gorgeous gardens split in two by a river. Her art studio is large, airy and separate from the house and once I'd greeted the girls, Alix led us straight there to get ready. We applied make-up, pulled on our stockings and slid on our gloves. Then as we pulled tight the satin ribbons of our basques, we began to feel our new burlesque-selves emerge.

'It feels as if we're in the cast of *Moulin Rouge*,' said Ele.

'Yeah! Or like we're about to perform in a West End play or something,' added Alix.

'Either that, or we look like the Blues Brothers, in drag, after a midnight bender,' Goldy joked.

'I feel kinda confident in this get-up though – like a new me,' said Bonnie as she placed her fedora hat on her head.

As the photo shoot began, we experienced the alien yet exhilarating feeling of moving and posing in front of the camera. It would have been excruciating if I had been alone, but as part of a group it was fun. We laughed a lot and the amity made us feel confident and sexy. Sam, the photographer, knew exactly what she wanted, giving us good direction and plenty of encouragement. She'd say things like, 'Think sexy ladies... Look at the camera... Hollywood smiles...'

We posed for pictures inside, with specialist lighting, then outside, alfresco in the garden. For one photo we formed a line and leant over the ivy-covered sides of a humpback bridge, and for another we used the bridge as a runway, strutting over it to the rhythmic clicks of the camera.

All in all, Sam took 368 photos but only six were usable. It turns out that it's exceedingly hard to take a group photo where everyone is happy with how they look. We may have felt like models – at least some of the time – but the camera told a different story. Still, six good photos were all we needed. If we could afford an advert in the paper they'd come in very handy. Sam had also taken a genius close-up photo of Goldy's torso. Her ample bosom ballooned out of the top of her basque in the most delicious way and we instantly knew it would be the perfect background for our poster design.

'I always knew your boobs would be famous,' I teased.

After the shoot, I came home to a scene of chaos. Rosie was sleeping under a blanket on the sofa looking unwell. The washing-up was stacked high and clothes and toys littered every surface.

'Hi hun, bit of a difficult afternoon…' Andy said as I walked in.

'What's happened?' I asked, picking up Grace, who'd toddled towards me.

'Rosie had a fit and I was trying to juggle her and Grace. We're OK though. The house is a mess – but we're fine.'

I felt terrible. 'I should never have left you, I'm so sorry, Ands. Is Rose OK?'

'Yeah, she's fine. I don't think it's a hospital job.'

'Good, well that's something.' I put the kettle on and set about tidying the kitchen. 'Maybe this isn't going to work.' I said, after a few minutes had passed.

'It will, Kar. It has to.'

'OK, but I just don't want you to think that your role in all this is going unnoticed. It's a lot, you having the kids all the time.'

Andy chuckled. 'As long as *I* don't have to get naked, I'm fine.'

I went to sleep that night with the clicking sound of the camera still echoing in my mind. Effervescent images of the Full Monty Girls flashed as if real in the darkness. Rosie twitched next to me in her sleep and I checked her breathing to see if she was having another fit. She was fine and I relaxed back into the soft reassurance of my pillow. *This is how it's going to be from now on*, I thought as I let out a deep sigh. 'Whether I'm twirling a bra round my head and flinging it into an audience, or changing Rosie's nappies and dealing with her fits, for a while at least, I'm going to be living two very different lives.' But these polar opposite worlds of Full Monty Girl and Mum, so opposite in nature, were linked by a core of devotion. Devotion to my precious Rosie. I'd felt so helpless as her difficulties had progressed and now, with my friends by my side, I was striving to give her a better future. I knew the road ahead was going to be hard and that I'd have to stay focused. But I wouldn't have to look far for the inspiration to keep me motivated… because my inspiration was lying right next to me, fast asleep. She was the fighter. She was the plucky one. She'd found a way to smile despite her challenges. If I couldn't do the same, what kind of mother would that make me?

CHAPTER EIGHT

COMMUNITY SPIRIT

It was a crisp, sunny morning, and still on a high from a rehearsal the previous night, I was in a buoyant mood. So when I spotted a post van trundling down the steep track towards our house I went out merrily to meet it, hopping barefoot across our gravel driveway to the front gate.

'Only one today,' said the postman, handing me a letter with a broad smile.

'Thanks,' I replied, as he returned to his van.

It had the familiar NHS stamp on the envelope and I opened it immediately, assuming it was yet another hospital appointment to attend. But my knees literally gave way as I read it. After the usual name/date of birth etc., it read as follows:

Problem 1: Severe autism.

Problem 2: Epilepsy.

The words screamed at me. SEVERE AUTISM. Severe? How can she have gone from mild to severe in just six months? There must be some kind of mistake! This was potentially catastrophic news for Rosie's prognosis and in that moment it felt like we were being sentenced. My mind raced, trying to come to terms with the magnitude of the words on the paper. Quotes from books and articles I had read flew to the fore from the darkest recesses of my mind, *'In severe cases the child may never speak and could have difficulty interacting with the world around them.' 'Progress is slow and sometimes non-existent for a child with severe autism and children can develop severe behavioural problems.'*

There must be some kind of mistake, I thought with rising panic. Severe autism? No, not Rosie. Not our darling Rose.

I went into the house to find Andy who was in the kitchen making coffee. When I handed him the letter he went white with disbelief. His reaction was the same as mine.

'Surely this is a mistake,' he said, slowly rubbing his face.

Suddenly, my panic was replaced by rage. 'Who would tell someone, I mean what heartless so-and-so would tell someone, that their beloved daughter had *severe* autism by writing it in a letter under 'Problem 1'?! Surely they would call you into the surgery and break it to you gently, with a prognosis and plan of action! You don't just put it in a blinkin' letter, Andy…'

My eyes danced across his face searching for solidarity. He was as calm as ever, but a stony seriousness had come over him, as if there was a deep stirring of anger that he would not (or could not) express.

'Ok. Look, let's not jump the gun,' he said slowly, careful not to let his feelings overtake him. 'It must be a cruel clerical error… I'm going to ring the hospital now.'

Grace toddled up to me, dragging her teddy behind her. I picked her up and we walked into the living room to find Rosie. She was in running mode, throwing herself against the wall at one end of the room then hurtling into the patio doors at the other. To anyone else this behaviour would look bizarre but I could tell from her squeaks of delight that she was enjoying the sensation. It was one of her favourite rituals and I knew she wasn't hurting herself. Still, I sat down on the floor and caught her playfully as she ran past me to break her out of the cycle, tickling her as she landed in my lap, which made her erupt with giggles. Grace, sensing the fun of the moment, piled on top of us both and I plied them both with kisses. I played with them as if nothing was wrong, but all the while, the contents of the letter tore at me as I waited for Andy to get off the phone to the hospital.

Finally, he came into the room and looked at me steadily, his olive-green eyes revealing shock and disbelief. My heart broke. He joined us and took Rosie onto his lap. 'Hello darling,' he said gently. 'Hello my lovely... my gorgeous girl.' He lay on his back and lifted her into a flying angel above his face, beaming at her. She gazed back at him adoringly. If the letter had been a mistake he would have told me the good news but he said nothing and I could tell by his eyes – and his silence – that the letter was accurate. Rosie was now classified as severely autistic.

Suddenly the whole vista of her future looked different again. Hope was slipping through our grasp like sand through the hands of a child. The future didn't just look bleak; in that moment, it looked terrifying.

As Andy was engaged with the children, I slipped outside and sat on the doorstep to take stock. The sun was hot on my face and the smell of horse manure and meadow grasses folded gently through the valley. I closed my eyes to focus on the clutter of thoughts that ran riot through my mind.

OK, so first, in the beginning, Rosie had eczema, then she got asthma, then they thought she had learning difficulties but not autism. Then they thought she had mild autism, then she got epilepsy – which still we can't get under control – and now they tell us that she is *severely* autistic. How much more is this little girl supposed to cope with? It's too much. 'Severe' means her life is going to be hard, very hard – and she will need full-time care 24/7 for the rest of her life. She's still in nappies. 'Severe' means she might stay incontinent forever. She doesn't eat well, she doesn't sleep. She has tantrums every day and she can't tell me why. She's never going to grow up and leave home like every other child I know. Andy and I never get time alone together in the evenings when the rest of the world have their little ones safely tucked up in bed. She sleeps with me every night because of possible fits. Perhaps she'll be in my bed forever? How is this going to affect our relationship? I was hoping this was all just a difficult phase and in time, with a good education and intensive therapy, things would improve – after all, she's only four years old. But this is it; she has the mental age of a baby and this is it. How are we going to cope?

Suddenly I felt familiar arms wrapping themselves around my waist. Andy had squatted down to sit behind me and I sank back, surrendering to the support and warmth of his embrace. I leaned my head back onto the burly safety of his shoulder and he kissed my neck.

'We're going to be all right, you know,' he said softly. It was typical Andy, always facing the world with optimism. I couldn't help but smile.

'And why do you think that?' I asked.

'Because we're strong.' He almost whispered the words but they rang with such conviction that I could feel the hairs on my arms stand on end as that strength re-entered me. 'And we're not taking it lying down. We're doing everything in our power to make a difference. That's what counts,' he continued.

'Thanks, hun,' I replied, opening my eyes again and looking out across the valley. Andy was right; at least we were searching for answers and ways to help Rosie.

'And if it all fails and she makes no progress at all, we'll be able to live with ourselves, because at least we tried,' I said.

'Yes, and even if she doesn't progress, we will have loved and treasured her anyway for the beautiful, inspirational person she is. I know we're going to give her a great life whatever happens.'

'You're right. We've just got to keep going.'

★ ★ ★ ★ ★

From the beginning of our Full Monty Girls fundraising enterprise I knew that it was going to take more than a one-night-only performance to raise the £10,000 we'd need to get Rosie to America. We also wanted to attend a three-day autism training seminar in Holland, which would cost just over £1,000. We estimated that the show would pull in about £2,000, I'd got a bank loan for £4,500 but I still needed about £3,000 by March to pay for the full cost of the flights, accommodation and the Growing Minds programme itself. Furthermore, I'd need to find at least £7,000 to cover the cost of running the programme from home for a year. This put the total bill at £17,000. I knew it was going to be a monumental challenge to raise this kind of cash and in the evenings, between sewing sequins onto suits, rehearsing for the show and dealing with the myriad of life's demands and delights, my mind whirred away in the background, trying to come up with new money-making ideas.

Happily, the Full Monty Girls fundraising idea was progressing at top speed. We now had a venue for the show called the Space, which was a chapel-like building with a stage just off Stroud High Street. We'd also set a date: Saturday the sixteenth of September. Now all we needed was a crowd!

We'd had word that many of the scattered rural villages of the Five Valleys were awash with our story and we marvelled at the speed of word of mouth. Although most of the family now knew about our enterprise, I hadn't told Andy's granny yet. I was a bit worried about her reaction to be perfectly honest and there had never been a 'good' time to spill the beans. I mean, how do you tell an eighty-six-year-old that you've decided to become a charity stripper? When I finally broached the subject her reaction stunned me, 'If that's what you want to do, then you must do it,' she said, her beautiful queenly voice warm with encouragement. 'I admire you for your entrepreneurial spirit, my darling. What fun!'

Then to our amazement our story reached the ears of a journalist from our local newspaper, *The Stroud News and Journal*. I nearly dropped the phone and squeakily told the reporter to 'Hold on a mo' when he rang, putting my hand over the receiver so I could mouth to Andy, 'It's the local news!' before saying, 'Hi. Yes, this is Kara,' as nonchalantly as possible as if journalists call me every day of my life.

'My name is Will Saunders, and I was wondering if I could come to your house to meet you and Rosie and help get your message and fundraising ideas out into the community.'

It was music to my ears. 'Yes, that would be a dream come true! When can you come?'

'Tomorrow? Say, 10am? That way we can get you into Wednesday's paper,' he replied enthusiastically.

'OK, great, I have a picture you can use if you want one because we've just done a photo shoot.' I smiled to myself and did a silent jig because I thought it made me sound professional.

'Fabulous! If you could email it to me when you get a chance that would be fantastic. Is it OK if we send our photographer up later today to take a picture of Rosie?'

'Yes, of course!'

'OK, great. Well, I'll look forward to meeting you tomorrow.'

'Yes, me too… and thanks for calling!'

'Bye for now.'

As I clutched the phone and danced around the kitchen in celebration, I could never have imagined how far our story was destined to spread.

★ ★ ★ ★ ★

On the Wednesday morning after the interview, I woke up extra early and went to the local Co-op at the bottom of the hill to get *The Stroud News and Journal.* I picked it up, flicked over the front page and there, staring back at me in printed ink, was a full-length article with the headline: 'Hoping for a Rosie future'. I couldn't help but smile.

As soon as I got home I rang my mum.

'Mum! You'll never guess what!' I squeaked excitedly clutching the newspaper in one hand. 'We're in the paper! We're on page three!'

'Oh, that's fantastic! Well done!' replied my mum, encouragingly.

'It's like we're Page Three Girls in *The Sun!*' I joked, instantly realising that this was not going to make her laugh, (Goldy, maybe but my mum, no).

'Err, well I hope not,' she said with friendly yet marked disapproval. 'You'd better not get yourself into one of *those* types of newspapers...' An image flashed into my mind of a semi-naked twenty-something beauty, boobs out and proud, posing provocatively for all of Britain to ogle at. I laughed.

'Well, that would give us the attention we need to get our story out to the nation,' I said to wind her up a bit, 'good idea, I'll give them a ring!'

'No you will not!' she replied, emphasising every word.

'It's OK, Mum. You don't have to worry,' I said soothingly. I knew she had big reservations about the whole thing, but I was certain that what we were doing was right. I also knew this: if *The Sun* had called me and wanted us to do a naked photo shoot I would have seriously considered consulting the girls and saying yes – even if my mum disowned me! Would that make me desperate? Well, the answer could only be 'Yes!' because I *was* desperate. I had a hell of a lot of money to raise and I'd have to seize whatever opportunities came my way with both hands, for Rosie's sake.

'But isn't it amazing?' I continued, trying to reignite my mum's enthusiasm for our media debut. 'There are 47,000 people in Stroud and everyone buys the *Stroud News*. Everyone in the whole town will know about us by the end of the week!'

'I just don't want people to judge you harshly...' my mother replied. I could hear the worry in her voice. She'd clearly been doing what most mums do in the dead of night – fretting about the well-being of their children.

'It's OK, Mum, really,' I reassured. 'Anyway, the article doesn't say, "Kara Westermann-Childs and friends have created a Full Monty-style strip show – what a bunch of hussies!"' She laughed. Finally. 'It clearly states *why* we're doing it. They've written a whole lot more about Rosie and her autism and what we want to do to help her... the Full Monty Girls part is just to grab people's attention, and hopefully keep it!'

'Yes I realise that... we just don't know how the wider community will react yet.'

'You're right. But so far the reaction has been great! Besides, if Andy's granny can grasp the idea and support us, I'm sure the rest of the community will be OK with it. I really think people are *getting* us, Mum – and getting behind us too.'

'Yes but that's just friends, family – people that love you...'

'Not any more… our story is spreading like wildfire – it's crazy.' I paused. 'Look, I know it's a risk, and *everyone* might think I'm a terrible mother, and *no one* might come to the show and I might be embarrassed to show my face in town for a few weeks… but I've thought about it a lot and I really think it's worth the risk. I'll send you the article. It's really good, and not at all judgmental.'

'The media can play dirty though; they can chew you up and spit you out,' she persisted.

'Yes I know. But the media can be a force for good, too. It's a good news story, about good people, for a good cause. I've got a feeling it'll be OK.'

When the call ended, despite her tempered reaction to my small media success, I couldn't help but let out an excited squeak as I put the phone in its cradle. Then I spread the newspaper out on the kitchen table and smoothed it affectionately with the palm of my hand. It was a good-sized article and in full colour. We had two pictures. One of the Full Monty Girls from the photo shoot in Candida's garden, and one of Rosie, her golden hair framing her beautiful, peachy face.

'That picture's going to melt people's hearts,' said Andy, leaning over my shoulder. 'She looks adorable.'

'I know. Isn't it cool?'

'Yeah. And look at you, all famous!' he teased.

'Yes, but what's everyone going to think?'

The moment of truth was just around the corner. Would the general Stroud population think we were the brave dedicated women that the article portrayed? Or was my mother right? Would we become known as a madcap bunch of exhibitionists who brought down the wholesome tone of the town, causing embarrassment and shame? There was only one way to find out... we'd have to face the post-newspaper-article music, venture into town and see what kind of reaction, if any, we'd receive.

Goldy and I decided to meet in town on the Saturday that followed the publication of *The Stroud News and Journal* piece. We reasoned that Stroud's bustling farmers' market was the best place to show our faces and see if anyone had read our story. The farmers' market is one of the social high points of the Stroud week and we knew it would be packed. Shoppers and foodies are drawn out of the woodwork by the promise of award-winning local produce and the chance to meet up with friends, swap pleasantries and soak up the vibrancy of the town.

Goldy knew pretty much everyone (and seemed to be distantly related to half of Stroud) and those she didn't know, I probably would. So when I pulled into Sunshine car park and located a space, I was not surprised to see her sitting on the bonnet of her car, casually smoking a roll-up, already deep in conversation with a couple of guys that had more than a passing resemblance to a couple of Hare Krishnas. (By the way, in case you're wondering why the car park has such an unusual moniker, it's because it's adjacent to Sunshine health-food shop, which, if you're ever passing, sells the best sourdough rye bread in the entire world.)

As I approached the trio, I could tell by the way the men were looking at Goldy that she was talking about the Full Monty. She was wearing a bright red outrageously low-cut vest top, a black flared jean skirt and of course those big black signature stomping boots. Her ringlets fell about her shoulders, drawing the eye to the line of her cleavage. With her new-found confidence she was embodying a caricature of herself. She was no longer Goldy – she was Goldy from the Full Monty Girls – and she was loving every second of it. She spotted me and gestured towards me, making her companions turn to look at me as I approached.

'… and this is Rosie's mum,' drifted into earshot. I smiled and instantly felt shy.

'Oh wow! Hi Kara,' said one of the men smiling broadly, his shaven head reflecting the sun. 'I read about your daughter Rosie and what you guys are doing to try and help her. I think you're amazing.'

'Oh, thanks!' I replied, taken aback by being called 'amazing' by a complete stranger who already knew my name. 'I can't really take credit for it,' I continued, going a little red. 'I mean, a mother would do anything to help her kids. It's the rest of the Full Monty Girls who deserve the credit; they're the selfless ones.'

'Well, I think you're *all* very brave,' said the other one, who was wearing an Afghani hat despite the clement weather. 'Now where can we buy a ticket?'

'They're not printed yet, sorry. But the show will be at the Space on September the sixteenth.'

'When they are printed out let me know and I'll tell all my friends. You girls are inspirational, you really are.'

Goldy cocked her head to one side. 'Why, thanks!' she said jokingly, twizzling her curls around her finger and fluttering her eyelashes. She jumped down off the bonnet of her car, indicating a close to the conversation.

'It was really lovely to meet you both!' I shouted happily, as we ambled out of the car park. 'See you at the show!'

'Well, we'll certainly see you! All of you!' one of them shouted back. We knew by his tone the comment was meant in fun, but our pace quickened and we giggled out of sight.

'Flipping heck. I know I'm stating the obvious but we are going to be naked in front of complete strangers!' I said in a rush of excitement and nerves so strong it made me hop.

'And stranger still, in front of all our friends!' replied Goldy. We looked at each other and laughed.

'We must be mad,' I said, as we turned the corner and headed into the crowded street of the farmers' market.

'Of course we are,' replied Goldy matter-of-factly. 'Best way to be!'

As predicted, the market was packed and for a while we mingled incognito in the crowd.

'Maybe not many people read the article,' I said with a sinking feeling.

'Give it five minutes,' said Goldy, giving my arm a reassuring squeeze. Then she laughed. 'Should have come down here in stockings and basques, that'd get tongues wagging!' I laughed too.

Then it started. People began to come over to comment on the article – and their response couldn't have been better. Everyone we spoke to was taken with our story and promised to come to the show. They wished us luck, told us how they could never do it and remarked on how brave they thought we all were. It was exactly the response we'd hoped for. People were very interested in Rosie and many stories were recounted about people they knew with autistic children, treatments to try, good schools, diets. Lots of people offered to help us in any way they could.

Suddenly, the community I had lived in all my life showed its warmth in a way that I could never have dreamed of. I knew Stroud was a nice place to live, unique too, but I had no idea that the Stroud people could be so supportive. And the formula was simple: in Stroud, if you let it be known that you need help for a good reason, extraordinary things begin to happen. The entire town will get behind you with the kind of earthy, plucky spirit you need to believe in yourself and make that dream a reality. It was a revelation. There had been a time only months before when I'd sat on the step of my house feeling so alone, desperate for solutions and deeply depressed. There had seemed to be no way out of the darkness and I'd felt like I was drowning. I'd told myself to hold on until September, as if time would inevitably change at least *something*. It was a simple notion that ignited a very small spark of transformation. Since then, Andy and I had found a therapy centre in America that spelled hope for Rosie and with more than a little help from our friends, we had come up with a plan of a kooky and audacious nature that would raise the profile of our story and help towards the cost of paying for it. With the help of the local press, our message had spread quickly and was well received. That tentative, positive step to at least try and help Rosie, whose autism seemed to claim her more every day, had snowballed.

Now here I was, standing in a bustling farmers' market in my beloved Stroud, surrounded by the support and positivity of a whole community. And it was *my* community. And bathing in its nurturing spirit, I felt more a part of the fabric of it than I ever had before. My mum needn't have worried. Not even a bit.

CHAPTER NINE

TAMING THE LION

There is something wonderfully comfortable about the familiar. Something safe and sacred about waking up in your own bed, for example, or pulling on your favourite jumper. It's the same with routine. There's something to be said for a good old established routine based around the relatively safe and predictable parameters of work and play. Routine can bring a sense of stability and grace in a chaotic world and a fighting chance to achieve long-term goals. But, like a double-edged sword, its repetitive nature can also have the potential to make life seem utterly and completely dull. So dull in fact that there's a danger of falling under its trance-like spell and sleepwalking through life like zombies – until out of the blue, something disrupts the status quo and jolts us awake.

Up until our idea to form the Full Monty Girls, my life had been swept along by necessity and expectation. I had never really taken ownership of my destiny – I'd just rolled with the tide and fallen into comfortable routines. Now, thanks to Rosie and my wonderful friends, I was walking my own unique path with a very specific goal. True, I didn't know if I could reach that goal or what might happen along the way, but it was *my* path and it had brought me to life. I found it exciting, thrilling, fascinating (and a little bit terrifying) that an idea, so singular in its infancy, could expand and snowball so quickly. Within one job, a thousand jobs lay and they multiplied daily, like rabbits in spring. Sometimes this was fun and energising, but sometimes it overwhelmed me and I flew from task to task like a plaything in a tornado full of demands.

Bonnie recently told me that, at the time, our friends were quite worried about Andy and me – they could see us heading for burnout, or worse, a breakdown, but felt powerless to stop it. 'I mean how could we stop someone trying to help their child?' she said. 'All we could really do was help in any way possible, share the burden of responsibility and be a friend.'

And we couldn't have been more grateful. It was extraordinarily humbling to us that people in our friendship group and now the wider community were willing to step out of their comfort zone and help. It gave us the energy and drive to carry on. And carry on we must.

It was now mid August and the summer had mellowed and matured. The light had changed again, soaking the countryside in rays of translucent gold. Wayside grasses, once strong and verdant, had become bleached pale by the sun – even the leaves on the trees had changed. They were still green but blemished now and dry so they rustled when the breeze disturbed them, filling the valley with a subtle white noise. Apples, blackberries, elderberries, sloes, rosehips, quinces and damsons sat ripening in the hedgerows and when I found time I took Rosie and Grace out on foraging expeditions. But family time was scarce.

We were just over three weeks away from the show and the biggest job on the agenda was to design a poster to put up around Stroud. As planned, the picture Sam had taken of Goldy's torso (bulging bosoms and basque) was selected as a background and we set about writing the text to be layered over it.

I had a degree in art and design so I knew exactly how I wanted the posters to look but, as you know, I didn't know how to work a computer back then, so Andy sat at the PC and tried his best to create my vision. I have a buried memory (now screaming back to me) of being a *tiny* bit of a nightmare… shouting in frustration at the screen and barking instructions like a deranged dictator when Andy couldn't manifest what I saw in my head. It seemed justifiable at the time, an inevitable by-product of the stress I was under, but I can now categorically state – with my tail between my legs – that I could have behaved better. (Sorry Andy, you really are a saint to have put up with me!)

Bad character traits aside, we were really proud of the resulting poster. It had the perfect amount of sauciness to catch the eye and deliver information, and the perfect amount of class to make people happy to pay £10 for a ticket.

Goldy and I cable-tied them to lamp posts, pinned them to noticeboards and asked permission to put them in the windows of shops and pubs. We were especially proud when we were allowed to put A1 posters in frames in The

Retreat pub, which was located down a side road off Stroud High Street.

'Bloody hell, Golds,' I said, as we stood back to admire them. 'They look so professional!'

The following Monday night, I got a call from Goldy.

'Guess what, Kar,' she said, clearly amused, 'I went to The Retreat to check on the posters, and they were gone!'

'Oh no! Nightmare! We'll have to get them reprinted now.'

'No! Hang on a minute,' she interrupted. 'I went to see the landlord and he told me they'd been nicked!' She shrieked with laughter, delighted at the prospect of them being hot property.

'Holy crow!' I replied laughing with her. 'We're still the talk of the town then!'

'Oh yes! My best assets are famous now, Kar, I can't go anywhere without being stopped by someone or other. My boobs have taken on a life of their own! And, what's more, I went round to a mate's house after the pub last night and he had one of our posters from the lamp posts on his wall!'

'Oh. My. God… Anyway, Golds, what were you doing round some bloke's house after the pub?!'

She laughed and said, 'Well, a Full Monty Girl needs to have her fun!'

'You little hussy!' I teased.

'No, I'm just a girl, with famous boobs, checking out the talent!' She paused to accommodate another hoot of laughter. 'Come round later and I'll tell you all the details. We've gotta get these dining chairs finished for tomorrow's rehearsal. I've got red stars to screw on to the backs… and Bonnie's painted them gold.'

'Wow, nice one! You guys are amazing.'

'So are you, darling' she replied happily. 'Now go feed your kids and I'll see you in a bit!'

'Excellent. And I want a blow-by-blow account of your antics! Besides, I've got a bit of news of my own…'

'Oh my. Not pregnant are you?' she asked, sounding surprised.

'I hope not!' I replied. 'But I've got a new idea brewing away…'

'Sounds intriguing… now go cook! Love you.'

I could hear her kiss the air loudly before putting down the phone.

Later that day, as we screwed the stars on the chairs, I spilled my idea: an art auction to be held in the town hall in Painswick in October. It would be a two-day exhibition of works, which I hoped would be donated by the many talented artists, both aspiring and famous, who were beavering away in the Five Valleys. The exhibition would culminate in an auction of the art in aid of Rosie's appeal. Goldy loved the idea and knew a small army of artists to approach. Then she told me all about her midnight liaison with her mystery man and how, after a night of passion, in the wee small hours of Sunday, she'd wobbled tipsily along the lane from Summer Street to home, smiling from ear to ear.

★ ★ ★ ★ ★

'Exposure' in one form or another was becoming the unlikely new theme of my life. We were finding ourselves on the front page of the local papers and we were invited to do interviews for the radio. We couldn't have dreamt of such good coverage and it gave us a much-needed boost of confidence.

Everywhere we went people recognised us. Being part of the Full Monty Girls made us feel like local celebrities and I'd be lying if I said we didn't enjoy the attention.

'Are you Rosie's mum?' people would stop and ask. 'How is she? What you're doing is very brave…'

At that time there had been a huge MMR/autism scare in the media. Autism had become a feared word loaded with negative connotations. I wanted to use my new-found media platform to break through that fear and highlight that living with an autistic person can be as life-affirming as it is challenging. I found that people had a lot of questions. There was a lot of confusion as to what autism actually was and I could see that spreading awareness was essential. I'd read so many articles about bullying, and had experienced people using the term 'special needs' or 'autistic' as a mild insult. I knew that if the general population could learn more about the autistic members of our society, they would be more understanding of their behaviours. The formula was clear: more awareness brings about a deeper understanding of autistic people within our communities. I didn't know it then but this mission was to become a mantra for my soul.

★ ★ ★ ★ ★

We had begun to come to terms with Rosie's new diagnosis of severe autism, but the sands quickly shifted again when her doctors, baffled by her continuing regression and atypical autistic traits (such as good eye contact and social curiosity), decided to pursue a possible diagnosis of Rett syndrome. Still classed as an autistic spectrum disorder, Rett syndrome is caused by a mutation in the MeCP2 gene. It affects mostly girls and is degenerative. So many of Rosie's symptoms pointed to it: decreased head circumference at four months, irritability, teeth grinding, regression, epilepsy. Andy and I were understandably extremely concerned. Rett syndrome is life-limiting and her prognosis would be extremely poor if she carried the faulty gene. Rosie was referred to a neurology professor at Bristol Children's Hospital who decided to go ahead with genetic testing. It would take at least six months before we would get the results, so we decided to carry on with what we had set out to do.

We were well aware, considering the severity of Rosie's autism, that our efforts could well come to nothing in terms of helping Rosie make developmental progress. Most of the skills she had learned – including her speech – had fallen away in the months that followed the onset of her epilepsy. I longed to hear her voice again even if it was just a couple of words, but the possibility seemed increasingly remote. That said, Andy and I refused to give up hope. As long as we were pushing forward with our plans we felt able to cope. For me, being part of the Full Monty Girls became a lifeline. It kept me going by giving me something positive to focus on.

It was during this time that Andy and I agreed to be filmed for a documentary that would track our life with Rosie over a number of years. Andy's sister Jessica, who worked in television news, wanted to make a tell-all film that would portray what it was really like for a family coping with severe autism. We knew that the filming would be intrusive, but spreading awareness was becoming more and more important to us, so we jumped at the opportunity.

The exposé *du jour*, of course, was the show itself and I was not alone in feeling a rising sense of panic, dread and delicious expectation as the big day approached. Every week a new section of the dance had been completed. Now our task was to figure out the dance moves to accompany the final song – the song that would take us to a state of complete undress! By this point the group had gelled completely. A brazen, playful openness had developed between us and we had lost many of the inhibitions we had started out with. No girlie subject was off limits and there was much playful banter. Like whether we sported a 'full bush', 'landing strip' or 'Brazilian', or how big/small/pert/wobbly or southward bound our boobs were. So by the time we ended up in the buff for the first time, none of us were remotely shy. In fact, there was a sense of triumphant liberation and we whooped and cheered as Jo wiped away tears of pride.

'I almost never thought we'd get here,' she sighed as we ran to retrieve our underwear. 'You were perfectly in time, ladies, sexy and oozing with confidence. You've got it… and you've earned your name. Now you really are the Full Monty Girls.'

After all the strictness and discipline, the tears, laughter, and frustration, Jo finally gave us the validation we'd craved. We had done it, our choreography was complete. It was a euphoric moment.

★ ★ ★ ★ ★

Before we knew it there were only two weeks to go before the big night, so we hired the Space for rehearsals so that we could get used to performing in the actual venue. Alix had decided to come to Stroud for a whole week, and Goldy and I met up with her every day for rehearsals. We also met up as a group in the evenings. By Thursday we decided we were ready to invite someone along as a kind of trial audience so Ele invited her friend Rodda, who had volunteered to be our compère. 'Nothing will ruffle Rodda,' Ele said after inviting him. 'Besides, as compère to the Full Monty Girls, it's only right that he has a preview!'

I was the first to arrive at the Space on the day of Rodda's preview, so I killed time by emptying my bootload of props onto the pavement before hauling them over the road to the venue's gothic back door. There I sat and waited for the girls. It wasn't long before Goldy arrived. I heard the sound of her car stereo well before I saw her. She was playing reggae at full volume and the street reverberated with the bass. She cruised around the corner and pulled up alongside me, her aviator sunglasses and hoop earrings reflecting the sun. I could sense she was in a good mood. As we emptied her share of props onto the street, her smile said everything.

'Your car's like a tardis!' I remarked, as three gold chairs, a bag of feather boas, a pile of hats, five costumes, five umbrellas and a stereo emerged from her boot. 'It's like Mary Poppins' carpet bag!'

Goldy ignored my comments. She had other things on her mind. 'So… this is it!' she said in an excited voice. 'Our first audience!'

'Yeah!' I replied, sounding more serious, 'Rodda is our

unsuspecting guinea pig. His reaction will tell us if the show is any good.'

'I imagine he's more *expecting* than unsuspecting,' Goldy replied, laughing.

'Yeah, Ele said he's been looking forward to it all week,' I agreed. 'Apparently he's boasting to everyone in the pub that he's getting a private show!'

'Precisely. He's the landlord of the Golden Fleece for goodness' sake! If we're rubbish, the whole town will know!'

'Well, let's hope we've got it right… no going back now!'

Just then Bonnie turned up in her beaten-up Vauxhall estate, followed by Ele in her shiny black brand-new VW Golf.

As they parked, Jo walked down the steps of the churchyard and approached us, red-faced with a cheeky, slightly embarrassed smile.

'You are not going to believe what I've just done,' she said wincingly, 'I've just pulled a Jo!'

'What have you done now!?' asked Bonnie playfully as Alix rounded the corner and joined us.

'Well, last week my mate Neil scared the crap out of me when I was parking my car by sneaking up and suddenly swinging the door open. So I wanted to get my own back… and just now, I saw his car pull up so I thought, *REVENGE!* I got down on all fours so he wouldn't see me in his wing mirror, crawled up to his car, opened his door and shouted: "AAAAAAGGGGGGGGHHHHHHHH!" only to realise… it wasn't his car and it wasn't Neil! It was this poor old chap! I frightened the life out of him!'

She had us all in stitches.

'Only you, Jo!' said Bonnie.

'What did the poor guy say?' asked Alix.

'Well, he was a bit kerfuffled, but he could see it was an honest mistake.'

'Oh, I do love you, Jo,' I said finally after we all caught our breath from the belly laughs.

'Come on, we'd better get some practice in before Rodda turns up,' said Goldy, getting us back on point.

'Oh, I saw him yesterday,' said Jo. 'He's beside himself with excitement!'

'Well, we better give him something to be excited about!' replied Goldy as she carried three chairs across the road at once.

'You really are freakishly strong, Golds,' I teased.

'Yeah. So don't mess – and let's get this show on the road!'

We carried the props through the back door and up some ancient, winding stone stairs to the main hall. It was a big space, rectangular in shape and flanked either side by tall, arched windows with faded, sage-green shutters. The worn wooden floor was pitted and polished and the whitewashed walls reached up to exposed beams high in the eaves. The stage was a good size, too, framed by red velvet curtains. An old-fashioned armchair and floor lamp had been left on the stage giving it an eerie feel – as if the ghosts of a past performance still lingered.

Bonnie opened the lid of an old piano that was positioned next to the stage and played the obligatory *Chopsticks* on it. 'Wow, this place has acoustics!' she said, her voice bouncing off the walls.

Ele, Goldy, Alix and I climbed the steps that led to the

stage and stood in line taking in the imaginary vista of an audience.

'So, two weeks from now, this will be us,' I said with a hint of disbelief.

Goldy chuckled and said, 'In your mind are they smiling, or throwing rotten tomatoes?'

'Smiling, I think,' I replied with a hint of reservation, 'but the insecure part of me sees flying tomatoes too!'

'It'll be fine…' said Ele evenly. 'I mean, what's not to like? Ladies dancing round a stage removing their clothes? *Good…* Naked? *Even better!*' We all laughed. 'And besides,' she continued, 'they'll all be here to support the cause more than anything and enter into the fun of it!'

'Looking good up there, ladies!' called Jo.

Goldy put her hands forward as if holding a dance pole and seductively circled it. 'Very nice!' she laughed. 'It would be *you* who'd feel so at home up there, Golds! Now get into your costumes and we'll have a run-through before Rodda arrives.'

We cleared the stage, then Jo passed up our chairs and we put them in their positions. The newly applied gold paint glimmered in the rays of the afternoon sun that streamed through the windows and we paused to admire them. Just seeing them there, ready for action, created a sense of expectation and as we dashed backstage to change into our costumes, our nerves began to rise.

We ran through the dance a couple of times, getting a feel for the stage and how we could make best use of its space. Then, three-quarters of the way through the third run-through, we heard the click of a door and the stomping of large feet ascending the stairs.

'Quick! It's Rodda!' squealed Jo, shutting off the stereo, and ushering us off the stage. 'Er... hello?' she shouted, rushing towards the stairs.

'Hello!' boomed a voice back.

'Yes. Definitely Rodda,' said Ele with a knowing nod.

'Oh my God, he almost caught us in the act!' said Alix.

'Yeah, it would have spoilt the impact a bit!' Goldy added.

We hurried backstage and flew into our costumes before braving the stage to greet Rodda.

'Well then, ladies, look at you!' he said, checking us out in our full regalia. 'Grrrrrr, you look fantastic!' I felt myself blush, but jumped down from the stage with the others to give him a welcoming hug.

Rodda is a big booming ex-biker turned pub landlord. One of Stroud's big characters, he is formidable, friendly, charismatic, well travelled and instantly likeable. Comfortable in his own skin, we felt comfortable in his presence and we chit-chatted for a while about Rosie, autism and about how he planned to introduce our act.

'So you girls are about to make my day!' he teased.

'Well, we do hope so,' I replied candidly. 'You're our barometer. Whatever reaction we get from you will give us a measure of how well we will go down with a big audience.'

'So be gentle with us,' joked Bonnie in her silky voice.

Rodda laughed. 'OK I will... so are you ready then, girls? Sock it to me!' he said, cupping his hands together and displaying a wide grin.

I spotted the old armchair that we'd taken off the stage and Alix and I dragged it slap bang into the middle of the hall.

'Right. Sit there, me dears!' I said in an exaggerated Gloucestershire accent.

'OK, the Full Monty Girls are a go-go!!' said Jo. 'Sit back, relax and enjoy, Rodda. This is your lucky day!'

★ ★ ★ ★ ★

This was our first real performance and we took to the stage with our hearts thumping. After getting into position (feet hip-width apart, heads down), Goldy and I exchanged an excited glance that reminded me of our very first rehearsal. We'd come a long way – and we knew it. Then, when the beat dictated, we looked up to see our first audience: one man seated – as happy as a king – in an old armchair.

As we got into the swing of the dance, our adrenalin kicked in and we began to have fun by smiling, winking, 'Ooooing' and 'Ahhhhing' at Rodda as our costumes came off piece by piece. Rodda became more and more wide-eyed, sometimes smiling, sometimes chuckling to himself as we performed. At the end of the dance, as we approached our big moment, he was literally pinned to the back of the chair as if on a roller-coaster ride. Then, in a second, it was over and we ran off the stage, suddenly hyper-aware of our nakedness. Jo jumped up, grabbed our gear and brought it backstage. 'If you can do that well on the night, you're going to bring the house down,' she said, her doe eyes shining. 'I mean, honestly, I'm so proud of you all. You're my babies!' She flicked her bleach-blonde hair over her shoulder and left us to dress.

'Aw, Jo. She's such a sweetie,' said Bonnie as she clasped her bra.

'We'd better see what the verdict is,' I said with a smile. We hurried into our clothes, then surrounded him, eager for the reaction from this larger-than-life, unflappable man.

'Ok, so what d'ya think, Rodda?' asked Ele, after she had given him a kiss on the cheek.

'Uh… uh, fantastic! I mean… wow! Um, you gir… it was… well, *incredible!*'

'Well I never – we've silenced the lion,' joked Bonnie. We all laughed as the normally composed bear of a man struggled to find his words.

'Well. I jus… I just wasn't expecting it. So professional, so… well. This doesn't often happen to me, but I'm speechless!'

'It's all down to Jo, and her great choreography,' said Alix, giving her a friendly nudge. Jo smiled bashfully, and we all beamed, on a high from what could only be described as the perfect reaction.

'This night's going to be a corker!' said Rodda, taking a few steps back before turning to leave. 'And I might just be the luckiest man in the world!'

'Well, we're glad you liked it!' Jo called after him as he disappeared down the stairs. We froze, motionless (still sporting those insane grins) until we heard the door click shut behind him. Then we jumped around the room, squealing with delight.

An amused look spread across Goldy's face. 'Well, if we can tame the lion… and turn him into a teensy little mouse, then we're on the right track.'

'Who's up for a bevvy down the Greyhound to celebrate?' asked Bonnie.

'Tell you what,' said Jo, 'one more run-through and we'll hit the pub like we deserve it!'

'And it's my round,' I said. 'I owe you all one... for everything really.'

'Don't be so ridiculous,' said Bonnie with a mock frown. 'We're all here 'cos we want to be...'

Goldy, already back on the stage, swung her umbrella onto her shoulder and said, 'Well you can buy me one, Kar 'cos I'm skint!'

'Cool, you're on!' I replied, joining her.

That evening, six women strolled laughing and joking to the local pub for a G&T. We had never felt so confident, part of something so special – you could see it in the way we walked: strutting, relaxed, buoyant, working our curves like we'd only just discovered their power. We had stunned the lion and boy did it feel good!

When I got home that night, I was left with the incredible feeling of what it was to be part of the collective force that had become the Full Monty Girls. Together we had gone through a myriad of emotions and had dug deep to find the confidence we needed to shine. We had sizzled and simmered, and now we were ready.

It was time.

CHAPTER TEN

THE BIG DAY

Have you ever had one of those nights before a big event – a wedding, a job interview, a holiday – when you know you *should* sleep, but you just lie there, tossing and turning in a semi-conscious malaise? You check the clock hour by hour, you count sheep, you sit up, lie down, put the pillow on your head but nothing is going to give you the sweet, restorative release of sleep. Well, Friday the fifteenth of September was one of those nights for me, because the next day, four remarkable women and I were going to face our fate and strip naked in front of an audience.

I watched the dawn light seep through the curtains and listened as the birds awoke one by one until the valley filled with life and light and sound. Then finally, I slept. Lulled by its harmony and my exhaustion.

Suddenly a phone was thrust onto my ear. 'Kar, wake up. It's ITV News!'

Within half a second I was bolt upright and wide awake. 'Hello?'

'Hello, Kara. This is ITV News. I understand you and your friends are about to do something very brave for your daughter today.'

'Well, yes, you could put it like that!' I chuckled, rubbing my eyes with my free hand.

'We'd like to come and film a segment for the six o'clock news. I know you must be very busy today, but do you have time to slot us in?'

I grabbed the clock. 8am. Then I got up and peeped through the curtains. Wincing at the strength of the early autumn sun, I sat back on the bed and tried to take in the magnitude of my wake-up call.

'Well, yes, we'd love to! Of course! It would be fantastic!'

'Great!' said the reporter. 'We love good-news stories! Our local correspondent Ken Goodwin is in your area today. We'd like to send him down to your house to meet you, your daughters and your partner, then we'd like to head down to the venue and film you and the rest of the Full Monty Girls in action!'

As we hashed out the details, the rumbling fear that had gripped me all night was replaced by bubbling excitement. We were going to be on TV! There would literally be thousands of people sitting down to tea, who'd flick on the news and see us! Perhaps it would inspire people to come to the show and support us. This was the ultimate advertising campaign; we'd only sold three-quarters of the tickets so it would be great to have a last-minute boost of publicity.

Andy was cooking sausages and eggs for breakfast when I emerged from the bedroom, phone in hand.

'Oh my giddy God. We're going to be on the six o'clock news!' I exclaimed gleefully, giving him a peck on the cheek. Rosie and Grace both ran towards me and I picked them up, one in each arm. 'You hear that, girlies, you're going to be famous for a day!' I spun round in a circle and they clung on smiling and giggling. 'Everyone will see how cute you both are… and how crazy your mother is!'

'Wonderful, more like!' said Andy, dishing out the breakfast with an easy smile as I seated the girls.

'Thanks, hun,' I replied. 'Do you mind if I dive in the shower? The news reporter is coming soon and we all have to be presentable.'

Suddenly a worried look spread over his face.

'What is it?' I asked coaxingly.

'They're not going to want to talk to *me* are they?'

'Yes, I think so… but they do seem really nice. And I'm sure it'll only be for a second. It will be the old "Do you mind your partner becoming a stripper?" question.'

To my relief, he laughed. 'Oh, the things you drag me into, Mrs!' he said, resigning himself to the inevitable tidal wave that was to become this day.

I headed into the bathroom and dived into the shower to wash off the fake tan that Goldy and I had applied on ourselves – and each other – the night before (with great hilarity, I might add, because we were fake tan virgins). Wrapping myself in a towel, I stood in front of the mirror and paused for a few seconds. I looked so different! My hair was now highlighted blonde and layered into a proper style (again a first). I'd plucked my eyebrows. I'd shaved! All the dancing and the chocolate ban had made me lose a stone and a half, which, let's face it, is always nice when you've spent the last four and a half years feeling more 'vo-lump-tuous' than 'voluptuous'. This whole crazy journey had changed me, inside and out, and had given me a reason to look after myself and care about my appearance. Now I had to take the ultimate test: to wear that new-found confidence on the stage. Naked.

I pulled a few burlesque faces in the mirror: A puckered Oooo, a saucy wink, a surprised gasp with the tips of my fingers over my mouth. I smiled to myself at the absurdity of it all. Then, ceremoniously, I let my towel drop to the floor. *OK, this is me*, I thought, taking an in-breath and staring at my body in the mirror, the beauty of it and the flaws: the long legs I possessed with the slightly knocked knees; ample boobs gently giving in to gravity; my sagging ex-baby-sack of a tummy, covered in stretch marks, in the shape of a big ironic smile. I grabbed it with two hands and gave it a little wobble. 'This is me!' I repeated, this time out loud and with a hint of resignation.

★ ★ ★ ★ ★

Over in Nailsworth, a distinctly browner-looking Bonnie was sitting on her bed with a big tub of body butter, calmly contemplating the day. As she smoothed the cream onto her legs an image flashed through her mind of the night ahead and the corners of her mouth lifted into a smile.

Bonnie's legs were the part of her body she loved the least. One word: cellulite. She had an enviable figure – the classic British pear. The bombshell… small waist, big breasts, childbearing hips, with the not-so-welcome tendency to carry weight on the thighs and bum. The pesky orange-peel-like dimpling was inevitable – the bane of the pear. In the six weeks leading up to the show, Bonnie's biggest challenge had been to learn to love her body, cellulite and all. This was no small thing. After all, Bonnie was a curvaceous lady. But her adventures in burlesque had helped her realise that the secret to sex appeal comes from within.

In the contemplative quietness of her room, before the chaos of the day possessed her and gave her to the night, she felt total acceptance of herself. No nerves, no butterflies, just utter calm. She was ready for whatever came her way – including the six o'clock news.

★ ★ ★ ★ ★

Goldy's day was quite simply going to be monumental. She was in the process of moving out of the house she had previously shared with her now ex-boyfriend Nige. She was on her hands and knees repainting a skirting board when I rang.

'What!' she shouted playfully down the mouthpiece once she'd located the phone under a dust sheet.

'OK, you're just not going to believe what's happened now,' I chortled excitedly.

'Well, if someone hasn't died I'm not interested! I literally hit the ground running this morning,' she replied in exasperation.

'No, this is worth it, believe me. We're going to be on the six o clock news!'

'WHAT!'

'Yes, exactly!' I said giggling, 'and they want to film us at the Space at one o'clock. Can you call Alix and let her know?'

'Yes of course! But I'd better get on with it, Kar, I'm almost disappearing into a pot of paint here!'

★ ★ ★ ★ ★

When I rang Ele, she was reading a magazine, wine glass of orange juice in hand and Radio Four burbling away in the background.

'Hi Els, haven't woken you, have I?' I asked.

'Oh, hello darling, no, no. I'm sitting back in bed reading *Cotswold Life*. I was up early this morning and decided to take a stroll across the valley to clear my head. I'm feeling a bit, well... nervy to be perfectly honest.'

'Where's Rich?'

'Downstairs making coffee. What's happening with you?'

'Well, brace yourself honey, we're going to be on the six o'clock news!'

'You've *got* to be kidding me!'

★ ★ ★ ★ ★

Back at home Andy and I tidied the house and awaited the imminent arrival of ITV's Ken Goodwin. He had been in the business for as long as I could remember, gracing our tea-time television with breaking news from every nook and cranny of the South West. If there was something quirky or interesting to report, they'd send out good old Ken, who'd always sign off in the same familiar manner: 'This is Ken Goodwin, for ITV News, cheese rolling on Cooper's Hill,' or 'This is Ken Goodwin, for ITV News, in Cheddar cave having tea with a witch.' Ken Goodwin was up for anything – he was nothing short of a legend.

Ken and his crew decided to stage the interview in our

living room and set up their filming equipment whilst I made them all tea.

'We want the whole family sitting together on the sofa like you would on any ordinary day,' said Ken.

I'd never done a televised interview before, so when it began, the presence of the cameras felt intimidating. But Ken was very personable and instantly put us both at ease by asking a lot of good questions. They struggled to get a good sound bite though because Rosie was either babbling to herself, humming or trying to wriggle off my lap. We must have done fifty takes before the cameraman finally gave up. 'OK love, I think we have enough footage to cut together a decent piece,' he said in kind resignation.

Later, when the crew came to the Space to interview the Full Monty Girls, you couldn't help but notice the excited amusement spread across Ken Goodwin's face as he clapped eyes on us, dressed in our revealing costumes.

'I've reported on a lot of things in my time,' he said with twinkling eyes, 'but I've never had to interview a group of charity strippers before.'

'Well, there's always a first time for everything,' said Bonnie, rippling with laughter.

'So, girls, we want to film you rehearsing on the stage while I stand close to the camera and say something like, 'I'm here with the girls at their last dress rehearsal… and in just a few hours' time, they will be getting their kit off for real, on this very stage.' Then I'll come up onto the stage, interrupt you and conduct a short interview. How does that sound?'

'Yep! Let's go for it,' said Goldy, sounding confident.

It took three takes to get what they wanted and we all had a scream. In between takes, he'd have shine-reducing powder applied to his face and would return to the camera, holding an oversized microphone, ready for someone to call 'Action'. To end the skit, we were asked to protest when he gave us the verbal cue, 'OK girls, I'll leave you to it,' so we had a bit of fun by throwing a red feather boa round his shoulders and asking him to join in! Ken loved it and signed off with, 'This is Ken Goodwin, for ITV News, having the time of my life in Stroud.'

When the camera stopped rolling he picked up an escaped red feather from the floor and said, 'That was great fun, girls. Can I keep this feather as a souvenir? It will remind me of the day I met five brave ladies working for such a worthy cause.'

'Oh course!' said Alix sweetly.

We all followed Ken and the camera crew down the backstairs to the exit.

'Thank you so much for coming out and giving us some coverage,' I said, shaking his hand. 'Can't wait for six o'clock now!'

We ventured out onto the street – still in costume – to look at their big white van parked prominently on the pavement. It had satellite dishes on the roof and ITV NEWS written in big letters on the side and there were people gathering to see what was going on. Suddenly, *we* became the spectacle and we found ourselves coming over all self-conscious. We smiled, joked about and pretended it was all in a day's work.

When we got back inside, Ele turned and said, 'I guess that means tonight, my darlings…we *are* the news!'

★ ★ ★ ★ ★

We stayed at the venue for a couple of hours to decorate the stage with red hearts, put chairs round the edge of the room and stock the bar with alcohol. Then, when our friends Dangerous Dave, Kim and Pete arrived to set up the PA and lighting, we ran through the show just one last time with stage lights flashing and full booming sound. That was when it began to feel real. All we needed now was an audience.

When I got home I went through the motions of cooking the tea, bathing the girls and settling them to sleep, but my mind was elsewhere. All my thoughts revolved around the show, and a jumble of projected images, inner pep talks and swarming doubts consumed me. If I tried to remember the dance routine my mind drew a disconcerting blank and I began to wonder if I was going to succumb to stage fright.

The six o'clock news proved to be a welcome distraction. It felt so surreal seeing us all on the TV and the phone rang off the hook afterwards with excited friends and family who'd tuned in. Then, before I could catch my breath, it was time to head back down the hill to the venue. The moment of truth had arrived and there was no going back.

Just before leaving, I made myself a cup of tea and went to sit on my front step to try and compose myself. *Three months ago*, I thought, *I was sitting in this exact spot at a total loss as to how to move forward in a positive way. I told myself to wait till September and for better or worse, things would be different. And I was right! Now we have hope, we've got a direction and life is about as technicolour as it can get!*

★ ★ ★ ★ ★

When it comes to getting ready for a show, the backstage area at the Space is tiny. There are two small dressing rooms, one with a toilet cubicle to the right of the stage and another down a thin corridor which runs along the back of the stage, linking the two. This second room was stuffed full of stage lights and old PA speakers so we all congregated in the room by the loo, hanging our costumes on every available inch of wall space. With five women, a choreographer, two hairdressers *and* the odd visitor crammed in, we became a blur of bodies: dressing and undressing, dusting each other with body glitter and sharing the mirror to apply our makeup. The room was a whirl of colour and flesh: black, scarlet, feather, lace, French knickers, tanned legs, bouncing bosoms and sparkling sequins. There was make-up being applied with shaky hands, basques being tightened, and stockings being pulled over nail-polished feet then attached to suspenders. There was laughter and admiration, insecurity and panic. The smell of hot hair and hairspray filled the air as our hair was straightened and coiffured into seductive burlesque creations. Adrenalin began to flow and intensified with the arrival of our audience. Their voices and laughter filled the air and mingled with the music, which thumped like the ticking of a clock, drawing us closer and closer to our impending performance.

We were a million miles from where we had started: three girls, a cup of coffee and Goldy's idea to ride naked down Stroud High Street like Lady Godiva. Now that sleepy dream had become reality – we were living it.

Andy was the only man allowed into the room and he'd pop his head round the door from time to time to give us an update on who had arrived and a head count.

On one such occasion, he passed back a beautiful hand-tied bunch of roses. 'Your dad's here, Golds... and he brought these,' he said passing the flowers to Jo who opened the accompanying card and read aloud, 'Good luck girls on your special night, love from David and Barbara.'

Goldy smiled proudly and took the flowers from Jo, propping them up on the windowsill.

'Also, your mum's here, Bonnie... and your sister – and Jon. And Valerie and Paul are here, Kar, with some of their mates. And there are two doctors and a nurse from the Children's Hospital who looked after Rosie.'

I was stunned. 'Really? That's amazing!' I said, with tears in my eyes. 'I can't believe they would come...'

'Obviously saw it in the paper,' he replied.

'Wow,' I said, as Goldy handed me a tissue.

'Don't well up now, love...' she said in a happy tempo, 'or your make-up will run!' 'Also... *I've* got you all a little something,' continued Andy, who stood aside to allow our good friend Beccy to come into view. She was holding five glasses and a bottle of champagne.

'Glass of bubbly to steady the nerves,' she said.

We erupted with gratitude.

'So who else is out there?' asked Bonnie, before applying a layer of bight red lipstick.

'Everyone you've ever known and their grandma... it's getting quite packed,' said Beccy, filling the glasses and handing them out one by one.

'OK,' said Andy, suddenly looking abashed. 'There's a bit too much flesh for me in here. I'm gonna go. I'll see you after.'

'OK. What's the time now?' asked Goldy, ever practical and poised.

'Nearly nine,' he replied. 'Ceilidh Jo and her band are on in five minutes and then you're on at ten.'

'Flipping heck!' said Ele. 'It's actually happening!'

The following hour whizzed by. The band finished with a genius folk cover of *Can't Get You Out of my Head* by Kylie. Then, as they cleared the stage, disco music was reinstated.

We could hear the crowd begin to gather as Beccy set the stage for us. Then she popped her head round the door. 'Five minute warning,' she said with an excited smile, 'and it's a full house!'

We stood together united. There is no other way to put it, we were absolutely bricking it, trembling with anticipation. We huddled into a circle and looked at each other with nervous smiles, squeaking with excitement and hopping up and down to shake out our nerves.

Suddenly the music died down and the excited chattering in the crowd began to stir into cheers.

'This is it, ladies!' I said, as we all put our hands together in the middle of our circle. 'Let's get out there and have the time of our lives!'

Then there was stasis, as we listened to the crowd and gathered our last ounce of courage.

'GOOD EVENING LADIES AND GENTLEMEN!' boomed Rodda's voice suddenly, as he made his way through the crowd, mic in hand. The crowd began to cheer loudly and we screamed with delight and relief.

'Listen to that, they *want* us!' exclaimed Goldy, wriggling in her basque to elevate her gargantuan assets even higher.

We lined up for our introduction onto the stage.

'Here we go!' said Ele, with the look of someone about to do a bungee jump.

'I HAVE FIVE VERY SPECIAL LADIES FOR YOU THIS EVENING...' continued Rodda with gusto, 'FOR YOUR PLEASURE!'

Clearly the lion was back on form.

The cheering built in volume and pace, and Bonnie playfully stuck a leg out of the stage door, producing a roar from the crowd.

'LADIES AND GENTLEMEN... PLEASE WELCOME... BONNIE... ELE... KARA... GOLDY AND ALIX! I GIVE YOU... THE FULL MONTY GIRLS!'

We strutted onto the stage as he called our names and waved at the audience with as much confidence as we could muster. Squinting to make out the size of the crowd through the flashing stage lights, we settled into our positions. There was a momentary hush as we waited for the music to start. I stared at my feet and held my breath. A couple of people from the back of the room shouted out 'Come on, Bonnie!' and 'Goldy!' All five of our hearts were pounding, our mouths were paper dry, and we waited, about to embark on a leap into the completely unbridled unknown. The eager audience began to chant and cheer to see the dance that had been the talk of the town for weeks. The urge to look up at the wall of sound was overwhelming, but we remained in position, straining for the introduction of the song. There was a moment when we wondered, *Will we hear it at all?*

Time seemed to stand still for an eternal moment, as it does sometimes when your world is hurtling beyond your control and comfort. Then it hurled us – full thrust – into the vivid whirl of movement, and light, and rhythm as the music penetrated the cheers.

There was nothing left to do but dance.

As we raised our heads in perfect time and faced our audience, one thought sprang into all our minds: 'OH MY GOD, I'm actually doing this! I'm going to get naked! NAKED – in front of all these people!'

The stage lights flashed hot and bright in my eyes as I tried to locate Andy but couldn't – there was too much to take in, too many people to scan.

'You don't have to be beautiful, to turn me on,' began the opening song *Kiss*.

The sheer number of gathered people stunned me. A sea of faces and mobile phones set to record. Everyone was smiling, whooping and cheering at the top of their lungs.

At first my legs felt as if they were made of concrete and for a moment I felt out of time, wooden and about as far away from sexy as you could get. But the power and support of the cheering crowd dispersed my nerves and gave me a sudden rush of euphoria.

'You can't be too flirty, Mama, I know how to undress me,' continued the song, as we strutted round the stage. We unbuttoned our suit jackets, and, as each of us reached centre-front, threw them open and slipped them off provocatively to reveal our basques and cleavage in one eye-popping movement. The crowd went wild, momentarily drowning out the music, as each girl came forward.

Then it struck me like an epiphany… it suddenly hit me that the audience loved us! There was a repartee between us and our audience and they were hanging on every move we made. The power of that synergy was electrifying, like nothing I had experienced before. Instantly, my moves became more fluid and as I caught eye contact with each of the girls, I could see they were feeling the same as me. We began to have fun, smiling to each other and the audience, as we dished out our moves perfectly in sync, perfectly in time.

'I wanna be your fantasy, maybe you can be mine,' sang Prince as we abandoned our nerves and unleashed our inner minxes. 'You just leave it all up to me, and we can have a good time.'

We unbuttoned our trousers, wiggling them off seductively to reveal our fishnet stockings, suspenders and French knickers.

'Ain't no particular sign I'm more compatible with, I just want your extra time and your… Kiss!' We spun in a circle and blew kisses at the audience.

The music changed to *Fever* and the mood of the dance turned from upbeat and sassy to smouldering and smoking. The lighting changed too. Sultry shades of blue and purple gave our skin an ethereal glow. We began to sizzle across the stage, bringing forward and twirling our gold chairs with controlled precision. Swinging one leg onto the red velvet seat in unison, we fluttered our eyelashes at the audience with cheeky knowing smiles and winked and pulled our well-rehearsed burlesque expressions of shock and delight, as people shouted our names and wolf-whistled over the swell of sound.

'You give me fever, fever when you kiss me, fever when you hold me tight.'

We detached our fishnet stockings from our suspenders one by one, which created a deafening roar from the crowd, and then we peeled off our stockings and pinged them mischievously into the audience.

'Everybody's got the fever, that is something we all know, fever isn't such a new thing, fever started long ago.'

Sauntering to the back of the stage, our chairs trailing behind us, we turned to unclasp our basques, drawing closer and closer to the audience as we opened each fastening. I caught Goldy's eye and could read her thoughts like a mirror. She was thinking, *This is it! This is my moment to shine and show all these people exactly how damn sexy I can be*. Her face shone and she moved like a temptress across the stage, every well-rehearsed twist and turn of her body revealing, in her own words, 'Just that little bit more naughtiness, outrageousness and hot sexy mama-ness'. Then as we stood just a hair's breadth from our audience, we slipped off our basques and revealed our bodies in nothing but our underwear.

'Now you've listened to my story,' sang Peggy Lee. 'Here's the point that I have made. Chicks were born to give you fever, be it Fahrenheit or centigrade.'

The noise from the crowd was deafening.

As the dance continued, I located so many familiar faces. Friends, past and present. Friends of Ele, family of Goldy and Bonnie, then finally Andy and our choreographer Jo, standing on chairs at the side of the room, whistling and cheering as if their lives depended on it. Some of our friends were crying, tears streaming down their faces, caught up in the moment and filled with emotion and pride. Bonnie's husband Jon was standing right at the front of the crowd, staring at Bonnie open-mouthed. He was completely in awe of her, as the tigress inside her that she'd kept only for him now slinked resplendently around the stage like an enchanting temptress. She shone with confidence. She was doing this not only for Rosie but also for every mother, sister and friend that felt insecure about her size and hid her body away.

'They give you fever, when you kiss them, fever if you live and learn. Fever till you sizzle, what a lovely way to burn.'

I glanced at Ele; she was moving effortlessly in the blue light like a mischievous duchess, accentuating every wiggle, every wink and gracefully revealing her slender body with diva-esque finesse. It was then that I realised the dance we had spent all these weeks creating was a sensation.

Facing the audience, we unclasped our bras and removed them whilst keeping one arm over our chests to conceal our modesty. The crowd went wild with anticipation, thinking they were going to get an eyeful of boob but we turned our backs to them and strutted away, only then lifting our arms skyward. It was the ultimate tease.

As the music changed again to the brassy burlesque tones of *The Stripper*, and with backs to the audience, we adorned our shoulders with feather boas, letting the scarlet feathers cascade down our bodies to conceal our breasts. Then we turned in unison and like cancan girls moved towards our awaiting sea of spectators with high straight-legged kicks.

I caught a glimpse of Alix and was stunned at her beauty both inside and out. Living in Brighton she'd had so little rehearsal time but her dance moves were in perfect sync with the rest of us. As she sashayed across the stage, her raven hair reflected the burnished light and her skin sparkled with body glitter. She'd travelled 150 miles to be here and I could see from her smile that she was glad she had. And when we stopped it was she who was the first to lift her feather boa skywards to reveal her body in nothing but a pair of lacy French knickers. The crowd erupted. Then it was my turn to bare, then Goldy, then Ele, then Bonnie. We stood together in our penultimate state of undress, displaying a sea of bootylicious bosoms, in every shape and size – and we lingered and smiled and soaked up the tsunami of support from the deafening crowd, before turning to locate our umbrellas for the final reveal.

Suddenly a surge of fear and excitement engulfed my entire body as the pending nudity was almost upon us. *OK, OK, here goes!* I said to myself, as we opened our umbrellas to form a screen behind which we quickly whipped off our lacy knickers. We held them up to show the audience that we were indeed naked and a frenzied cheer rippled through the crowd as they anticipated the finale of the show.

Everything had come down to this one moment; all our fears, all our courage, the message we had sent into the world that we, the Full Monty Girls, dared to bare all to give a special little girl the chance of a better life. This was the moment where all our worlds collided in the simplicity of a naked form.

In the end it was easy.

Pulling in our tummies, we lifted our umbrellas high and bared all for what felt like a glorious liberating eternity. Then the lights went down and it was over.

We ran off the stage in the darkness saying, 'Oh my God! OH MY GOD!!!!!!!!!!! WE DID IT!'

The sound that was coming from the audience now was insane. Every single person was cheering at the very top of their voice and the floor shook as they stamped their feet, shouting, 'MORE! MORE! MORE!'

Backstage, against that backdrop of sound, the closeness we felt as a group was incredible. We had come through a journey of monumental fears and letting go. We had experienced something so wild and liberating. As we rushed into our underwear for the encore, we all said the same thing, 'That was without a doubt one of the best moments of my life.'

★ ★ ★ ★ ★

It was two o'clock when I finally got home and I quietly tiptoed into my house so as not to wake anyone up. My ears rang loudly in the silence – a remnant of the sheer volume of the crowd. In the darkness, I crept across the living room to the window seat and sat in a pool of moonlight. I looked across the sleeping valley: mute, still and suffused with inky shades of grey. After all the adrenalin that had pumped around my body, I knew I'd be lucky if I got a wink of sleep, so I let my mind replay every tantalising second of the show. I almost couldn't believe we'd done it! A calm, blissful, euphoric relief poured over me. And there was emptiness, contained by the bittersweet realisation that I had given my all and it was over. As my mind wandered, I got to thinking how something as small and fleeting as a thought – which starts as nothing more than a ripple in the mind – can change a person's life forever. If the thought is a good one and it's given the power and momentum to thrive, then past, present and future collide in a moment that can be nothing short of explosive – a perfect mélange of the three elements that define time itself. It had never been clearer… if we dare to dream and give ourselves to making those dreams a reality, wonderful and totally unexpected things can happen. All it takes is a little imagination and faith… and between the goalposts of idea and achievement, you begin to experience the story of your life.

As for the future of the Full Monty Girls? There was no denying it, we were hooked. And I couldn't stop myself from wondering… it can't just be a one-off really, can it?

CHAPTER ELEVEN

LIVING THE DREAM

On the morning after the show, I woke up with a big smile on my face, still euphoric from the night before. The success of the show had exceeded all our expectations. Not only had we reached our goal but we'd smashed it, raising over £2,000 for Rosie in the process. It was a wonderful sense of achievement. But as the day wore on and I started to come back down to earth, I couldn't help but feel a sense of loss and emptiness creep into my being. After all the hype, the sense of camaraderie and the endless activity, it was over. There was no getting away from it – I was going to miss being a Full Monty Girl.

'You've got the Full Monty blues, love,' said Goldy when I called her. 'I've been on the phone to Bonnie and she feels exactly the same way. She's completely deflated. Happy, but... you know...'

'Yeah,' I sighed, 'I thought I'd be relieved and don't get me wrong, I am. But I feel kind of empty too.'

'I know... I didn't think about the comedown. If I

could click my fingers now I'd be back on that stage in a heartbeat.'

★ ★ ★ ★ ★

The show might have been over but I still had a lot of money to raise and I knew there was no time to rest on my laurels. There were more conservative fundraising ideas to bring to fruition such as the art auction, and we'd been offered the chance to run a café (which we called the Rosie Café) at Stroud farmers' market. I was exhausted, though, so I decided to allow myself a couple of days to rest before dusting myself off and carrying on. I'd also decided to stick to my word and give up smoking. A couple of days of relaxing would be the perfect opportunity to quit.

The art auction came two short weeks later. Held at Painswick town hall, it showcased the diverse talents of the artists and craftsmen in the area. I was humbled by the amount of works donated. There was sculpture, furniture, knitwear, woodwork, quilting, pottery, paintings and jewellery. Even Rosie painted a picture to be auctioned and by the end of the night we'd raised over £4,000. Added to the money raised by the Full Monty Girls and my original bank loan, Rosie's fund well exceeded £10,000. Now we could pay for both the three-day seminar in Holland *and* the comprehensive five-day training programme in America. We booked our flights and bought a build-your-own wooden chalet to serve as a classroom for Rosie, which we planned to erect in the garden upon our return from Holland. It was incredible to see our dream being put into action. Thanks to pretty much everyone we knew and many people we didn't, we now had the power to give Rosie a fighting chance.

★ ★ ★ ★ ★

In theory, travelling to the Netherlands was achievable. It was only an hour and ten minutes away by plane – a mere hop over the North Sea, but the thought of leaving the security of our Cotswold hillside and taking Rosie abroad filled me and Andy with dread. We hadn't attempted to go further than Cornwall with Rosie, which more than once had ended in epileptic fits and an early return home. Because of this, we knew that venturing overseas could turn into a nightmare. The thought of her potentially needing hospital treatment in Holland was more than a little unnerving. Fortunately, we weren't travelling alone: Goldy, Lily, and Andy's sister Jessica would be joining us. Goldy had volunteered to babysit for Rosie and Grace (whilst Andy and I attended the lectures) and Jessica, who had begun filming for her documentary, wanted to bank some footage of our experiences. We were pleased to have the backup. This meant there would be an extra pair of hands if Rosie had to be rushed to hospital.

I had packed Rosie a carry-on bag for the flight, rammed with things – both practical and distracting – in the hope of keeping her engaged and in a good mood. Nappies, a change of clothes and anti-epilepsy medication were practical choices but beads, straws, pens, paper, play dough, picture cards, books, chocolate, biscuits, crisps and a bottle of juice played equal importance in my 'bag of tricks'. Basically, anything and everything that could hold Rosie's attention for a few minutes was going in my bag and I laughed to myself as I sat on top of it trying to force the zip shut.

The airline was very helpful and put us first in line to be seated on the plane. Rosie settled down with some beads and everything appeared to be going well – until the other people boarded and we hit a snag. When everyone else had settled into their seats, the top of their heads could be seen above the back of their chairs. To you or me, this would mean very little, but to Rosie, it meant one thing: rows and rows of hair, just begging to be played with! It was as if all her Christmasses had come at once! I hadn't anticipated this glitch and before I could stop her, she had plunged her hands into the perfectly styled bouffant of the lady in front of us. To make matters worse, before I could react she'd buried her face in it, letting out a high pitched, 'Ding-ding-a-ding-ding-a-ding.'

It all happened so quickly, I was mortified!

'Rosie, no!' I cried, prising her hands away.

Needless to say the poor passenger nearly jumped out of her skin! She turned round with a look like thunder and muttered something to us in Dutch.

'I'm so sorry, she's autistic,' I said apologetically.

'OK, OK,' she replied, satisfied with the explanation, but clearly not amused.

'I think we've got our work cut out for the next couple of hours!' said Andy, under his breath.

Amsterdam was only the first leg of our journey. The training seminar was in the seaside town of Zandvoort, twenty miles west of the city so we – the merry band of travellers – negotiated bus, train and taxi, determined to reach our destination before nightfall.

First impressions of Zandvoort during late October were, I have to be honest, grey, cold, soulless and wet. The resort in which we were staying (which I'm sure is very charming in summer) was bleak and deserted at this time of year, except for the attendants of the seminar. The chalets (painted grey) were camouflaged against the grey sky, driving rain and the steel-grey North Sea that stretched out beyond the surrounding sand dunes. In fact the only colour that interrupted this monotone scene was the sight of people, in primary-coloured rain macs, dashing to the shelter of their chalets.

In contrast to the scene outdoors, inside the chalets it was warm and cheery. The first thing we noticed when we arrived was a large welcome pack on the kitchen table containing food. Goldy immediately began to unpack it, looking for a snack for the children who were by now desperately hungry.

'Yum, we've got holey cheese, crispbread and salad stuff,' she said while opening a large packet of Dutch-style kettle crisps.

'Any teabags?' asked Andy.

'Yep!' Goldy replied. 'And milk. Here you go, Ands, I could murder a cup of tea.'

With the children now settled with their snack and Andy making tea, Goldy, Jessica and I began to look around. The chalet was clean, well-equipped and there was lots of space, but I could see that from Rosie's perspective there were hazards everywhere.

'We'd better move all these plants and ornaments out of reach,' I said, swiftly blocking off the stairway with a heavy armchair.

'Totally,' said Goldy helpfully. 'And let's sort out who sleeps where.'

'I reckon you, Lily and Jessica in the two bedrooms upstairs and us four down here in the side room,' I replied. 'What d'ya think, Jessica?'

'Sounds sensible,' Jessica agreed. 'But first things first: let's have a glass of wine and eat something. I'm starved.'

'YES!' I replied, enthusiastically eyeing up the bottle she'd produced from her luggage.

'Hold your horses!' interrupted Andy, holding a tray of tea and juice. 'Drink this first and warm up. These next few days are going to be busy and I don't want anyone to catch a cold.'

The next afternoon, before Andy, Jessica and I attended an orientation meeting, Goldy told me that while we were away she planned to make the most of the on-site leisure facilities and take the children swimming.

'Golds, you're crazy to do this on your own,' I said, admiring her courage but knowing she was bonkers to even think it.

Goldy, ever the optimist, couldn't see what I was fussing about. 'Why?' she asked with amusement.

'Because two toddlers and a severely autistic child spells trouble! I wouldn't attempt it in a month of Sundays!'

After we'd left, Goldy, undaunted by my pessimistic attitude, set off for the pool with Grace on her hip, Rosie in the buggy and Lily trotting along beside her. She was delighted to find the pool relatively empty – only a couple of other families and a few lone swimmers were there so they virtually had the place to themselves.

'This is going to be a cinch!' she told herself.

The water was warm and inviting and both Lily and Rosie could walk around well within their depth so she let go of their hands and allowed them to paddle about in the water on their own.

'Isn't this nice,' said Goldy to Grace who was sitting happily on her hip. 'It's like we're on a little holiday, isn't it Gracie?'

She then noticed Rosie, heading across the pool at breakneck speed.

'Rosie!' she called. 'Come back here you cheeky monkey!'

Of course Rosie ignored her.

Goldy scooped up Lily with her free arm and waded after Rosie, who appeared to be fast approaching a rather hairy-looking Dutchman, sitting at the edge of the pool.

'ROSIE!!!' she called again, but again she was ignored, the gap between them widening. Rosie reached the unsuspecting man and clambered onto his lap.

Pinned to the spot and not sure how to respond the poor man's eyes widened in shock.

'Rooooosssssiiieeee!' cried Goldy, still too far away to intervene as Rosie plunged her hands into the man's very hairy chest.

'Oh my goodness! I'm so sorry!' she said, finally catching up and plucking Rosie from his lap.'

The man shook his head in disbelief.

'Autistic!' she said, hoping he would understand. 'Autistic!! So sorry!'

The man smiled weakly but it was clear from his blank response that he didn't understand her.

Those English can't control their children, he probably thought.

Either way, as embarrassing as it was at the time, the comedy of the situation couldn't be denied and when she later told me her story, we couldn't stop ourselves from laughing.

'Autistic people will follow their obsessions! To hell with social airs and graces!' I giggled. 'That's why I always go to places with Rosie *and* another person.'

'I can see that now,' Goldy conceded. 'But still… I did it, Kar. I took them out all by myself and we came back in one piece. That's what counts.'

'Well, I've got to hand it to you, Golds, you're one determined lady.'

Goldy laughed. 'Anyway, how was your orientation?'

'Well, we met the founder of Growing Minds. A guy called Steven Wertz. I had butterflies queueing up to meet him. Don't know why!'

'Probably because you want this to work so much.'

'Yeah probably… he's this big bear of a man, Golds – a bit like a bearded version of Rodda. Really friendly. He's got one of those big personalities that fill a room, you know? Anyway, we start tomorrow with the lectures, so we'll just have to see.'

We sat silently for a while, then I got up to start making dinner.

'Oh, and another thing,' I said, turning to face her. 'Andy told Steven that Rosie's here in Holland and asked him if he'd drop by and meet her. You know, tell us his thoughts on her autism and all that… he's coming tomorrow after the seminar!'

'Wow!'

'I know! Andy's thrilled, what with Rosie being such

an enigma and all. Maybe he can shed some light on her condition and tell us how she'll respond to this kind of intervention. Sometimes she seems so unreachable – or maybe unteachable is a better word…'

'Well, the hairy man from the pool would have disagreed,' laughed Goldy. '"Highly sociable" would have been *his* description!'

★ ★ ★ ★ ★

That night I went to bed with a racing heart. At the end of the day would any of our efforts ever make a difference, or were we just chasing the dream of a future that Rosie could never have? I had read that ten per cent of autistic children will not respond to any type of intervention. Could Rosie be in that ten per cent? Of course connecting with Rosie non-verbally was easy. She knew she was loved. There was an unspoken bond between us that would transcend any challenge we faced together. But as far as functional communication went, we had nothing. Could we build a bridge that would connect our worlds and facilitate a real flow of communication? Was she remotely teachable? I was worried that the answer would be 'no'. Reaching Rosie was without a doubt the biggest challenge of our lives.

The next morning, ten minutes into his first lecture, Steven Wertz said something that revolutionised my understanding of autism forever:

'There are people you could look at and say, "Severely autistic", or "Mentally impaired"… but when we work with these people for a little bit of time, we can see that they have a good mind – and they want to use it.'

Later that day, we spruced up the chalet in anticipation of Steven's arrival. I couldn't help but feel a little nervous and when he knocked on the door, my stomach leapt, but if Steven sensed the maelstrom of emotions riding on his visit he didn't show it.

Andy did his best to explain our concerns about Rosie and Steven listened warmly, observing her running around the room as Andy spoke.

So far Rosie had ignored our visitor. Perhaps she was listening to our conversation and adjusting to Steven's presence; perhaps she was lost in her own little world. Either way, she suddenly stopped running and abruptly turned to face him.

Steven reacted in an animated way. His kind-looking face suddenly lit up and his whole body jumped in delight at her gaze. Pleased with his reaction she approached him and touched his beard.

'Rosie! Hello! Well, it's lovely to see you,' he said sincerely. His voice was deep and his American accent carried the hint of a New York twang.

Andy, Goldy and I watched their interaction. He knew how to engage her and keep her attention in a way that I'd never seen before. He asked her to tap the table and helped her respond, praising her efforts and co-operation. He exaggerated his reactions to her, in response to her curiosity in him. He adjusted the volume and pitch of his voice to see which best attracted her attention. It was inspirational to see the way he worked. After a few minutes Rosie returned to her rituals so Steven turned his attention back to us.

'You have a beautiful daughter,' he said, pausing to accommodate our smiles. He had a way of speaking, never fast, often with a measured pause, which gave every sentence gravitas and meaning. 'We're also looking forward to you coming to spend a week with us in Florida,' he continued. 'Rosie has some dyspraxia, some motor control issues and we have some work to do with her communication... but she engages easily and she certainly knows her own mind!'

He broke out into a sudden booming laugh and we laughed too, partly from surprise. After a few minutes he rose to leave and Andy expressed our gratitude for his visit.

'It was a pleasure to meet your family,' he replied graciously.

After he left, I ran and hugged Andy in a rush of optimism.

'Now we have hope!' he whispered.

All the while Jessica filmed us. More a producer by trade, she quickly mastered the camera equipment, recording every detail of our trip, from Steven talking at the seminar, to Rosie, Grace and Lily running round the chalet.

It was easy to see the passion she had in the project and despite being family, she was very professional, knowing exactly what footage she needed to portray Rosie's story.

Over the next three days at the seminar, Steven described the techniques the Growing Minds Programme uses both for the classroom and everyday life. Topics like 'Handling challenging behaviour', 'Helping children with dyspraxia' and 'How to harness a positive attitude to encourage motivation and communication' were covered in great detail. Teaching methods were discussed too. The main ones being Son-Rise and ABA (Applied Behaviour Analysis).

Briefly, ABA is a practical technique with ongoing assessment where the child is expected to complete a programme of tasks ('discrete trials') within a designated timeframe. Each trial has three clear steps: an instruction from the teacher, a response from the child and a reaction from the teacher. If the child completes the task there is an immediate reward (reinforcement), like praise, food or time with a favourite toy. If the child needs help they are prompted by the teacher and then rewarded for effort and co-operation. Better and faster responses to requests mean bigger rewards, which the child picks up very quickly. This fast-paced request/response/result tactic is fun for the child and keeps them engaged and motivated. A programme of trials covering a broad range of targets is repeated at intervals during the day until a new skill is mastered and they can move on.

Son-Rise on the other hand uses an enthusiastic, play-oriented method, focusing on socialisation and rapport-building. The method embraces an attitude of total acceptance of the child – just the way they are. In doing so, rather than *trying to stop* a child's repetitive ways, they *join in* with them, including their exclusive and ritualistic behaviours. Joining the child in their world and embracing their interests gives the teacher the opportunity to build a connection, which creates a platform to further their education and development.

The Growing Minds Programme uses both these techniques and tailors an IEP (individualised education plan) to specifically help each child access education, channelling their strengths to work through their challenges.

During the lectures (and fortified by further research and observation during the years that followed), I began to piece together what Rosie might be experiencing. Autism manifests itself in many ways depending on how severely it affects the individual, but for people with severe autism like Rosie, sensory processing issues can play a big part in how they perceive the world around them. A neurotypical (non-autistic) brain will automatically pick out the most important sensory information from its surroundings, making it easy to function safely and effectively in the world. Autistic brains, on the other hand, are wired a little differently…

If you were to stop and listen for a second, you might hear the hum of your fridge, the whirr of your computer, cars driving past your house, an aeroplane, perhaps, or birdsong. There might be people talking in the room or on the street outside, or the sound of children playing. Imagine taking them all in at once. No filters, just sound. Intense, isn't it? Previously, your brain has been selectively filtering out some of these background sounds so you can focus your attention on reading this book. Someone with severe autism experiencing difficulty with auditory processing doesn't always manage to filter incoming sounds in order of relevance. This can make it hard to focus on the 'right' thing when in a setting that demands your full attention, like in a classroom, for example.

Then there's visual processing to contend with. When you're out and about, you know to make, let's say, the car driving towards you a visual priority over the detail of a crack in the pavement, or your image reflected in a shop window as you walk by. You don't have to think about it; your brain will do it all for you. In this case, it will save you from being run over. With visual processing difficulties, every detail in your visual field can hit you between the eyes and beg for attention. It's the same with all incoming senses: smell, touch, taste, atmosphere… If you live in a world where anything and everything can take priority and distract you from your purpose, the world can become confusing, overwhelming, frightening – even dangerous.

Lastly, imagine that your brain has difficulty organising a response to the world around you. You could have the will to express yourself or the desire to move your limbs but if the part of your brain responsible for organising your thoughts and accessing and assimilating information has trouble functioning correctly, achieving what you set out to do or say can prove to be a challenge. It must be frustrating beyond words, don't you think?

For months I had observed Rosie go in and out of sensory overload several times a day. Sometimes she was focused, engaged and interactive, then – whoosh – the world and its demands would suddenly overwhelm her and she'd retreat into her own little world or have a meltdown. Now, armed with new understanding from the seminar, Andy and I were beginning to see her behaviour in a clearer light.

By the end of the third day in Zandvoort it was also clear that teaching Rosie was not going to be straightforward. The saying goes that when you meet one person with autism, you meet *one* person with autism, and I was beginning to see why this was true. The autistic spectrum – so varied in the way it manifests itself – would never lend itself to a prescriptive one-size-fits-all education programme, and we felt hugely grateful to have the opportunity to go to America, learn more and get some much-needed practical advice.

★ ★ ★ ★ ★

The final day ended on a high. There must have been twenty or thirty people at the seminar and most, including us, were gathered in the foyer of the venue saying our goodbyes. We were all charged with information and energised by the experience. The standout method we all buzzed about was the Son-Rise technique of 'joining the child in their world'. It was something we could all implement straight away to connect with our children and we felt empowered by it.

'I can't wait to go home, see my child and try it out,' said one of the participants, receiving universal agreement from the others. As I too nodded, I glanced out of the hotel doors and spotted Goldy, braving a chilly seaside stroll with Rosie, Grace and Lily.

'Oh, I can see my daughters!' I exclaimed to one of the group, before rushing outside to call them in.

When we got back inside, the entire group gathered round Rosie to admire her. I couldn't help but swell with pride as I unstrapped her from her pushchair and held her in my arms. Her cheeks were flushed red from the cold and some of her blonde hair had escaped from her hat, framing her face angelically.

'Everybody, this is Rose!' I said ceremoniously.

Rosie, unaware of her audience was looking in the opposite direction. She buried her face in my neck and said, 'Tug tug tug a tug a tug tug,' in her usual high-pitched tone.

'Tug tug tug a tug a tug tug,' replied the group in unison, eager to try out our newly learned technique.

Rosie immediately spun around to locate the sound

and clocked the sea of eager smiling faces. She grinned at them in delight and said, 'Yay!'

'Yay!' repeated the group. She broke into a giggle and put her head coyly onto my shoulder. It was the perfect end to the seminar and now a treasured memory.

The hope that we gleaned from that short interaction became another turning point in our journey with Rosie – an injection of confidence that we were on the right track. And in that moment, Zandvoort no longer felt grey and soulless; it was as warm and welcoming and inspiring as the people around us. We were united by one mission: to help our autistic children reach their potential, the hope of a better life for them burning in our hearts. We knew that the journey might be long and fraught with emotion but we also knew that the fighting spirit of our beautiful children would shine a light and with it bring happiness and humour – and we would all need it because we could now see their challenges all the more clearly. We'd always known how extraordinary and special our children were. We'd also known how hard they had to work to achieve the things that most of us take for granted. But we could now see with renewed clarity how resourceful, determined, innovative, perceptive, truthful, passionate, authentic, unique, original and nothing short of inspirational autistic people are – wherever they are on the spectrum.

★ ★ ★ ★ ★

As we travelled back on the plane, the exhausted children peacefully asleep on our laps, I began to think about Rosie and how people must perceive her – like the hairy Dutch guy in the pool and the lady with the perfect hair on the outbound flight. During the brief encounters she has with strangers, there is no time to explain why she behaves the way she does.

There's no time to say, 'My daughter's essentially just like you, she just has extraordinary neurological challenges to deal with!'

And of course *they* can't be expected to look beyond her strange behaviour to see the person behind it. There's simply no time, in this fast-paced, technicoloured whirlwind of a life, to pause for thought. That's just the way it is. Distracted by the demands of our own lives, we sometimes forget that the bottom line is – whether we're tolerant of each other or not – we're all in this world together. Seven billion people, trying the best we can to deal with the cards that life has dealt us. Perhaps, though, what's written on the cards is as unimportant as it is all-consuming. It's almost too easy to get lost in the detail of our daily lives and lose sight of the fact that often, things are not quite as they first appear to be. A person is not – and never will be – their disability, their illness or the image they project to the world. Neither their wealth, their lifestyle choices nor their religious persuasion. When all these images and labels are stripped away, we become equal: a blank canvas upon which life paints a picture.

In the case of autism the picture can evoke a myriad of responses – believe me, I've seen it all: shock, fear, disgust, pity, amusement, disapproval, curiosity…

My new-found clarity and enthusiasm spurred me forward on my mission to try to spread autism awareness, so when people meet an autistic person like Rosie they will have a better understanding of the condition and be able to see the person behind the label.

★ ★ ★ ★ ★

Within a week of our return from Zandvoort we took delivery of Rosie's classroom. It came in a hundred pieces, ready to be assembled, but sat under a tarpaulin in the November rain for a good fortnight while we waited for a dry spell to erect it. Then, like scenes from an Amish barn raising, Jon and our good friend Wx (pronounced 'Weeks') arrived at first light to help Andy build the basic structure. Bonnie and Goldy also came along, as well as Jessica, who wanted to film the event for her documentary. There was a cheerful mood in the air from the flurry of activity and I remember saying to Goldy that it felt like we were in an episode of *The Little House on the Prairie*. As the sun set on the day we all congregated with hot cups of tea to admire the work. The structure was elevated a foot and a half from the ground on stilts and looked like it was floating. This gave it a surreal quality, like it was the birthplace of a dream waiting to be realised.

In the weeks that followed, Andy continued the project alone, insulating the walls, laying the floor and hanging the doors and windows. He finished just as the first flurry of snow heralded winter, turning the greens and browns of the dormant valley pure lily white.

Now weatherproof, we painted the outside bottle green and the inside peach. Then we installed heating, put up shelves on one wall and screwed a huge mirror to another. The final job (before we brought in her toys) was laying a linoleum floor, but before we rolled it out, I grabbed a small brush and painted these words on the floorboards in emulsion: 'Rosie. I'm going to build a bridge to you. If you want to cross it, you can. No pressure. You can be whoever you want to be! The sky's the limit! Xxxx.'

With the classroom ready for action, Goldy and I took three-hour shifts to spend time playing with Rosie. By playing I mean, we *tried* to play, whilst Rosie wilfully ignored us and pursued her Rosie-ish interests. Her favourite activities at that time were running up and down the classroom (bumping the walls at either end) and standing at the window. Here she had two rituals: moving her lips across the said window's smooth cold surface, and watching the tree branches sway in silhouette against the winter sky. We attempted to practise the 'join your child in their world' technique that we'd learned at Zandvoort and copied her rituals with enthusiasm. To an outsider we must have looked completely insane!

'Do you feel silly?' asked Goldy after one session.

'Yes, I do a bit,' I admitted. But frankly, I didn't care. If this was going to be what it took to get my daughter to engage with us then so be it!

And our efforts began to pay off. Rosie would occasionally stop and notice our presence and over time we began to see that she was enjoying our attention – even seeking it out! It felt like a monumental breakthrough.

We continued our shifts in the classroom every day until Christmas. Then, before we knew it, spring arrived with its colourful rush of new life. To me this meant one thing: it was time to pack our bags again, this time for America.

CHAPTER TWELVE

THE AMERICAN DREAM –
AKA THE BIG AMERICAN
REALITY CHECK

For a small British family travelling abroad with an autistic child, going to Holland was one thing, but going to America was quite another.

Holland was just a couple of hours away by plane, so won hands down for easy(ish) access. And despite our cultural nuances, Holland, like England, was European, steeped in history and sat under predominately grey skies. OK, Holland had pot-smoking, red light districts and good hot chocolate, and true, they all spoke Dutch, but when we visited Holland it felt more familiar than foreign.

Then there's the good ol' US of A. The country of hope and prosperity. The land of the free! Despite our obvious differences in cultural attitude (like their optimistic positivity and our rather dry cynicism), as nations we appear to share so much. We watch the same movies, speak the same language, follow the lives of each other's celebrities and have a strong political alliance. So before I set foot in this vast country, I assumed that we'd complement each other like tea and cake. I assumed wrong. Not that we clash, we're just more like tea and hot dogs. In fact America turned out to be as foreign a place as any I'd been – and the culture shock took me completely by surprise.

If we were a motley crew the last time we travelled, this time we were a rabble. There were the four of us, of course, and my sixteen-year-old sister Meg (who would babysit for Grace whilst we attended the Growing Minds Programme with Rosie). Then there was Jessica, here to capture more footage for her documentary, who this time had brought with her an impishly handsome and inspired cameraman called Tom.

We all met up at the airport and Tom wasted no time in filming us as we explored the departure lounge. Because of the filming and Rosie's obvious eccentricities, we weren't exactly blending in. People were staring at us, nudging each other and talking in whispers. Neither Tom nor Rosie were in the least bit fazed by the spectators but Meg and I exchanged a few knowing looks because it couldn't be denied – the attention, though a little awkward, was novel and quite fun!

The pathways between the duty-free shops and cafés were made of large azure-blue tiles, flecked with silver. When Rosie noticed them her face shone and she immediately became absorbed by the way they sparkled. It didn't take her long to work out that the silver flecks twinkled more intensely with movement so she leant forward, cast her eyes to the floor, and broke into a run. The tiles sparkled wildly as they whizzed beneath her feet and I ran alongside her, making sure she didn't bump into anyone. Tom filmed Rosie running, then, pointing the camera at the floor, he ran up and down too, filming the sparkly floor as Rosie was experiencing it. I was impressed by his insightfulness.

'His aim is to try to understand Rosie's world and to capture her experiences from her point of view,' Jessica explained.

'I like him already,' I replied. 'Plus, he's a bit of a dish, isn't he?'

'He is a bit,' she said laughing. 'Anyway, Kar, how was your journey up from Stroud?'

'Well, we're four hours into a twenty-hour journey – and we're still alive,' I joked, well aware that twenty hours of attempting to keep control of Rosie in a multi-sensory shit-storm where she could (and probably would) fill her nappy, have a tantrum and generally exasperate her fellow passengers was enough to fray the nerves of anyone.

That said, just like on our outward-bound flight to Holland, the staff at Heathrow bent over backwards to make things easy for Rosie and offered to board us onto the plane first – which we gratefully accepted.

While we waited, I took Grace to see the plane from the window. As it came into view she squealed with excitement.

'Mama… plane!' she said, pushing her chubby index finger against the window.

'Yes, that's *our* plane!' I replied, trying to ignore the rising butterflies in my stomach (I hate flying). I squatted down to her level and put my arm around her. 'It's lovely, isn't it? Like a big bird!'

'Mama. Paint coming off,' she replied.

'Humm, so it is!'

Children have a habit of saying it like it is.

I swallowed nervously, then I noticed Tom filming me, and Jessica smiling from a few paces behind.

'OK, you got me,' I laughed.

'Not so keen on the old flying thing then, Kar?' she said warmly.

'Well, I'm just not sure it's natural...' I confessed. 'I mean look at it! A great big chunk of metal travelling through the air at hundreds of miles an hour. It's every kind of wrong!'

The flight was as challenging as we had expected. We had to work hard to keep Rosie amused and, as predicted, she had tantrums, wanted to climb on people's laps and created her usual brand of beautiful mayhem. But somehow or other we made it across the Atlantic with no more damage than a frazzled brain, tempered with sweet relief. We had arrived – and the sense of achievement was palpable. So palpable in fact that the air hostess (who had taken a particular shine to Rosie) gave us a bottle of champagne at the end of the flight!

However, the rosy glow soon wore off after we clocked eyes on the security staff at Miami airport. I'd naïvely imagined an all-singing, all-dancing, all-American greeting from a middle-aged fat man wearing a Hawaiian shirt, shorts and aviator sunglasses. Instead we came across armed men and women in uniform who had militant expressions that said, 'You piss me off and I'll shoot you.' I couldn't help but feel intimidated. The presence of weapons conjured up memories of 9/11 and I didn't argue when they refused to fast-track us through security for the sake of Rosie.

'Bloody hell,' I whispered to Meg, 'this is *not* what I expected to see from a country famed for its optimism.'

'It couldn't be less like Heathrow, could it?' Meg whispered back.

After we were released from passport control we collected our luggage and headed for the exit, excited to get our first gulp of Florida air. Jessica, Tom and Andy went on ahead and Meg, now holding Grace, skipped up beside me and Rosie in a holiday mood.

'I'm going to Miami,' she sang, quoting the Will Smith song, *Miami*, in a full American accent. She danced forward a few steps, 'Welcome to Miami.'

'I'm going to Miami!' I sang, joining in the fun. 'Oh God, here we go!' I squeaked excitedly as we headed out of the door.

Again, I don't know what I had expected to find... I'd envisaged a scene of swaying palm trees, a soft breeze and the smell of tropical seas, but the reality couldn't have been more different. We found ourselves in a covered bus terminal in the choke and sweat of what felt like ninety-degree heat and one hundred per cent humidity. The mix of diesel and thick, wet urban air hit our lungs like a wall. Heat seemed to be radiating from every surface and the noise of yellow taxi cabs and buses revving and beeping filled our ears.

The terminal was open to the elements along one side, allowing the turquoise sky to pierce the smoggy atmosphere through great concrete pillars and I remember thinking that we could easily have been in India. I paused for a second, stunned. Jessica (who had travelled the world for her job) looked unfazed. She quickly found the right bus for us to board and we muddled inside, glad to escape.

A broad-faced African American man was driving the bus. He must have been about seventy, had greying hair, a weather-beaten face and kind beady eyes. As he whisked us away from the terminal and into the stinging afternoon light, I thought to myself, *Where the flipping heck have we arrived?* He must have read my thoughts because when he helped us and our paraphernalia off the bus, he gave me a little reassuring wink.

As Andy and Tom queued for our hire car, Jessica, Meg and I bought ice creams for the girls and we sat on a bench in the sunshine. It was a beautiful day and a heat-haze shimmered across the surface of the parking lot that stretched out before us. There was a group of teenagers standing nearby dressed like hip-hop gangsters, which set my nerves slightly on edge, and I glanced at them periodically to make sure they were at a safe distance.

'They look a bit dodgy,' I remarked, thinking aloud.

'Nah, that's probably the dress code for teens over here,' Meg replied reassuringly.

'Totally. You're right. Good point. But it's almost unreal isn't it? The scenery, the people, the heat... I feel like I'm in another world!'

When Andy pulled around the corner in a snow-white Dodge Caravan, that feeling intensified. He was driving a slice of American heaven. It had blacked-out windows, seven seats, air conditioning, a TV in the back and a sliding door. We piled in, Tom in the front to map-read and the rest of us in the roomy back section. This was by far the coolest car I'd ever travelled in and Andy upped the 'rad' factor by putting on a Ragga CD. We wound down the windows, donned our sunglasses and sped away – at the breakneck speed of five miles an hour! Then we stalled. (Well, it's just not British to be *that* cool.)

Andy's first job was to negotiate an elevated, entwined maze of intersections and from this vantage point we could see for miles across the flat landscape. Most of the roads followed a grid-like pattern: pencil straight and lined with buildings. Skyscrapers rose from the ground like silver monuments to wealth and there were broken buildings too, neglected by time and circumstance. There were smartly dressed people in smart cars cruising the city and homeless people pushing shopping trolleys of tat along the underpasses. I was shocked at the contrast of rich and poor and couldn't help but wonder if the American Dream was supposed to contain this much polarity. That said, I was mesmerised by the vibrancy of the place. Florida's light is clear and sharp – like that of the Pyrenees or St Ives – which makes everything look alive. Billboard signs, palm trees, cars, buildings, roads, people – everything pulsated with colour. Traffic lights suspended across the roads on wires swung passively in the breeze, American flags were hung everywhere and big blue road signs ushered us into new and terrifying streams of traffic. None of us could work out what the signs saying 'merge' meant, which we all found very comical. To his credit, Andy took the whole thing in his stride and drove us calmly out of the city and onto the freeway towards Orlando with only one hand on the wheel, just as he does in England. It was reassuring. If *I* had been driving, it would have been a white-knuckle ride.

Once out of the city, Tom and I swapped seats so I could sit next to Andy and help keep him awake for the rest of the drive. We had a three-hour journey to our destination, a small seaside town called Jupiter which was roughly twice the size of Stroud. We were all exhausted and I could barely keep my eyes open – which renders me grumpy at the best of times.

'It won't be long now,' said Andy, spotting my gloomy face.

'Good,' I replied trying to sound upbeat. We fell into silence for a while and I watched as the umpteenth oversized billboard rose into view and was left behind us.

'I'm not sure if I like America,' I confessed.

Andy chuckled to himself. 'You're just tired. You always get pessimistic when you're tired… and it's all so new! I do know what you mean though, Kar… it's just really, *really* unfamiliar, that's all.' He squeezed my knee. 'Bet you'll feel different in the morning.'

It was dark when we arrived at our condo, which looked about as uninviting as a council flat in Croydon. Letting ourselves in through the back door and with hardly a glance at our new home, we carried the children up to bed, slumped down next to them and fell asleep.

The following morning, we defied jet lag by waking up at first light, which I thought was pretty good considering our body clocks were six hours behind local time. The black cloud of pessimism had lifted; Andy was right, everything did seem different after some much-needed sleep. Sunshine streamed through the cream slotted blinds of our bedroom window. I rolled out of bed, found the cord and pulled it to reveal a delicious surprise. Our Croydon council flat was actually part of a beautiful condominium complex on the edge of a sparkling lake!

The lake was surrounded by four huge buildings, each a mirror image of the other. They were cream and attractive, with balconies on every floor and brown-tinted windows. Each block had a Spanish-style turquoise roof and the whole complex was connected by a path that circled the lake. There were palm trees swaying lazily in the breeze and bushes full of frangipani flowers injected hot-pink smudges of colour against the endless blue sky.

'Oh my God! Look everyone!' I exclaimed. 'We've come to paradise!'

Our bedroom 'window' was in fact patio doors edging onto a large fenced balcony with a mosquito screen surrounding it. It was perfect, safe for Rosie and Grace, but with an outdoorsy feel. Andy sat up in bed to survey the view.

'Blimey! This is unbelievable!' he said rubbing his eyes.

Grace sprang out of bed and tottered sleepily onto the balcony. 'Look, Mama, water!' she stated.

'Yes, and look over there!' I replied. 'I spy a pool! Shall we go swimming later?'

Rosie, not yet ready to absorb her surroundings, lay on the bed and sleepily played with her eyelashes, humming to herself.

There was a soft knock on the door and in walked Meg and Jessica.

'Morning guys!' said Meg. 'Cuppa for ya.'

'Ah, amazing,' I replied. 'How did you all sleep? And *where* did you sleep!'

'Meg and I have got the next-door bedroom,' said

Jessica, 'and Tom slept in the corridor at the top of the stairs.'

'Oh no! Poor Tom!'

'I know! He's too much of a gentleman to sleep in our room… Anyway chaps, we need to mic you up and get filming straight away if that's OK. Just you guys getting up and your reaction to the surroundings.'

'Flip! Oh, OK. But let me just brush my teeth first. Have you seen that view?'

'Amazing, isn't it,' said Meg as I headed into the bathroom. 'Have you noticed all the OAPs speed-walking round the lake?

'No.'

'It's hilarious, Kar! They've been out there since half past six dressed in white shorts, polo shirts and caps, it must be the "in" thing!'

'Yeah?' I called to her as I searched for the bathroom light switch. Then I saw myself in the mirror. 'Oh God, Jessica, I look like shit!'

'Don't worry. You look fine. It's all about real life anyway, and you're *supposed* to look a bit ruffled in the morning.'

'I suppose so…' I replied reluctantly. 'But ruffled is not the word. It's more like zombified!'

Jessica attached a small microphone to the front of our tops and clipped a battery pack to the back of our trousers.

'Wow! It's like being on *Big Brother*!' I declared with amusement.

'You'll forget it's there in a minute,' she said smiling. She could see that Andy and I, although more than willing to be filmed, were a little taken aback by the intrusive nature of the filming schedule. She was treading the delicate path of director, who needed the right footage to tell her story, and family member personally involved in the lives of her loved ones – in many ways an impossible position to be in.

Tom entered the room with his camera.

'Right. I know it's not spontaneous, but we need a little footage of your reaction when you got up this morning, opened the curtains and saw that view…'

And so the filming began.

★ ★ ★ ★ ★

It took the best part of the morning to get organised. Seven people squeezed into a two-bedroom condo was a cosy proposition! Andy, Jessica and Tom decided to nip out for some supplies, so Meg and I unpacked, fed the children and generally mooched around the condo until every cupboard had been inspected, every breakable ornament had been stashed and safety measures had been put in place.

The condo was spacious and open-plan downstairs, with the kitchen-come-living-room leading through sliding glass doors to a porch-like outdoor seating area with a view of the lake. As with the upstairs balcony, this too was surrounded by a mosquito screen, making it safe for the children and therefore relaxing for us. I could see why the people at Growing Minds had recommended it.

Rosie, wearing an ethnic dress of paper-thin cotton, merrily explored the condo, her face flushed and sweating from the Florida heat. Grace, dressed in similar attire – and similarly wilting – padded purposely about the place, unpacking her toys and getting lost in imaginary play.

'I hope they get some ice lollies,' I said to Meg when we finally settled on sun loungers in the porch.

'Mmm. Me too,' she agreed, closing her eyes. 'And crisps, and marmite.'

'Yeah, and eggs. Rosie was not too impressed with that complimentary toast I tried to give her this morning. Oh, and good coffee… and something Americany.'

'Yeah, like burritos, and iced tea…'

'… and New York bagels.'

It wasn't long before Andy was back, laden with bags of food that answered most of our culinary fantasies.

'You wouldn't believe it, Kar,' he said. 'People here are so nice! I didn't have enough cash to pay for the shopping, so this guy, who looked like someone out of *Miami Vice*, insisted on paying the difference!'

'Wow, this place is starting to grow on me,' I replied.

'Told you!' he teased, as he tore open a box of ice lollies and began to hand them round. 'It's boiling out there and it's only half past ten.'

'I know, I love it! Where's Jessica?'

'Still out with Tom getting AA batteries. Something to do with the filming.'

'Oh cool. I felt a bit intimidated by the camera this morning, did you?' I asked, pulling a one-cheeked smile.

'Yeah, I did a bit,' he replied. 'It's quite strange being followed around everywhere – but I reckon we'll get used to it. Anyway, let's not worry about that now. Let's have a lolly and cool down.'

Later that day we headed down to the local beach. Tom filmed Rosie as she ran down the boardwalk, across the sand and up to the water's edge. The water looked choppy – like a storm out at sea had found its way to shore – but the big waves didn't put Rosie off. She was desperate to enter the water so I held her hand tightly and we waded in fully clothed. The current was strong and I knew that if I let her go she could easily get swept away. But Rosie, unaware of the danger, delighted at the feeling of her body being jostled about by the rhythmic crashing of the waves.

'It's as if she wants to merge with the sea!' I called out, now holding her with two hands.

Tom, spotting the drama of the moment, took off his shirt, kicked off his trainers and waded into the sea in his shorts. Like an action man, he stood in the swirling swell, holding the camera steadily on his shoulder. He captured Rosie's lack of fear as she communed with the surf and my struggle to keep her from being swept away. Then, to illustrate Rosie's point of view, he filmed the water frothing around his waist and the gravelly hiss of white noise that accompanied the churning waves. It was a symbolic moment: it was as if I was trying to stop Rosie from being swept away on a tide of autism and Rosie, unaware of my intentions, was lost in her senses, revelling in the chaos.

Then I turned and spotted Jessica on the water's edge looking at Tom. She was ever so slightly swooning.

We had three days to get over any jet lag and prepare for our week with the Growing Minds team, so we flipped into full holiday mode, splitting our time between the pool, the beach and our condo. This routine was only interrupted by trips to our local shop, Publix, which we all loved because it was nothing like supermarkets in the UK. Here, crisps were called 'chips', semi-skimmed milk was sold as '2%

milk', and everything was branded differently. The novelty factor never wore thin!

Going out and about as a family has never been easy for us Morrises (even on a good day) so Andy and I had learned to adopt the tactic of each taking sole charge of one child, then swapping from time to time. Grace, now an articulate and co-operative toddler, was easy to care for and would happily get involved in everything we wanted to do. Rosie, on the other hand, had her own agenda. She needed one hundred per cent attention and she kept us on our toes – lest merry hell break loose! We had learned to function pretty well like this and didn't think much of it – until now. The reflective eye of Tom's camera made us realise how challenging daily life really was for us in comparison to other parents. It put a spotlight on how organised and vigilant we had to be just to get through the day without incident and as we watched other families relaxing together on their vacations, we began to see exactly why our little family was so unique.

As the three sun-filled days passed by, Rosie's epilepsy weighed heavily on my mind. I confided in Andy and he felt the same. An undercurrent of anxiety was present in us both; it had been at least three weeks since Rosie had last had a cluster of fits and we knew that the odds of her staying fit-free were dwindling by the day. If she had a fit, the week-long session would be good for nothing, the documentary would have no usable footage and all our fundraising efforts would have been in vain. To add further pressure, no medical insurance company would touch us with a barge pole. If Rosie needed to go into intensive care in an American hospital it would probably take us a lifetime to pay off the bills. We knew we were living on a knife edge and that fate could call us out at any time, but we felt strong in our resolve to help Rosie and that notion alone kept us going.

So it was a wonderful relief, like being blessed with sunshine on your wedding day, when Monday morning came fit-free. I almost couldn't believe that everything was going to plan! We'd worked so hard to get to this moment and we'd risked so much – but would it be worth it? A lot was riding on these next five days and as we headed across palm-fringed countryside towards the Growing Minds facility, my stomach leapt with butterflies.

CHAPTER THIRTEEN

THE AMERICAN DREAM
PART TWO– THE
MOMENT OF TRUTH

I've always been a slave to a vivid imagination. I think in pictures, so my mind is filled with images that document the past and presuppose the future. In the case of recalling past events this can be very useful, but when it comes to the future, my mind is filled with images that describe the unknowable; a trillion paintings that can never be realised. I really don't know why I do it. I mean I *should* know better – and I do – but I can't stop this visual torrent any more than I can stop time. It's just the way I'm wired.

So as we rounded the corner and headed up the driveway to the Growing Minds facility, I had a strong image in my mind of what we'd see. Predictably, I was way off base – but this time pleasantly so. We hadn't arrived at the generic therapeutic facility that I'd cooked up in my imagination, we'd come to a house – the home of Steven

236

Wertz – a modest white ranch-style bungalow that sat neatly against a vibrant backdrop of tropical fauna and flora.

As we bundled out of the car, Tom's camera kit and all, Steven immediately came outside to greet us. He was accompanied by his colleague Stephanie. She was petite and casually dressed in combat trousers and a white T-shirt. She had a thin friendly face, radiant skin and the most explosive head of curls I had ever seen. She would be spending the most time with Rosie and wasted no time in getting to know her newest pupil.

She squatted on her haunches to greet Rosie, who responded by angelically singing. 'Laaaa laaaa la laaaa la.'

'Laaaa laaaa la laaaa la,' repeated Stephanie, perfectly imitating the melody, her soft brown eyes searching for eye contact with Rosie.

Rosie, impressed by Stephanie's reaction, looked straight back at her. 'Achoo!' she said, faking a sneeze with comic stylisation.

'Achoo!' repeated Steven and Stephanie in unison. Steven laughed. It was a big belly laugh only common in extremely jolly men like David Bellamy and Father Christmas and I remembered why I liked him.

'Well it looks like we're going to have a fun week!' Steven declared, signalling towards a small extension on the side of his house. We entered and Rosie immediately ran through a small living room area and into a purpose-built classroom at the back. 'Well, I think we'll just get started,' said Stephanie, following her.

We hung back.

'OK, great. We'll stop here,' said Steven, gesturing towards a blue three-piece suite before offering coffee.

'It's so nice to see you all here,' Steven continued, not at all ruffled by the presence of Tom's camera and getting straight down to business. 'I've watched the video you sent to us and of course I met Rosie at your chalet in Zandvoort, and I've gotta say… this girl knows what she wants – but hasn't yet worked out how to get it.'

'I think that's part of the reason why she gets so upset…' said Andy earnestly.

'You don't say!' interrupted Steven, letting out another booming laugh. Then he fell serious and said in a softer tone, 'Rosie uses crying behaviour to try and get what she wants. We need to help her find a more effective means of communication that won't result in the both of you running around trying to work out what she needs by deduction.'

'Yeah, we're good at that,' I said half jokingly.

'We noticed!' he retorted, laughing again – this time with melodic intonation.

'Anyway,' Andy continued, 'if we can give her a way to communicate better with us, I mean that's what we're here for… we want to teach her how to talk to us.'

'Well, that's what we're going to address this week, amongst other things… I find your daughter fascinating. She's somewhat feisty, she's got musical ability – great rhythm and the girl can hold a tune! Plus she's sociable and likes the company of other people. We're going to start to play to these strengths and harness her interests to enable her to make better sense of her environment and interact better with the people in her life.'

'Sounds good!' said Andy enthusiastically. I nodded in agreement and sipped my coffee feeling a little out of my depth.

It was in this moment, barely ten minutes into the day, that Rosie began to have a tantrum. Something had upset her and the sound of her distress came through the wall and tugged hard at my heartstrings. I wanted to go to her, offer her some comfort, but Steven was clearly unmoved by her outburst and continued talking.

'We're going to have Rosie begin to respond to some simple requests and have her practise them over and over again until she has them mastered. The more demands you place on her nervous system – and the more she has to respond to those demands – the more organised and capable she will become. It's all about practice…'

The screaming continued and I began to feel uncomfortable about it.

'… and we're going to help her to organise those responses on demand and on time,' Steven continued, taking no notice of the crying, which was hugely loud. 'We're aiming for five hundred responses a day.'

'That is *a lot!*' Andy exclaimed. 'Rosie never responds to any requests. We're truly at a loss as to whether she understands anything we say to be honest. Five hundred responses a day sounds impossible, considering how long it takes just to meet her basic everyday needs.'

'Well, we're going to show you how,' replied Steven, kindly.

We continued to talk for a while. Steven explained the basics of some of the techniques we would learn over the course of the week, but as Rosie's tantrum persisted, so did my sense of anxiety and I took in little of what he said. Finally, after a good half-hour of Rosie wailing for Britain, Andy addressed the elephant in the room.

'I'm thinking that Rosie… the crying might be because she is thirsty, or that she wants to be picked up and held.' There was a marked concern in his voice that told me that he too was disturbed by her distress.

'I know she might have had her idea,' said Steven cheerily, 'but I have my idea.' Again, Steven's laughter rippled around the room and I realised that he had seen this scenario a hundred times before. He was completely unruffled by Rosie's distress, which reassured me just enough not to jump up, grab Rosie, and run for the hills! My instinct to comfort her was overwhelming – almost physical – but I could tell that he was seeing some kind of bigger picture, so I told myself to trust the process, stay put and see it through.

Steven took a scrap of paper and a pencil and drew the simple outline of a bottle on it (even though she was four, Rosie still drank from a bottle because she couldn't co-ordinate the use of a cup). Then he wrote the word 'bottle' at the bottom of the paper in large letters and asked us to prepare one for her, which we did. We then followed him into a narrow observation room where we could view the classroom through a two-way mirror. (We could see her, she couldn't see us.) From there we watched – and Tom filmed – our heartbreakingly upset daughter, stomping crossly around the room with tears streaking down her face, which was scarlet with rage. In stark contrast to Rosie, Stephanie looked radiantly happy and relaxed. She had been with Rosie this whole time but she appeared to be utterly and genuinely unconcerned by Rosie's behaviour. I knew that if Rosie has thrown this kind of tantrum at home, Andy and I would be frantic in our mission to calm her down. I mean, any loving parent would, wouldn't they? A ten-minute tantrum is fine but after half an hour you start to question everything.

Steven entered the classroom area and put Rosie's bottle on a high shelf out of her reach. He then put the picture card he'd drawn into Rosie's hand and physically prompted her to give it to Stephanie. Stephanie took the card and said, 'Bottle!' before handing her the bottle with a big smile.

Rosie stopped crying straight away. 'Achoo!' she exclaimed, almost jumping with surprise.

'There you go, you asked for the bottle! That was some really nice work,' said Steven gently. Rosie looked at him still stunned by the turn of events, then she lay on the floor, began to drink and promptly fell asleep, exhausted. Andy and I looked on in amazement.

'That was incredible,' said Andy, when Steven came back to the observation room. 'It really gave us hope that we can teach her.'

'The fact of the matter is, she wants things,' Steven replied, waving us back into the living room. 'We wanna teach her how to use a picture-exchange communication system called PECS, so she can ask for what she wants.'

'We'd love that,' I replied, 'but all the professionals back home say she's not ready for PECS yet... for starters she can't physically pick up a flat object like a card.'

I was worried that he might be setting the bar too high.

He looked at me square in the face and then a hint of a smile peeped out from behind his beard. To me, that smile spoke volumes. He was clearly not one to underestimate the capability of anyone with a disability – however severe.

'Well, if she can't physically pick up a PEC, we'll adapt them so she can,' Steven replied confidently.

I nodded and smiled. I wanted to believe him but I have to confess I thought he was being a bit ambitious. Andy and I love our daughter unconditionally but in the cold light of day Rosie's abilities were at the lowest functioning end of the autistic spectrum. She was unable to communicate, doubly incontinent, she couldn't feed herself and was incapable of following even the most basic of instructions. She didn't even respond to her own name, so how could she be expected to grasp the concept of PECS? I believed that it would take a small miracle for Rosie to gain this kind of skill set but we'd come here hoping for a miracle, so I said nothing of my doubts to Steven. I had to see him try.

Over the course of the day, we worked with Steven and learned about the various techniques we would be using at home in her classroom. Her day would be divided into short alternating bursts of 'table time' and 'floor time'. At the table she would be expected to work and carry out requests in the style of ABA and on the floor she would take the lead in play.

'There is no way she is going to sit at a table and work,' said Andy doubtfully. But Steven explained how she would soon learn that working brought her rewards – like food, praise or time with a favourite toy.

We were dubious. Not least because for most of the first day, whatever Stephanie attempted to do with Rosie, she cried one long tantrum of defiance.

As the day drew to a close, Andy and I were feeling frazzled to say the least and when Rosie emerged from the classroom at 3pm she looked like she'd been through a mangle. She located me quickly and climbed onto my lap for a cuddle. My whole body exhaled with relief. At last I could comfort her. In stark contrast to us Morrises, Stephanie looked as radiant as she did when she had entered the classroom in the morning. It was extraordinary! She looked like she'd spent the entire day relaxing at a local spa. Steven was the same. He looked like he'd just come back from a couple of weeks in the Bahamas! This brought up a lot of questions. Were they morally right to be so unruffled by Rosie's distress, or had we made a terrible mistake in bringing her here? Because in our eyes, all we'd seen her do that day was suffer. What were they seeing that we couldn't yet see? And how could they be so confident?

'What if all this crying somehow breaks her?' said Andy as we drove back to our condo.

'I know,' I replied glumly. I paused for a long time trying to make sense of the day. 'But we need help, Ands… and Rosie needs help. And so far going purely on our own instincts and the advice of the health pros has gotten us nowhere.'

'I know, but I just want to protect her. It's my responsibility as her dad to keep her from harm.'

I squeezed his knee and glanced behind me to check on our precious girl. She was sitting happily in her car seat, holding a book to her lips and humming a melody as if nothing had happened.

'Ands, you're an amazing dad…' I said – and I meant it. '… and I think she's OK. None the worse for the ordeal. I know she came out of that classroom looking awful but she's fine now, you should see her.'

'OK. But if that happens again tomorrow, I don't know what I'll do,' he said, still clearly shaken.

But the following day it did happen again and Andy and I only made it through the day because we were starting to understand Steven's theory. We were beginning to see that we were inadvertently shaping Rosie's behaviour by the way we responded to her tears. By running around trying to find something to pacify and comfort her, we were holding her back from developing more effective means of communication.

No parent likes to come to the realisation that after all their best efforts and good intentions, they are failing to meet the needs of their child. It's a painful revelation that we both found hard to take. Ironically, we had come to America to see how we could change our daughter and had learned that it was *us* who needed to change. So we swallowed our pride and let ourselves be guided into a new parental style, allowing every aspect of our old beliefs to be torn down, analysed and stripped away. I had never felt so raw and broken down.

By the end of day two I felt utterly devoid of direction and didn't even know how to interact with my own child. My parental compass had stalled and it felt like hell. Andy was struggling too. It was very intense and demanding, and felt completely alien. All the while Rosie cried ceaselessly in her classroom, which blew our stress levels through the roof. Tom recorded the whole shebang and I hated the presence of his camera whilst we were going through such a tumultuous time. This created further tension as Jessica tried to balance being intrusive enough to get the footage she needed against the privacy we craved to process our thoughts and discuss our feelings.

So it was a wonderful relief for us all when the end of the day came and we were able to put everything aside, go home and unwind. Meg would tell us about her day with Grace, we'd cook dinner and then head to the pool until the last drop of light had faded from the equatorial sky.

As the week continued, under the watchful guidance of Steven and Stephanie we began to learn new ways of interacting with Rosie. By not responding to her crying and praising good behaviour we began to see a light at the end of the tunnel. By the second half of day three, the incessant crying that had been the theme of the week had begun to diminish. Not completely, but enough to give us hope.

We would observe Rosie sitting at the table. Yes, actually sitting there – albeit reluctantly! And after days of having her tears gently ignored, she was attempting to follow Stephanie's requests by carrying out simple tasks like putting a coin in a bowl, or identifying a picture card from an array of two in exchange for time with play dough or a favourite book. You couldn't help but admire Stephanie's calm, persistent manner. She wasn't just implementing the teaching techniques, she was living them. The Growing Minds philosophy had become part of her life, which was inspiring.

Andy and I gradually spent more time in the classroom, having a go at teaching Rosie ourselves. Both Steven and Stephanie guided us in every detail, from technique and method, to body language, tone of voice, and timing. Steven's wife Kaitryn gave us counselling too, which was extremely helpful. There were a thousand things to take in. But amongst the tears and triumphs we finally found that we were having fun.

Before we knew it our old 'selves' were being replaced by new and improved versions of Andy and Kara, with new attitudes and an optimistic outlook for the future. We were still stinging a little from the process but it was nothing we couldn't work on.

The best moment of the week came on day four when Rosie slid a PEC across her work table to request a spoonful of avocado. You could almost see her brain tick. It started with her sitting opposite me, looking between the avocado in my hand, and the 'avocado' picture card that lay on the table in front of her. Slowly, she drummed her fingers on the card. I didn't respond. Then she slapped her hands on it a couple of times. That action didn't yield results either. Finally she slid the card purposefully towards me and was instantly rewarded with a spoonful of avocado and a bucketload of praise. It was the first time she had attempted true communication since her regression. It was a beautiful moment of pure magic which made everything worthwhile, and watching Tom's footage still brings tears to my eyes.

As our final day drew to a close I couldn't stop a lump from forming in my throat as we said our goodbyes. The hope we had carried here from Zandvoort had been realised. Teaching Rosie *was* possible. And it felt bloody wonderful.

★ ★ ★ ★ ★

Early the following morning, we packed our car, returned the keys to our condo and began our journey home. Our flight from Miami wasn't until the evening but we wanted to visit the famous Miami Beach area before we left, so we decided to set off early. We arrived just before midday and cruised around in the comfort of our air-conditioned hire car to take in the scenery. The beauty of the city was breathtaking. From the curved art deco architecture to the bustling streets of hyper cool people, the place had a tropical, multicultural, carnival atmosphere that made you want to celebrate life. We found a side street, parked the car and Andy strapped Rosie into her pushchair whilst I rummaged in our bags looking for our beach stuff: swimsuits, towels, sunscreen, water, food, toys, nappies… you name it and it was coming with us to the beach. Then, with Grace on my hip, we headed into the crowd and straight into what felt like the set of a movie.

It was a scorching day. A soft breeze came in off the sea and the palm trees lining the road looked as tropical and divine as the white sand and turquoise sea beyond them. We crossed the road and came across a long path that ran the length of the beach. Here we found what can only be described as a dazzling display of the perfectly bronzed 'beautiful people' using the path like a tropical runway. There were flawlessly toned beach babes on rollerblades, dressed in barely there brightly coloured bikinis, or tiny hot pants, or cut-off jeans – all sporting mirrored aviator sunglasses or huge dark Hollywood shades. The male specimens on this perfection parade had either a surfer look – shaggy sun-bleached hair, six-pack and long shorts – or they looked like they had just stepped off the set of a rap music video, working their swagger with oversized boom boxes balanced on their shoulders. Whatever their individual style, these people knew how to work their picture-perfect bods with the kind of coolness that could never be attained by a bespectacled square like me and we couldn't help but stop and stare for a while.

To contrast this biological splendour there was an old homeless man sitting yards away from the path under the inadequate shade of a palm tree. He was dressed as Father Christmas. Clearly inebriated and scarred by life, he had worn the outfit for so long that only a hint of red could be seen through the grubby brown it had now become. He had a big dirty-white beard and long matted hair, and next to him was a shopping trolley full of cardboard, tin cans and rags. Seeing this disparity between poverty and glamour only added to the feeling of being on a Hollywood film set and I almost had to pinch myself – just to be sure that he wasn't Eddie Murphy in disguise, filming the sequel to *Trading Places*.

We headed onto the beach. Here a thousand multicoloured towels covered the sand each providing their owner with their own little slice of paradise for the day. We worked our way around them looking for a gap big enough for the seven of us, eventually finding one next to a *Baywatch*-style lifeguard hut. Looking around, I realised that we (the rabble) stuck out like a sore thumb! If we weren't obviously British, then we were obviously *not* American – a fact I was comfortable with until I unpacked the swimming costumes and realised that mine was missing.

'Oh no, Meg!' I declared with alarm, 'I've forgotten my cozzie.'

'You what!' she said, dropping her towel to reveal her beautifully brown figure in a navy polka-dot bikini. (A young Kim Kardashian springs to mind.) 'What underwear have you got on?'

'Comfy ones for the plane.'

'Are they matching?'

'No! We're talking purple granny knickers and an old red bra. I mean my boobs have literally no support!'

'Oh, Kar! What are you going do?' said Meg as she spread her towel out on the sand.

'Well the water's just too inviting and the kids are boiling and sticky so I'm just going to have to go for it!'

I got the girls into their swimming costumes and reluctantly peeled off my clothes to reveal my mismatched, saggy lingerie to a beach full of gods and goddesses. I was sporting the most embarrassing underwear ever, on the coolest beach in the world.

'Only the British!' I laughed, putting my hands on my hips. Meg, Jessica, Tom and Andy couldn't help but laugh too, nor could a couple of bronzed beauties to my left. 'Well there's nothing for it, I'm just going to have to work it *Baywatch*-style!' I said, resigned to my fate.

'Yeah, go for it, sis!' said Meg encouragingly. We grabbed a child each, ran to the water's edge and waded in. The water was every bit as warm and tropical as it looked and Rosie and Grace both loved it. It would have been the perfect end to a very challenging week but I should have realised that autism would have the last laugh. It always does and I should have known better. 'Bikini-gate' had lulled me into a false sense of security that the most embarrassing thing had already happened. I couldn't have been more wrong...

As Grace, Rosie, Meg and I bobbed about happily in the water, Andy came down to join us. He waved happily then waded through the water towards us. Suddenly his face dropped; he was staring at the water next to Rosie. I followed his gaze and there it was: a floating poo bobbing on the top of the water for all to see. I looked at Rosie and there she was, cheerfully straining away. Up popped another little specimen, which created a small flotilla of poo, merrily sailing in on the tide. Meg's mouth immediately dropped open in shock; Andy on the other hand was nothing short of horrified.

Now, Andy could have subtly got a bag and played it smart and low-key. He could have caught the poo and removed it without anyone noticing. Instead, he panicked and despite knowing that we too had spotted it, he began to point at it and declare, 'Floating poo! Oh my God, Kar, *floating poo!*'

All the people within twenty yards of us spun around and watched in horror as Andy waded towards it, cupped his hands, caught it and ran from the sea like a man possessed.

Meg and I looked at Rosie, who had clearly finished her business and was now happily splashing in the waves, completely unaware of the furore she had caused. Then we looked back at Andy and shook with laughter as he reached the shore and tore past Jessica and Tom repeating, 'Poo alert!' dodging sunbathers across the beach to find a bush or a bin. It was all rather priceless.

To top it all (just in case the granny underwear and floating poo hadn't attracted enough attention), after we'd cleaned Rosie up in the beach shower and got her dressed, she decided to have a full-blown autistic 'speciality' tantrum. Andy, who had lost the will to live by this point, calmly took her for a walk down the beach and she screamed full volume all the way. When it was time to go I have to admit that our fellow beachgoers looked a little relieved.

'We're just too cool for Miami beach,' I said to Meg jokingly as we strolled back to the car.

On the plane journey back to England, after the children had gone to sleep, I got the chance to reflect on what had turned out to be one of the most transformative weeks of my life. It had been nothing like I had expected. I'd thought we would learn some new stuff, Rosie would cope, Tom would film a lovely life-affirming documentary about autism and everything would be straightforward and positive. In reality, Rosie had freaked out because she'd had to learn that crying gets you nowhere, we'd freaked out as we faced our parental demons and Jessica had struggled to get half-decent footage out of a family in the tumultuous throes of transformation.

Surprisingly, the week hadn't just been about learning new things – it was the things we needed to *unlearn* that were suddenly important. It was a revelation I had not expected and a painful one at that. Because, at the end of the day, we tend to hold on with vice-like grip to who we are, the good and the bad, because it makes us *us*. Unlearning habits formed and rethinking opinions and beliefs we have held for so long can make us feel that we are losing a part of our identity, part of what makes us unique. But sometimes, someone or something comes along and *makes* us change and when that happens our old selves have to make way. I was starting to see the bigger picture. It had been hard at first, there had been tears and tantrums on the way to moving forward, but I knew this journey to America had changed the shape of our future forever.

So I made a resolution... I vowed to continue to make the changes in me in order to help facilitate a change in Rosie. And it was already working; Rosie proved that, when she pushed a PEC across the table to ask for some avocado.

CHAPTER FOURTEEN

THE JOURNEY CONTINUES

Over the next four years things began to change for our family. It took six weeks for Rosie to grasp the request-response-reward concept of ABA, and then slowly she began to make progress, gaining a host of new skills and even acquiring some spoken words!

Every weekday morning I'd work in the classroom with Rosie while Grace attended nursery, and Goldy would work with her in the afternoons as I babysat Lily. She continued teaching, day after day, for four years. Her dedication to Rosie was inspirational. Without Goldy I just couldn't have done it. It's as simple as that.

We shared some magical eureka moments in the classroom. There was the time when Rosie imitated me and waved at herself in the mirror, and a literally jaw-dropping occasion when she spontaneously asked for crisps. Another breakthrough moment occurred when Rosie, after literally months of practice, finally learned to stack wooden blocks and built a tower of five all by herself.

And there were difficult times too, when I'd break down in tears over the slow pace of her progress. And sometimes, secretly, I'd long for the simple pleasure of being a normal mum – one who drops their child off at school in the morning, picks them up at three and gets to hear them rabbit on about their day. It's the little things like that which you grieve for from time to time.

The following year, after the genetic testing for Rett syndrome had proved negative, we planned another trip to America. I had the ambitious idea of taking our show on tour to raise the funds so we reformed the Full Monty Girls with a new member. Alix felt she was too far away to commit to a run of shows, so Emma, a local care worker for young adults with special needs, joined the group. She was tall and striking (she still is) with dark hair cut into a jaw-length bob. She had a quick and quirky sense of humour and a love of all things vintage and kitsch. Goldy and I met her by chance in the gym and despite not knowing any of us when she joined, we instantly gelled as a group and worked well together.

To prepare for the new shows we changed our outfits and re-jigged the music, opening the show with the theme tune to *The Pink Panther*, leading into *Lady Marmalade* by Patti LaBelle. It felt wonderful to be back in rehearsals, with that familiar feeling of camaraderie and excitement as we worked on the new choreography.

The first show of our tour was in London. A stand-out memory of our journey to the venue is Emma's sat nav directing us through central London instead of the ring road. We must have driven through Piccadilly Circus three times before we found the right road and the girls laughed at my shrieks of panic as I negotiated the traffic past pushy black-cab drivers that kept beeping at me in frustration. In fact I drove so tentatively, a Turkish cab driver wound down his window and asked, 'Eh, missy. Why you dr-r-rive so slow?'

I didn't live that one down for a long time.

The show itself was in a warehouse down a back street on the Tottenham Court Road. We were to be the final act of a travelling collective called Baseline Circus. It couldn't have been more exciting to be backstage with professional performers. There were aerial silk dancers, burlesque artistes and fire-eaters. Our act went down a storm and we raised £1,000.

Shows followed in Brighton and Bristol, put on by my good friends Rowan and Roz, and finally we had a homecoming Christmas show in Stroud back at the Space. The venue was packed with familiar faces, all in the mood for a bit of Christmas cheer. Goldy and I even got on the stage and sang *Santa Baby* to a whooping crowd. Let's just say we're better strippers than singers!

The local press continued to support us, with *The Stroud News and Journal* taking on Rosie's appeal as their own official campaign. Then national journalists started to contact me too and I sold our story to a few weekly magazines like *First* and *Love it!* After that *The Sun* wanted to do a story and invited us to London for an all-expenses-paid photo shoot. My poor mum was horrified, but we couldn't have been more excited as we piled onto the 6am train to London. We were on a complete high and sat like a gaggle of teenagers, chatting loudly in a train full of grave-faced suits commuting to the capital for work. They probably hated us.

At the London studio we had a team of make-up artists, stylists and a photographer. We couldn't believe it was all for us! We were in hair and make-up for almost two hours, and when we posed in front of the camera dressed in our Full Monty regalia we felt like stars. Of course they wanted the obligatory *Calendar Girls*-style naked shot at the end of the shoot and of course we obliged. It was easy really; we were getting used to being in a state of undress and we knew only too well the attention it brought to our cause.

After that, our story spilled into the international arena and we were paid for exclusive articles in the French version of *Closer* magazine and *The National Enquirer* in America. All the money we made went towards our trip to America with Rosie. Articles were also published in Greece, Japan, China, Russia, South Korea, Turkey and most prominently on the front page of an Italian broadsheet. We were even asked to pose for a spread in a porn magazine in Australia! Of course, we politely refused.

In the world of television, we were invited to the Sky studios to be interviewed for Channel Five News. We were also asked to appear on *This Morning* and *Richard and Judy* on two competing networks. We chose *This Morning*, and performed a snippet of our show live to the nation and got to sit on their famous sofa for a burlesque chat. As usual, things never went off without embarrassment. As we helped ourselves to some breakfast in the green room at the *This Morning* studios, Philip Schofield – AKA 'The Silver Fox' – came in to meet us. Unfortunately for me, I had my mouth so stuffed full of croissant that I could hardly speak! Typical.

Every week something new would happen: an interview, an article, a request for a show... we couldn't believe how fast things were escalating and how well we were being received. As a group, we had never expected this much attention and we revelled in the fun! On a more personal level, I was fulfilling the dream I'd had since the start of spreading awareness about autism. Autism and nudity was an unlikely pairing but somehow it worked. The Full Monty story captured people's imagination and became the platform upon which I could talk about autism. People often emailed me to say how inspired they were by our proactive approach with Rosie. Sometimes they told us their stories too, which I loved.

Interest from America continued, and we were asked to film a show for an American news programme called *Inside Edition*. We did a bit of a radio tour too, donning the studio headphones for BBC Radio Gloucestershire, BBC Bristol, Heart Radio, LBC, Stroud FM, and Kerrang Radio who hosted *An Evening with the Full Monty Girls*, where we performed live on air for ITV's Mr Impossible. It was all very rock and roll.

★ ★ ★ ★ ★

That same winter, Andy decided to take me out for dinner to celebrate the anniversary of the day we'd met. Unbeknown to me, he decided to mark the occasion with a surprise. So in the late afternoon, he leapt into the car and raced to the nearest large town, Cheltenham. As he reached the outskirts of town, a huge traffic jam brought the hope of fulfilling his intentions to a halt, so Andy, being Andy, valiantly mounted the kerb and drove on as far as he could via the pavement. Then, when he could go no further, he abandoned the car and ran to the jewellers, catching them just in the nick of time.

That night, on the way back from our meal, he parked the car on a country lane and said, 'Let's go for a walk.'

It was a beautiful night with a clear, star-filled sky and a high moon that cast a silver light on the hills in the distance. A hard frost made the grass crunch and sparkle underfoot as we made our way across a nearby field.

'This is beautiful. What a lovely idea, hun,' I said, putting my arm round his waist.

'Well, it's our anniversary and I wanted to do something special to celebrate it,' he replied suddenly stopping us both in our tracks.

Then he faced me and said with a gentle tone, 'Kar, I've loved you from the first moment we met, and I can't believe how lucky I am to have you in my life. We've been through so much. Being with you has been the best thing that's ever happened to me... and I can't imagine my life without you in it.' Then, to my total astonishment, he got down on one knee and proposed.

Of course I said yes. And I cried. And when we visited Tesco on the way home I shouted, 'We're getting married!' to anyone within earshot.

★ ★ ★ ★ ★

The following spring, after our planned trip to America and with Rosie's progress continuing, we took the local education authority to court in order to secure government funding – but we lost our case. So again I found myself losing sleep whilst racking my brains to come up with another money-making idea. One night, I had a sudden spike of creativity. An idea exploded in my mind which caused me to sit bolt upright in bed. But there was a catch: to achieve this dream I would need a hundred women willing to strip naked… oh, and a helicopter, a photographer and a field to use for the day! My idea was to produce a naked charity calendar with a twist: the front cover would feature an aerial photo of my hundred naked women lying in a field forming the word 'AUTISM' in giant capital letters. I knew it was an audacious plan, but I also knew that staging an event on this scale would create a lot of publicity which I hoped would translate to sales.

True to form, the local press backed me yet again, putting a good-sized article in the paper appealing for volunteers. By the end of the week, eighty-seven volunteers had signed up and I knew it wouldn't be long before we'd recruit the rest. Each woman had her own personal reason for wanting to take part. Some had relatives with autism, one was hitting seventy and wanted to give the middle finger to old age, while others just wanted a challenge. They were young and old – grandmothers, mothers, daughters and friends. They were of every size and stature and from all walks of life. I was truly humbled by the response and loved hearing their stories.

Our eighty-five-year-old landlord, Peter, who owned the farm where we lived, let us use the field next to our house to stage the event. All we needed now was a helicopter and a photographer.

'If I've learnt anything from my experiences so far,' I told myself, 'it's that everything comes together if you work hard and keep the faith.' So I went ahead and set a date for the first of September.

Meanwhile, the Full Monty Girls prepared to pose for photos to feature on the inside of the calendar. Thanks to Ele, we were given the use of her friend's beautiful gothic mansion for the day and thanks to Goldy, a renowned local portrait photographer Georgie Brocklehurst volunteered to take the shots using her beautiful vintage 1950s camera. Props included: fake snow, vintage tea sets, flowery material, iced buns, cupcakes, scones and a hundred beautiful white roses donated by generous local florist, Mixed Monkey.

We posed together in group shots for August, September and December. August featured a tea party theme. September featured us sitting naked on a wall in the garden – much to the delight of the gardener! And December captured a wintery scene, complete with the fake snow donated by Snow Business. For the other months we posed individually. Ele wore nothing but high heels while stepping out of her friend's vintage Rolls Royce; Bonnie lay in a marble bath of freezing cold water (poor thing), adorned with floating roses; Emma did 'Death By Roses', an aerial shot of her lying on a rose-covered floor as if she'd tragically leapt from a balcony (very Twilight-esque); and I posed in an original white Charles Eames rocking chair, sitting sideways with pointed toes and a beautiful spray of roses in my lap. But perhaps the best and most iconic image of all was that of Goldy, standing with statuesque poise, holding a floral spray in nothing but her big biker boots.

Two weeks before the 'hundred naked ladies' event, I still hadn't found a helicopter or a photographer willing to fly in it, but not wanting to cancel, I pressed ahead with my plans regardless. Then, in a eureka moment, I decided to email every media outlet I knew with a press release. Almost immediately I got a response from a news agency who was not only interested in my story, but their boss, the former editor of a big national newspaper, offered to pay for a helicopter *and* supply a photographer to take the aerial shot. All he wanted in exchange was the copyright to the pictures. It was a perfect transaction – they were even generous enough to allow Jessica's cameraman a free ride in the helicopter to film the event for her documentary!

On that same day Channel Five News also got in touch. This time they wanted to come to Stroud to film a feature that would be aired throughout the day on the following Monday, which would be the launch date of their new news programmes. We couldn't have been more excited – but it got better... to top all that, they wanted Goldy and me to come to their London studios at Sky and conduct a series of live interviews to go with the feature. This was publicity I could only have dreamed of. Suddenly it was all systems go and I launched myself into what was to become one of the busiest weeks of my life. It would also be one of the best. Because, after all the excitement and rushing around, the following Saturday I would be a bride, walking up the aisle to marry my Andy.

The night before the event, Jessica and I took a hundred matchsticks and worked out how to clearly spell the word AUTISM with them. Then at 6:30am, Goldy and I met bleary eyed in the field to stake out the word in giant letters using bailing twine and twigs. It was spotting with rain by the time we'd finished and I looked anxiously across the valley in search of black clouds.

'It'll be OK, Kar,' Goldy said optimistically, 'it always is.'

And it was. By midday, the weather was better. Not perfect, but not raining and a hint of blue sky broke through the clouds from time to time, warming the air just enough for the women not to freeze after they'd stripped off.

At twelve noon my ladies began to arrive, each wearing nothing but a towel, a pair of shoes and an excited smile. The sloping field was covered with wild flowers and as they strode through the long ripening grass, they reminded me of a curious version of *The Sound of Music*. The mood was buoyant and relaxed as everyone found their positions along the bailing twine, and we sat wrapped in our towels while Jessica filmed and some of us were interviewed by Ruth Liptrot who was reporting for Channel Five News. Then we waited for a call on my mobile phone to let us know that the helicopter had taken off. It must have been less than five minutes before it rang.

All we had to do was disrobe en masse, lie down and wait. It has to be said, being naked with a hundred women in a field is an exhilarating feeling. The feeling of liberation – jubilation even – as our towels dropped one by one onto the grass seemed to fill the whole valley with extra colour and light. Then everyone took their positions and we waited for the helicopter to arrive.

Two minutes later we heard the sound of a helicopter approaching. We lay still in readiness but it flew over – then sped away.

'Someone just got an eyeful!' said Emma, who was lying next to me on the letter U.

I jumped up. 'Don't get up! Don't move ladies!' I shouted. 'I don't think that was our helicopter!'

'It was probably Prince Charles on his way home!' one of the ladies shouted back.

Everyone laughed.

Again, we braced ourselves for the *actual* helicopter which arrived less than two minutes later guided by our friend Cookie, who had bagged a ride to give directions. It flew over us loud and low, and we could feel the air from the blades as they whirred in a halo. It circled us carefully before flying over again and we stayed still to allow the necessary photos to be taken. On the third swoop we waved our arms frantically then jumped to our feet and cheered. Then, as quickly as it came, it disappeared from view, leaving us all on a naked high.

The resulting photo was awe-inspiring and exactly what I'd hoped for. Not only would it be perfect for the cover of my calendar but that week it featured in *The Metro* newspaper, *The British Medical Journal* and graced the front cover of *The Stroud News and Journal*.

★ ★ ★ ★ ★

On Monday, Goldy and I drove to London with the first copy of our calendar, ready to unveil it live on national television. We'd arrived early and were crossing the road from the car park to enter the studios at Sky when a slick-looking black car came into view.

'Oh my God, that's *got* to be someone famous,' I said, tugging at Goldy's arm.

To our excitement it pulled up right next to us and we stopped to see who would emerge. The door opened and out stepped the eminent news presenter John Suchet! Of course we recognised him instantly and were a little star-struck when he walked over to greet us.

'Aha! Two naked ladies!' he said, smiling.

'Mr Suchet, lovely to meet you! I think you might be interviewing us later about our naked calendar,' I said, thrilled that *he* wanted to talk to *us*.

'Oh am I?' he replied. 'I'll look forward to that! I think you ladies are fabulous.'

'Thank you!' said Goldy. 'But if you didn't know you were interviewing us, how did you know who we were?'

'I recognise you from the *last* time you were on the news!' he said warmly.

As he walked away, Goldy and I looked at each other in astonishment.

'You see that,' I said to Goldy. '*He* knows us. *He* – John Suchet – recognises *us*!'

'God, he's hot though isn't he?' said Goldy, with a cheeky smile.

Once inside, we were met by a producer who briefed us on our itinerary.

'Right then, ladies, you've got three interviews,' she said with a smile, 'one at midday, one at five and one at eight o'clock this evening. Why don't you grab a coffee, then I'll call you in for hair and make-up.'

Later, whilst we were in the make-up department, and as they sprayed my face with foundation, I heard a woman with an extremely familiar voice enter the room. She was ushered into the chair next to me and continued her banter, 'Princess Diana' this, 'Dody Fayed' that. This woman was about as outspoken and confident as a person could get.

I know that voice, I thought to myself, but I couldn't place it. I didn't have my glasses on either, so I couldn't see who it was. Then the penny dropped. It was the feminist icon Germaine Greer.

Later, to our surprise, she was sitting in the green room reading the paper when Goldy and I walked in to get another coffee. She was really friendly and struck up a conversation straight away, cursing the newspaper she was reading, branding it 'boring' and 'full of rubbish'. In that moment it occurred to me that I was holding the calendar in my hand. I was curious to find out what she, a world-renowned feminist, would think of our efforts. Would she think I was liberated and proactive, or vulgar for becoming a burlesque stripper to help my child? And what of the hundred naked women forming the word AUTISM? Would she see it as exploitation?

'Go on, hand it to her,' I thought, daring myself.

At that moment the producer came in.

'If you'll just come with me, ladies,' she said kindly, 'we need to mic you up! Then you can come back and finish that coffee.'

It was now or never. *Go on! Do it!* I told myself.

'Germaine, if you're not keen on the papers, why don't you look at this,' I said handing her the calendar. 'It's something we're doing to help my autistic daughter.'

'Oh right, thank you,' she replied, as we left the room.

'I can't believe I just did that!' I squeaked to Goldy as we headed up the corridor.

When we got back, it turned out that she was genuinely interested in our story and asked a lot of questions. However, I was never quite sure what she thought of the nudity, until a couple of years ago, when I spotted her posing naked for an article in a newspaper.

The interviews with the lovely and deliciously dishy John Suchet went off without a hitch. But the shock was yet to come…

When the news piece was put on YouTube it went viral and clocked up nearly thirty million hits! My dream of spreading autism awareness was being realised.

When we headed back from London that night, it dawned on me that I had only four days to prepare for the wedding. I'd been so wrapped up in organising the calendar, the wedding had taken a bit of a back seat.

'You've got two choices,' said Goldy. 'You can either panic, or enjoy running around like a headless chicken for the week.'

Not wanting to be a bridezilla, I chose the latter.

We were having a white wedding on a shoestring, and in true 'Andy and Kara' style, we had no idea how it would come together. Four days to go and we still didn't know exactly how we would feed our guests! There was so much to do that my mind boggled: there were flowers to get; a (very rudimentary) marquee to put up; decorations to make; food to prepare; children to care for; wedding rehearsals to attend…

Our biggest expense was the outfits which were, thankfully, already organised and waiting to be picked up. I'd found my dress in Cheltenham in the January sales. It had been a try-on dress with 70% off the original price due to a grubby hem and make-up stains around the front. Once dry-cleaned, I knew it would be perfect. It was made of thick ivory taffeta silk and it was plain and classic in shape, with a corseted bodice and a thin line of crystal-beaded detail around the waist. Also on the sale rail, I found mismatched ivory dresses for my bridesmaids Rosie, Grace and Lily, and a tiny beige suit for Bonnie's son Ronan, who was to be our pageboy. In another cost-cutting exercise we hired Andy a morning suit – also from Cheltenham – and when he stepped out of the changing room at the suit-hire shop I couldn't believe my eyes! Apart from the time when he accidently wore my Full Monty stripping trousers to his granddad's funeral (which, when we realised, caused a bit of a chuckle in the church), I'd never seen him in a suit before. I was stunned at how handsome he was. I know I'm totally biased, but to me he looked like a young George Clooney on a red carpet stroll.

Aside from our wedding attire, we'd hired the marquee and ten white plastic table-and-chair sets from a friend for just a hundred pounds – perfect for our reception, which was to be held in our garden. For extra seating, we bought two dozen hay bales and for decoration we put up bunting and tied pastel-coloured balloons everywhere. On the tables we had mismatched vintage tablecloths, wild flowers arranged in jam jars, floral paper plates, and wooden cutlery. It was a perfect country wedding set-up, a vision of happiness.

The day before the wedding, my family gathered to decorate the church where we were due to marry. Harescombe Church is one of the oldest, smallest and most remote churches in Gloucestershire. To us that meant one thing: it would provide a safe setting for Rosie to run free while we said our vows. Consecrated in 1315, on the outside it is simple in design with a straight tower at one end, all constructed from local Cotswold stone. Inside, it has limewash walls, wooden pews and pulpit, and a simple altar. My mum, sisters and I set about filling the church vases with flowers, while my dad hung dark pink hydrangeas around the arched entrance and my stepdad Max wove ivy and other greenery around the gate. It looked idyllic. The vicar, a lovely lady called Elizabeth, was very accommodating to our circumstances and told us not to worry when we explained that Rosie might run around and create chaos.

'Let the children run free, and the atmosphere be light,' she said. And that was just how it was.

Throughout the service the children ran happily up and down the aisle. Rosie sang the *Eastenders* theme tune by the altar at the top of her voice and Grace kept running up to us saying, 'Mummy, are you married yet?'

It couldn't have been more joyous.

The church was packed with family and friends who broke into rapturous cheers when the deed was done and we became husband and wife. I couldn't believe how lucky I was to be marrying that same boy who I'd kissed in the autumn rain some eighteen years before. We'd been through so much together, and our love had only grown with us through our challenges.

Rosie coped amazingly with the hustle and bustle of the day. She ran around the reception sitting on people's laps for cuddles, touching their hair with chocolaty fingers and jumping up and down to the music.

Everyone was looking out for signs of progress. Had all the effort of the fundraising and trips to America paid off? She delighted everyone by saying several words like 'biscuits', 'water', 'chips' and 'hello darling!' She also wowed everyone by not having a single tantrum all day. She was totally different to the constantly screaming, never-sleeping, bewildered child that they remembered. There was every reason to celebrate and everyone knew that this wedding wasn't just about the love between Andy and me... it was just as much the celebration of a family who were finally coping again.

After the wedding and up until Christmas, Goldy and I were given a stall at the farmers' market to sell our calendar. Together with online sales we made over £10,000, which paid for our third trip to America with Rosie. Then, to cover the cost of running the programme for the rest of that year, I continued doing the Rosie Café at the farmers' market, and picked up a few jobs catering for other local events.

People from the wider community organised some fundraising activities too: a cancan dancing troupe called Rosie's Angels was formed; there was a sponsored bike ride to Cornwall; a Halloween disco; a sponsored walk; a half-marathon; a sponsored aerobics day; and a local fire brigade did a car-wash-for-cash event. We were astonished by the amount of help we were receiving and the local support spurred us on. And we had to go on... Rosie's epilepsy was still proving impossible to control, and keeping her home education programme going was our only option.

Again, I appealed to the local authority to fund Rosie's programme and despite the backing of her medical team, I lost the case. I'd spent long hours compiling my arguments and I'd represented myself in court so the defeat was a heavy blow. In the aftermath I felt dispirited and exhausted; the workload of fundraising, teaching and playing lawyer had stretched me to my limit and within a week I was laid up in bed with pneumonia. It was the first time I'd experienced true burnout – and it wouldn't be the last.

The following year – with the need for more funds ever pressing – Goldy, Bonnie and I came up with the idea of forming an all-male striptease ensemble called the Full Monty Boys. We held auditions, took on the choreography – and I have to say, it was one of the funniest, most outrageous undertakings we'd done to date. Members of the group were: Goldy's ex-boyfriend, Nige; Bonnie's husband, Jon; clown and ex-paratrooper, Paul; local DJ, Jake; BMX bike champion, Dan; and fitness instructor, Willam. In contrast to the tongue-in-cheek burlesque tone of our shows, the lads' performance was an energetic, testosterone-fuelled, visually impressive combination of macho dance moves and acrobatics. They even formed a human pyramid midway through their striptease, which never failed to impress the crowd!

That same year, we reformed the Full Monty Girls for a third and final time with a new member, Nancy, who replaced Emma. We then scheduled four more shows – three locally and one in Sheffield courtesy of our lovely friend Kay.

My favourite show among them, though, was an old age pensioners' Hat Lunch at the village hall in Oakridge, not far from Stroud. I did warn the organisers about the naked nature of our show but they wanted to support our cause and insisted we came along – at two o'clock in the afternoon on a Thursday! There were no stage lights, no PA, no alcohol-fuelled crowd; just us, a small stage, a

CD player and a room full of ladies over sixty in lovely hats, sipping tea with the vicar. When we began our performance, I looked out onto our straight-faced audience (some of whom I'd known as a child) and thought, *We're going to shock them into an early grave*, but after a couple of awkward minutes, the vicar (who was female I might add) smiled and began to clap along in time to the music. Everyone followed suit and the more naked we got, the more enthusiastic they became. By the time we were fully naked they were cheering and applauding rapturously. After the show, when we came out to meet our audience, an old lady of eighty-three approached me. 'Best thing I've seen in ages,' she said. 'Things can get terribly boring round these parts you know.'

Our final fling was at a swanky gala party at Beaufort Polo Club. My friend Clare had organised it, inviting some distinguished guests including the popular author Katie Fford and the Mayor of Stroud. I couldn't resist the urge to ping my bra at him when the time came to remove it. It was just too tempting.

All in all, our collective efforts enabled us to take Rosie to America for assessments for four consecutive years. Then, finally, I won funding from the local education authority and our fundraising marathon was over – just like that. I'm not going to lie; it was a huge relief. Together, we'd been on the adventure of a lifetime. We'd given the whole of our hearts to helping Rosie and watched our story circle the globe. To hang up our stockings at last felt like landing safely back on earth after a trip to the moon.

EPILOGUE

AUGUST 2020

As I write this, I'm sitting in a caravan near the runway of Birmingham airport in the garden of a house we now call home. 'Why on earth would you up sticks and leave the supportive bosom of Stroud?' I hear you cry. Well, the reason, as always, begins and ends with our lovely Rosie. When she was eight, her epilepsy improved enough to allow her to go to school so we searched the county – then the country – looking for a provision to meet her needs. We eventually found a groundbreaking ABA school on the edge of Birmingham and the rest is history. I can't describe what a wrench it was to leave our beloved valley or the community that had helped us like family for so long, but in many ways Rosie's journey in autism defines the direction of our lives and we have learned to roll with the adventure.

Rosie is now nineteen years old – a proper adult! These days her wispy-blonde hair is dark and straight but she still holds the same beauty. She's now brighter, more focused, sleeps well and is better equipped to regulate her moods. She's also more connected to the world and the people in her life, which is a joy to see.

However, as always seems to be the case with Rosie, things haven't been without their challenges. In 2013, as Rosie grew into adolescence, she developed scoliosis. In January 2015 she had major surgery to secure metal rods either side of her spine to straighten the curve. I could write another book about that little episode, but to cut a long story short, we're nearly six years down the line and thanks to our wonderful NHS, she's recovered well.

Also in 2013, Rosie's consultants entered her into a genetic study called the DDD study (Deciphering Developmental Disorders). Rosie will always have a diagnosis of severe autism but they wanted to see if they could find the *cause* of it as well as finding out why she has additional problems like microcephaly, scoliosis, hypertonia, and epilepsy. Incredibly, after five years of looking for what can only be described as a needle in a haystack, they had a breakthrough! It was found that Rosie has a mutation in a gene known as IQSEC2. She is one of just over a hundred known cases worldwide and is likely to be the only one in the world with her exact mutation. On the one hand, the discovery of just how rare Rosie's condition is came as a shock, but it also made everything finally slot into place. Like Rett syndrome, the IQSEC2 gene is located on the X chromosome and shares some similar symptoms. In fact there are now a small handful of children who, like Rosie, tested negative for Rett syndrome but were found to have an IQSEC2 mutation further down the line. Because it's so rare and there's no concrete prognosis, parents are left with more questions than answers about their child's future. However, many IQSEC2 children, Rosie included, are participating in clinical studies and the field of genetics is making gargantuan strides forward, which gives our little IQSEC2 community hope.

From an educational standpoint, Rosie's progress has stalled, regressed and pushed forward many times. She goes through phases when she says a handful of words and phases when she is silent. Andy and I have learned not to let this cloud our belief that there's a lot more going on in her mind than she can express. Occasionally (and literally years can go by between these occasions), she will say a string of words so clearly it shocks us. One of my favourite examples of this was when she told me that she loved me. As soon as the words left her lips she repeated them over and over again: 'I love you, Mummy,' 'I love you, Mummy,' 'I love you, Mummy.' It was as if she knew that after the moment had passed she may never be able to recall them again. There are no words to describe how precious those kind of moments are.

So did we manage to coax our child out of her autistic world? No. Did we break new ground or come across the holy grail of a 'cure' that so many parents long to find? Definitely not. But we *did* find out that a good education, hard work and a positive attitude can change lives. We discovered that this simple formula gave us a way to survive the most challenging end of the autistic spectrum, and that's no small thing. In fact it's paradigm-altering because it's the difference between struggling and thriving as a family unit.

Of course, reaching Rosie will continue to be an ongoing endeavour, fuelled by love and driven by the inspiration she brings into our daily lives. Her remarkable ability to find joy and humour in a life beset with challenges is astounding. It's a big reason why we're still smiling.

Grace, now sixteen, has also grown up to become a beautiful, remarkable young lady. Andy and I have enjoyed the simple pleasure of seeing her develop like most kids do and she is now an independent, strong-minded teenager who is full of life. Of course, we have tried to give her as normal a life as possible, but growing up with Rosie has definitely influenced Grace's perception of what life's all about. After witnessing everything Rosie's gone through, Grace has become a patient, kind, tolerant and understanding person, and the enthusiasm and heart she brings to everything she does is a testimony to how strong she has become in her own right. Is Grace's everyday life shaped by her sister's disabilities? The answer can only be yes... but Rosie has given her a gift in return – the gift of compassion. Unsurprisingly she has become quite the fundraiser herself! Over the years she has raised more than £2,000 for charity – an enormous achievement, which makes Andy and me exceedingly proud.

In 2010 Jessica finished her documentary, also called *Reaching Rosie*, to critical acclaim. It went on to win the 'Best Short Documentary' award at the European Independent Film Festival in Paris. I was lucky enough to be there as she collected her award, which was incredibly exciting for us both. In 2011 the documentary was bought by the news network Al Jazeera and has been a regular feature ever since.

Looking back, we have to pinch ourselves that we were ever part of the Full Monty Girls. It feels like a dream.

Occasionally we reminisce and look at the photos or press articles of our crazy adventure, but mostly we're looking forward.

Alix eventually moved to Stroud, and now has a beautiful daughter; Emma is busy being a care worker, moonlighting as a DJ in and around Stroud; and Nancy is a mother of two.

Ele now lives in London, working for the music giant, Spotify. She and Rich eventually went their separate ways but she went on to find new love in New York. Of course, Ele met her new beau, Jeremy, in a fabulously glamorous setting, at a picture-perfect moment in time. They had an uber-cool winter wedding in Soho and have gone on to have two gorgeous little boys. She's still the most well-connected person I know and I love her all the more for it.

Bonnie is still married to Jon and still has a wonderfully big and generous heart. She's now a midwife and we get together from time to time, laugh a lot, eat good food and drink Jon's excellent homemade Italian-style wine.

Goldy is still a bit of a wild child. She went on to have another baby and has stayed in the Stroud valleys. Still best of friends, we're often on the phone and in and out of each other's lives. She never tires of telling me about her crazy antics – just so she can laugh at what a prude I am.

As for me? Well, after we moved to Birmingham I began to write this book! It took six disciplined years of stealthily snatching blocks of writing time to fit in and around the more pressing job of being a mum. There were many times when I only got the chance to write when Rosie had an epilepsy day. In bed, she would lie in the crook of my arm recovering from a cluster of seizures and I would balance my laptop on my knees and gently reach over her head to type. Letter by letter, word by word, we got there in the end. Three years ago I also opened my own pottery studio. I now teach and make my own work to sell. I feel so lucky to have a job I love and grateful that I have a little chunk of the day that's just for me. My life now feels like a world away from my burlesque days but the spirit of it hasn't deserted me. Sometimes, when I'm running an errand or doing the weekly shop, a flashing image enters my mind. And I remember the lights, the music, and the deafening roar of the crowd. Then I lengthen my step, wiggle my hips and hold my head high. Because, when all is said and done, I'll always be a Full Monty Girl. Heart and soul.

And what adventures does autism still have up its sleeve, I sometimes wonder? Only Rosie holds the key to that. But if the last nineteen years are anything to go by, we're in for quite a ride.

CREDITS

Where do I start! It took a whole community to do what we did for Rosie. Without everyone's collective efforts I can't imagine where we would be now. A huge thank you to everyone who came to our shows and to all the many people who donated time and money to our appeal. Big kisses for Andy, Nige and Jon for the many, many, MANY nights of looking after our offspring while we practised and performed – we couldn't have done it without you. Special thanks go to the wonderful NHS doctors, nurses and surgeons who have cared for Rosie over the years and to Steven Wertz and his team for showing us how to help Rosie reach her potential.

I'd also like to thank Marilyn Ward, Susan Shields, Grace Morris, Ceri Goodall and Vanessa Walker for proofreading, and Roz Loveday for editing and proofreading. Thanks Roz, for the many long nights we spent sitting into the wee small hours, wrestling with semi-colons and hyphens! I couldn't have got this book off the ground without you. Lastly, thanks to Wx and Alex for having the patience to listen to me read my book out loud – one final time – before I skipped off to the publishers with it.

With much love and gratitude to…

The Full Monty Girls
Goldy Manzi-Fé, Bonnie Cicuttin, Ele Knowles, Alix Chalk,Emma Hannaway and Nancy Cawkwell.

The Full Monty Boys
Nige Wilson, Jake Kirton, Jon Cicuttin, Paul Bradley, Dan Neale and Willam Fox.

Choreography
Jo Goodall and Alistair Bull.

Supporting Acts
Rosie's Angels (Selva, Rosebud, Sophie, Beccy, Bonnie, Nicky and Melissa). Fi-Fi. Man Can. The Feel Good Floozies. Venus Noir. Lola Pops. Bam-Bam Blue. Miss Crimson Kiss.

Bands and DJs
Ceilidh Jo & Co. The Mad Cows. Jamie Rainbow. Pete Daisy. Oood. Freeno. Emma. The Stroud School of Samba. Jo Reeve – AKA Elvis.

Lighting and Sound
Dangerous Dave, Kim Holden and Pete Johnson

Music for our Shows
Chas Burns

Photographers

Sam Cribin, Georgie Brocklehurst, Jeremy Clifton-Gould and Nicholas Bechgaard

Props and Backdrops

Snow Business, Mixed Monkey, Dan and Juliet Chadwick, Mark Playne

Also, huge thanks go to: Kay Morriss, for organising the Sheffield show; Rowan Schofield, for the Brighton show; Bassline Circus and Ryan Wilmot, for the London show; Clare Cooke, for the Halloween rave; Roz Loveday and Oood, for the Bristol show; Marrion and Elizabeth Gardiner, for the Hat Lunch; Clare Honeyfield, for organising our final show, and giving us stalls at the farmers' market to sell our calendars and run the Rosie Café.

Rodda Thomas, for being our first audience, the best compère and for scoring us the catering job at Miserden Cricket Festival; Pob and friends, for the sponsored cycle ride; Fi Fi's Hair Boutique, for all those fab hairdos! Anthony and Liz Fisher, for all your help with the art auction; David and Barbara Manzi-Fé, for all your support through the years; Liisa Newton and the ladies at The Fitness Mill, for the sponsored aerobics event; Emma Dicker, for the Trade Plas fundraiser; Jo Manzi-Fé, Kizzy Martin and Chloe Martin, for the sponsored walk; Nailsworth Fire Brigade, for the car-wash-for-cash event; all the artists who donated works to sell at Rosie's art auction; Sam, website design; Emilie Dadswell, poster design; Michael Eavis, Glastonbury festival and all the volunteers who donated their wages to Rosie's appeal; Jessica Morris, for putting up with us during the filming for *Reaching Rosie*; INS news, for the helicopter; all the media outlets who supported our campaign – especially *The Stroud News and Journal*, *Stroud Life* and *The Citizen* who were there for us every step of the way!

With thanks to Made in Stroud, Amberley Post Office, Moonflower, Stroud Bookshop, Eclipse, Brilliant Disguise, Erotic Boutique, D Furley Newsagents, Spencer Thorn Bookshop, Dessous Chics, Secret Lady, The Shetland Shop, The Prince Albert, C2, Non Such Bookshop, and Gather Me Flowers, for helping us sell our calendars.

To the fabulous 'hundred naked ladies': Goldy, Bonnie, Emma, Ele, Amy, Tracy, Clare Cooke, Lizzie Chadwick, Beccy Partridge, Becky Martin, Rach Oldfield, Nicola Clifford, Angela Helbrow, Lorna Watson, Karen Visor, Calay, Adele Parret, Michelle Mast, Karen Blanche, Annette Morris, Reli St Claire, Rosie Sanderson, Marie Bellini, Lorna, Cima, Josie, Sally Unwin, Julie Pease, Jackie Ticehurst, Cherry Connolly, Jenny Beard, Liz Brown, Megan Melish, Karen Hunt, Liz Banyard, Joanne Cry, Fiona Hawker, Meredith Fisk, Meredith's friend, Irene Martin, Zana Helbrow, Tammy Bell, Georgina Wood, Jeniffer Newman, Christine Milne, Kelly, Trish, Tinsey, Joanne Brown, Caroline Smith, Naomi Cooper, Katey Paradine, Laura Wick, Ingrid Thorn, Luck Marks, Amy Freeman, Damaris, Jess, Anna, Jo Green, Lis Parker, Brenda, Florence, Annmarie Thouless, Abby Ferkin, Liz Weafer, Sarah Standing, Natalie Foster, Lu Griffiths, Claire Watt, Emma Cox, Julie Mordin, Tina, Pam Jenkins, Sarah Stepheson, Bel Savage, Rachel Slevin, Alex Archer, Stephanie Rose, Kim Button, Debbie Thwaie, Jessica

Morris, Diane Gardiner, Sue Cox, Liz Segal, Pat Britton, Kay Rotta, Bindi Downey, Jil Costello, Geraldine Atkins, Julia Foster, Carly, Gay Overs, Rachel Souter, Viv, Cathy Howe and friend, Karen, Hayley Selway, Ceilidh Rowe, Nicki, Sharon Foot, Florencia Martinez, and Sarah Sullivan. Thank you for being a force to be reckoned with!

To the show-goers, the private donors, the believers, the kind-word-givers, the movers and shakers, and the moral supporters. We couldn't have done it without you.

Everyone else... you know who you are!